MW01037060

"The most challenging ques[...] exist?' or 'Who do you say J[...] it mean to be human?' Iain [...] nest (his metaphor for unbib[...] surgical air strike. Here is so[...] it is to be human, and about the practical implications for all areas of life."

—**Kevin J. Vanhoozer**, research professor of systematic theology,
Trinity Evangelical Divinity School

"Iain Provan is a trusted guide for thinking biblically about all of life and about the most pressing issues of our time. The short topical essays presented in this book are accessible, but they pack a real punch. They may be read individually in bit-size pieces and digested at leisure, but cumulatively they will provoke the reader to consider deeply how Scripture ought to inform our minds and hearts today."

—**Bruce Hindmarsh**, professor of spiritual theology and history
of Christianity, Regent College

"In the moral and ethical maze of our time, this gathering of Iain Provan's insights will help to upend assumed and cherished cultural narratives and ground the thinking of the church in biblical and theological narratives instead. His insight that the primary theological question of our time is 'What does it mean to be human?' is, I believe, correct. The core answer to this question lies in Christian humanism grounded in the biblical texts and the incarnation. This kind of work will hopefully curb the descent of the West into dystopia."

—**Ross Hastings**, chair of theology, Regent College

"The most pressing question of our day—which we find posed in news, in print, and in social media—is 'What does it mean to be human? Are we really just spirits "merely clothed in physicality" that can be discarded? Or is there more to being human?' Iain Provan answers this question with great insight into the biblical witness but also with profound engagement with contemporary issues. This book is a treasury of wisdom and insight. You will not want to be without it."

—**Ian Paul**, author of *Revelation: An Introduction and Commentary*

"In Iain Provan's *Cuckoos in Our Nest*, rich reflection on the story of Scripture meets clear-headed, up-to-the-minute analysis on the most pressing issues of our age. This book is as helpful and penetrating as it is timely. For all who want full-orbed, biblical guidance on what it means to be human—and the implications of biblical anthropology for living in the modern world—you could not find a better guide. Highly recommended!"

—**George H. Guthrie**, professor of New Testament, Regent College

Cuckoos in Our Nest

Cuckoos in Our Nest

Truth and Lies about Being Human

Iain Provan

CASCADE *Books* · Eugene, Oregon

CUCKOOS IN OUR NEST
Truth and Lies about Being Human

Cascade Books
An Imprint of Wipf and Stock Publishers
199 W. 8th Ave., Suite 3
Eugene, OR 97401

www.wipfandstock.com

PAPERBACK ISBN: 978-1-6667-6870-1
HARDCOVER ISBN: 978-1-6667-6871-8
EBOOK ISBN: 978-1-6667-6872-5

Cataloguing-in-Publication data:

Names: Provan, Iain W. (Iain William), 1957– [author].

Title: Cuckoos in our nest : truth and lies about being human / by Iain Provan.

Description: Eugene, OR: Cascade Books, 2023 | Includes bibliographical references.

Identifiers: ISBN 978-1-6667-6870-1 (paperback) | ISBN 978-1-6667-6871-8 (hardcover) | ISBN 978-1-6667-6872-5 (ebook)

Subjects: LCSH: Theological anthropology—Biblical teaching. | Theological anthropology—Christianity. | Theological anthropology. | Christianity and culture.

Classification: BT701.3 P76 2023 (print) | BT701.3 (ebook)

05/15/23

This book is dedicated to my parents:

Rena Provan 1931–2021

Bill Provan 1930–2022

Rest in Peace

Contents

Part III: Furthermore

Part IV: Foreign Bodies

Acknowledgements

VARIOUS FRIENDS AND FAMILY members helped me greatly with this project in reading drafts of chapters or the entire book: my wife, Lynette, and then Scott and Monica Cousens, Brett Landry, Ed Gerber, David Wood, Eddie Larkman, and Jonathan Spainhour. I am grateful to them all, but the normal caveats apply—I am entirely responsible for the final product.

Abbreviations

Introduction

*"I find bird-watching so fascinating because it forces you
to decide what you are looking at. I am honing my art of
discernment."*[1]
(Henry Norcross)

"You see, but you do not observe."[2]
(Sherlock Holmes)

THROUGHOUT THE HISTORY OF the Christian church there have been particular moments of significant theological crisis. In the fourth century, for
example, there was a period when the full divinity of Jesus Christ became a
matter of controversy, before the Athanasian party defeated the Arians and
Trinitarian orthodoxy was enshrined in the Nicene Creed. In the sixteenth
century the question of how sinful human beings are put right with God
was widely debated. The differing answers given to this question contributed to a schism in the Western church, with the newly emergent Protestants
determined to defend a biblical version of "justification by faith." At all
such moments in history considerable numbers of churchgoers, firmly
embedded in their cultural contexts and comfortable with their "norms"
of thought and practice, have at least initially displayed a disturbing pro-
pensity simply to "go with the prevailing culture." They have done so either
because they have failed to understand how seriously their culture stands
at odds with truly Christian faith, or because they don't care. The defenders
of the true faith "once for all delivered to the saints" (Jude 3) have often
found themselves members of a minority, resisted, dismissed, and attacked
by the majority even of their fellow churchgoers, who have regarded them
as "troubling Israel" for no good reason (1 Kings 18:17).[3]

1

In my judgment the church today is in the very midst of another theological crisis. However, the pressing question now is not "Who is Jesus?" or "How can we be saved?" It is instead, "What is a human being?" In many communities that claim the name "Christian," even among people who would be able to provide the right answers to the first two questions, we find no such clarity when it comes to the third. In fact, it seems that many church members are currently deeply *compromised* in their understanding of what a properly Christian view of the human person *is*, and what this *means*. This is true at the individual level; it's also true of groups like denominational and pastoral leadership teams and the boards and faculties of universities and theological colleges. Whether such individuals and groups realize it or not, their views on "anthropology"—which is the technical term for this area of theology—derive (in part or even substantially), not from Christian Scripture, but from other sources. And as in past "crises," so also in the present moment those who attempt to bring the church back to right doctrine and practice are resisted, dismissed, and attacked for their troubles. They are caricatured as mere "conservatives" who lack humility in claiming a monopoly on the truth. They allegedly find themselves "on the wrong side of history" on the anthropological question, and they must give way to more enlightened "progressives."

This book is intended to speak into this theological crisis. I have a very particular audience in mind: I hope to help readers who are serious about following Jesus Christ to understand how they *should*, as faithful Christians, answer the question, "What is a human being?" and how they *should* live as a result. This is what I aspire to achieve in the first three-quarters of the book. At the same time, I want to help equip these serious Christians to recognize the non-Christian roots of the powerful, competing ideas of "the human" that they encounter every day, both in contemporary society and (unfortunately) in contemporary churches, and to have the courage to reject these unbiblical ideas. For especially when they are already embedded within a Christian community, these ideas do damage to Christian faith and life. This is the focus of the final quarter of the book.

The European cuckoo provides my chosen metaphor for describing these unbiblical ideas about humanity. This cuckoo, which migrates to Europe from Africa every spring, is a "brood parasite." It does not raise its own young, but instead sneaks into another bird's nest and replaces an egg with one of its own. This egg looks very much like the host's eggs, so it is difficult to spot. The host bird therefore raises the cuckoo chick believing that it is one of its own. Unfortunately the cuckoo is, from the moment of birth, an assassin. It systematically goes around pushing any other eggs or chicks out of the nest, ensuring that its own song is the only one that can be heard by its adoptive parents.

Having taken over the nest in this way, it receives the adoptive parents' sole attention, growing as a consequence to two or three times their size.[4] In all of this the cuckoo is "a cunning master of misdirection."[5]

Unbiblical anthropological ideas are like cuckoo chicks in the Christian nest. They have been smuggled into it by birds whose natural habitat is elsewhere. They can be difficult to spot, and they can therefore easily be regarded as a legitimate "part of the family." But in reality they are foreign bodies in our Christian nest and a threat to the survival of the family. If they are not removed, they can grow to such a size that they take over the entire habitat. This is what unchallenged falsehoods about "being human," embedded in our Christian nests, can do to our churches. They can "misdirect" us to our doom, such that the church is no longer really the church.

I have a particular audience in mind, then—but obviously I'm very happy also to have persons read this book who don't currently share (at least consciously) my Christian convictions. I'd like to think that fair-minded, external readers will still be able to derive some benefit from engaging with my argument. Indeed, I'd like to think that such readers might realize, as they go along, just how far they already hold a Christian view of the human person—perhaps because they are products of a Christendom that has historically shaped their own view of the world. The question then, of course, is how they can reasonably hold those Christian views of "being human" *without* being a Christian. But this book is not mainly addressed to my neighbors who find themselves currently outside of the Church. It is primarily addressed to serious, but perhaps confused, troubled, and even beleaguered fellow-Christians.

So what exactly will you find as you read the book? It is divided into in four parts. Part I prepares the way for what follows by exploring how any person hoping to arrive at a reliable answer might sensibly approach our central question, "What is a human being?" It also outlines what specifically *Christian* enquiry uniquely brings to this search for truth. Part II proceeds to lay out the fundamentals of a Christian anthropology, and Part III develops various implications of holding to these fundamentals. Parts I to III of the book focus, therefore, on the *truth* about being human, although in doing this they highlight some of the lies as well. But it's Part IV that *focuses* on the lies. It is here that we explicitly consider numerous important "cuckoos" seeking entry to, and perhaps even already inhabiting, our Christian nest. That is, it's in Part IV that we look in depth at the nature and the provenance of some important contemporary anthropological ideas that are not Christian. So don't go looking for explicit cuckoo language until you get to the last couple of pages of Part III.

All the chapters in the book are short, and I've written each one in what I hope is an accessible style for a broad readership. Each one is designed to make a concise argument about one aspect of a properly Christian anthropology. The idea is that you can read a single chapter at one sitting, then put the book down and think about its content before moving on. If you would like to have some specific, reflective questions to mull over, or put before a discussion group, while you think about each chapter, you can find these on my website (iainprovan.ca) on the "publications" page. All of this enables the book to be read individually, day-by-day, by the interested lay-person, or week by week in preparation for a church Bible-study group, or in those groups themselves. Each chapter, especially in Parts II and III, can also be used as the basis for a sermon, and related chapters in each of those parts can also be paired for this purpose. Readers should also be able to use the book effectively in church educational programs. It has been designed, essentially, as "catechesis," in pursuit of the recovery in all areas of our church life of a robust and truly Christian view of the human being.

Readers will not find long endnotes in this book, nor a large bibliography. This is by design, in order to keep the volume slim and straightforward. The endnotes that do exist are mainly designed to provide you with scriptural and other, very brief (but necessary) references. Even then, I have prioritized wherever possible interesting, illustrative material that can be found easily on the internet and does not require access to a library. I recognize that there is a downside to this decision. Since my chapters are deliberately short, they cannot do more than lay out a relatively brief (but hopefully reliable) map for traveling through the landscape of a Christian anthropology. It is inevitable, then, that various aspects of each part of my argument will raise questions in your mind, and that you will want further help in processing these questions. Fortunately, I've written numerous other books of a more traditional scholarly type that will help you further with many of the topics covered in this volume. The Select Bibliography fully describes these other books, which *do* possess extensive notes and bibliographies that will take you even deeper into particular topics. And the endnotes will identify which ones are particularly relevant to the topic that has just been covered in a particular chapter. Also, for those interested in a video series that would work well as a supplement to this volume, I recommend the ten-session "ReFrame" series available for free download at https://www.reframecourse.com/.

With all of this said, we'll begin!

PART I

Finding Out

1

A War of Myths

"Take up the whole armor of God, that you may be
able to withstand in the evil day, and having done
all, to stand firm. Stand therefore, having fastened
on the belt of truth." (Ephesians 6:13–14)

IN THE MIDDLE OF 2020, right in the eye of the COVID-19 storm, Anuja Sonalker—the CEO of a Maryland-based company selling self-parking technology—expressed this opinion concerning human nature: "Humans are biohazards."[6] She said this while enthusing about human-less, contactless machines: "Humans are biohazards, machines are not."[7] In other words, her view of the human being is integrally bound up with a wider vision of society. In this vision, machines lacking various kinds of human limitations will happily play an increasingly central role in the way the world works. Ms. Sonalker is only one of many influential people currently hoping to create in the future very different societies to the ones to which we're accustomed. In these societies the "problems" created by our physical embodiment will progressively be overcome by advanced technology, particularly artificial intelligence. The levers that will produce these outcomes will be (and already are) unprecedented alliances between global technology giants and various levels of government. Together these "saviors" will make life better in pursuit of keeping us all "safe" (the new favorite word of our Western politicians).

But what does "better" mean? How is "better" being measured? A moment's reflection will reveal that all these saviors are measuring "better" in terms of deeply held (though often unexpressed) convictions about what is essentially human. But is it *in fact* better that humans should massively reduce their physical contact across the whole spectrum of their lives, from shopping and banking, through healthcare and education, and on into governance and all the rest? How and why is this truly better for us, as individuals and communities?

This same interest in transcending our embodied limitations is also found among those influential and wealthy people globally who are currently promoting "transgenderism." Their goal is to wean the rest of us away from a traditional "dimorphic" understanding of sex—humans are male or female—to a very different idea. This new idea is that "who we really are" has little or nothing to do, necessarily, with our biology. It is in fact perfectly possible (they claim) to be born in the "wrong" body. This makes space, then, for the creation of synthetic sex identities by way of drugs and surgeries. Individuals decide for themselves which kinds of bodies they would prefer, in line with their intuitions and feelings about their "real" selves, or perhaps simply as a matter of arbitrary choice.

Consider the role of the Pritzker family, for example, in promoting this agenda—one of the richest families in the United States, wielding significant social and political power in that country and beyond. Jennifer (born James) Pritzker has used the family-initiated Tawani Foundation to help fund various institutions that support this new idea, including the World Professional Association of Transgender Health (WPATH).[8] In 2021 another family member, Illinois Governor J. B. Pritzker, signed into law a sex-education bill for all public schools in that state, introducing this new idea into the curriculum even for young children. This curriculum holds that by the end of second grade, for instance, students should be able "to define gender, gender identity, and gender-role stereotypes" and "to discuss the range of ways people express their gender and how gender-role stereotypes may limit behavior." By the end of fifth grade, they should be able to "distinguish between sex assigned at birth and gender identity and explain how they may or may not differ."[9]

Here again a particular view of humanness is integrally bound up with a wider vision of society. In this case it includes a clear idea about the appropriate content of school curricula. A human being, on this view, is an immaterial spirit that happens to possess a body—a body that may or may not be considered satisfactory by its spirit-owner. Like a piece of clothing, this physical body can (and should) be discarded in pursuit of personal authenticity. With the help of technology, a different fashion can (and should) be chosen. Then everything will be "better."

But is it really true that human beings are essentially spirits merely clothed in a physicality that can easily be discarded? Who says so, and how do they know? Surely we *should* want to *know*. For if the people who make this claim are mistaken, then the rest of us—if we simply indulge their feelings on this matter—are failing entirely to look after their real interests. In that case, we are certainly not participating in making any-thing "better." We are in reality making things much worse, by adding to someone's pre-existing mental anguish the mutilation of their body, infertility, and a lifelong dependency on drugs.

The stakes are high, then, when it comes to the question that lies at the heart of this book. What *is* a human being? The answer that we give to this question *matters*. It matters *individually*, affecting how I look at my-self, what I agree to do to myself or have done to me, the goals I set myself, and so on. It also matters *communally*, affecting how I look at and treat other people, what kind of society I am trying to help to build, and so on. In fact, the answer to this question about humanness affects everything else that is important in life.

It's surprising, then, that most people do not spend much time think-ing about what it means to be human. They seem to believe that "it's just obvious." But it really isn't obvious at all. The reality is that this question is, and always has been, *disputed*. Whether we realize it or not, we are all caught up, all the time, in what one author has referred to as "a war of myths."[10] He does not mean by "myth" something that is untrue. To the contrary, "myth" in this context refers to big ideas—truth claims—about reality. We are all caught up, all the time, in a battle between competing ideas of reality—for example, how to think about disease ("humans are biohazards"), or about sex and gender ("we can choose our own"). And it is critical that we *decide* what to believe about reality, including the reality of our humanness, and that we are clear about *why* we are making that choice. Otherwise, we shall pass through life simply marching unwittingly to the beat of somebody else's drum. We shall find ourselves living the unexamined life that, according to one ancient philosopher, is not *worth* living. And there will, inevitably, be significant consequences.

This is a book that presents a particular argument, in the heat of the ongoing war of "myths," about the nature of our humanity. I'd like to per-suade you that a particular way of thinking about our humanness is true, and to exhort you to take your "stand" on this truth as you put on "the whole armor of God" for the battle (Ephesians 6:13–14). But as one ancient Roman bureaucrat once famously asked: "What is truth?"

2

The Question of Truth

"What is truth?" (John 18:38)

THE MAN IN QUESTION was Pontius Pilate, and his words are recorded in the Gospel of John in the Christian New Testament (NT). "Everyone who is of the truth listens to my voice," Jesus of Nazareth tells him.[11] "What is truth?" Pilate replies.[12] Perhaps the question is cynical, betraying that Pilate does not believe in the existence of "truth." Maybe it's more of a genuine question: among the various claims that are made about truth, which ones are actually true? In both of these scenarios, anyway, Pilate's question is not only ancient, but also highly contemporary.

First of all, for many people today there is allegedly no such thing as truth in the singular—what I'm going to refer to now as Truth (with a capital T). At least, that is what people *say*. "We believe only in truths in the plural"—your truth, my truth, and so on. This has become a common way of speaking in our global culture, and we encounter it everywhere. A rather famous example is provided by the 2021 Oprah Winfrey interview with Harry and Meghan, the Duke and Duchess of Sussex. In this interview Oprah invites Meghan to "speak your truth" about life in the UK Royal Family. Meghan is apparently a great fan of the American social psychologist Brené Brown, who encourages her followers to "walk into your own story and own your truth." Meghan's own philosophy of life reflects these commitments. As she says to Oprah in the interview: "Life is about storytelling, right? About the stories we tell ourselves and what we buy into."

So people often *speak* nowadays in ways that suggest that they don't believe in Truth. Of course, whether this is itself actually True is quite another matter. Falsely accused of a crime, even thoroughly postmodern people do not tend to cry out, "But that is not my truth." They still shout: "That is not in fact (objectively) True." And more generally, sane people tend to pay serious attention to the factual shape of reality—its True nature—in conducting their lives. They know that if they don't, reality will hurt them. When all is said and done, a cliff is a cliff, and stepping off a cliff-edge is not going to end well for you, no matter what your own "story" tells you about it. A fire is a fire, and whatever "your truth" may be, sticking your hand in the flame will usually hurt. Indeed, everyone knows that what Meghan is really doing in that Oprah interview, when allegedly speaking "her truth," is making assertions about *the* Truth, and at the same time strongly implying that other people are lying.

So there is considerable self-delusion in this contemporary mindset about truth. And necessarily it's *selective* self-delusion, because you can only get away with just so much of this approach to life before you bump up, painfully, against rock-solid reality. In Truth, you need considerable power, money, and protection even to prolong the attempt. These are in fact the common means by which people delay the moment when reality comes painfully crashing back into their lives.

My point is that people *do* believe in objective Truth, no matter what they say. They sometimes just choose to ignore some of it—always to their own cost, eventually. And then they resort to the language of "my truth, your truth" so that no one else can disturb their "story" by way of annoyances like argument and evidence. In other words, in the end this "postmodern" approach to truth is merely a clever strategy designed to remove any possibility that you might find yourself in error, and in need of a change of mind. Its purpose is to avoid the discovery that the "story you are telling yourself" is false—or at least, only partially true.

So perhaps Pilate's question, and its modern equivalent, is more of a veiled assertion than a question—an assertion that no one in the end Truly (!) believes. But maybe, secondly, it's a more *genuine* question. Among the various claims that are made about the Truth, which ones are actually True, and how could I possibly *know* that this is the case? I believe that there *is* such a thing as Truth (I might affirm), and I am committed to grasping hold of it. But how can I be reasonably sure that I have done so?

Maybe Pilate had it easier than we do when it comes to this important question, because he lived in a simpler world. We live, we are now told, in a world marked by post-truth (or post-reality, or post-factual) politics. It is a world driven by twenty-four-hour news cycles that dominate both traditional media outlets and social media sites. And these news cycles are delivered in ways that inhabit a spectrum, from truthful, through to considerably biased, through to completely fake news. The central appeal of post-truth politics is not indeed to facts at all, really, but to emotion. If emotion can be sufficiently aroused, it will resist all factual rebuttal. The facts will cease to matter, and even experts talking about the facts will cease to matter.

This is not only true of politics. The same kind of appeal is central to
modern advertising in general. This is why the images on your TV or computer
screen show you puppies cavorting around the place even while the voiceover
is describing the hundred ways in which an advertised drug can harm you.
The advertisers want you to remember the puppies, not the words—to recall
the feelings, rather than the facts. And it works. Otherwise, companies would
not devote huge sums of money to their advertising budgets.

What is the person seeking the Truth to *do* in this kind of world? How
should we proceed? We need to think carefully about this question. For the
consequences of taking a wrong step here might well be serious—far more
serious than the inconvenience of ending up with a disappointing product
purchased in response to a TV advertisement.

The importance of thoughtfulness is well-illustrated by the 2016 case
of Pizzagate. This story began with a widely advertised but false claim on
social media about the emails of John Podesta, Hillary Clinton's 2016 US
election campaign manager. The allegation was that these emails contained
coded messages connecting several high-ranking Democratic Party offi-
cials and some restaurants with a human trafficking and child sex ring.
Among the restaurants implicated was the Comet Ping Pong pizzeria in
Washington, DC. I'm sure we all agree that right-minded people should
vigorously oppose human trafficking and child sex rings. Certainly this is
what Maddison Welch, a twenty-eight-year-old man from North Carolina,
believed. So in December 2016 he drove to Washington, entered the Comet
Ping Pong, and fired three shots from a rifle that struck the restaurant's
walls, a desk, and a door. He had read online that the restaurant was har-
boring child sex slaves in its basement, and he wanted to rescue them. Upon
discovering that in reality the Comet Ping Pong possessed no basement,
Welch acknowledged that "the intel on this wasn't 100%," which is putting
things rather mildly! "I just wanted to do some good and went about it the
wrong way," he said.[13] On this occasion, the consequences of "the wrong
way" for this soft-spoken and polite young father of two daughters, whose
heart was breaking "over the thought of innocent people suffering," were
terrible. He served four years in prison.

In this world of information- and disinformation-overload, when the
stakes in the game of life are so very high, how are Truth-seekers to proceed?
The next four chapters reflect on this issue of what philosophers call "epistemology." In these chapters I shall propose that the critical question we need
to ask here is this one: "Whom shall I admit to my circle of trust, and why?"
And I shall discuss various sources of knowledge, including science, leading
in the end to the crucial importance of trusting in Jesus Christ and in the
Holy Scripture he has given us. I believe that these immediately upcoming

chapters will be important for many readers. But in a broad readership of the kind that this book seeks to address, some of you will perhaps feel that you already have a good grasp of *how* we should approach knowledge in general. If so—and if you're anxious to get on now to *what* Holy Scripture says about "being human"—feel free to proceed directly to chapter 7. You can always circle back to chapters 3 to 6 later, before you begin Part IV.

3

The Circle of Trust

"Some trust in chariots and some in horses."
(Psalm 20:7)

AMONG THE VARIOUS CLAIMS that are made about the Truth (which we'll now just call "truth" in the normal way), how can we know which ones are actually true?[14] It seems so easy even for sincere, caring people who are *committed* to knowing and living by the truth to make mistakes. So how should we proceed? The best answer to this question is grounded in the idea of "the circle of trust"—a way of speaking that I'm borrowing from the 2000 comedy movie *Meet the Parents*. It's useful phraseology because it emphasizes the role of the *community* in our knowing, rather than simply the *individual*.

We are obviously capable, individually, of discerning *some* truth directly by way of our senses (e.g., sight and hearing) and without anyone else's help. We see and hear things, and we touch, smell, and taste things, and in these ways we gain quite a bit of firsthand knowledge about reality. And for the most part we *trust* our own perceptions of the world accumulated in this way. We could hardly do otherwise and still function in the world. Even though we know that we can sometimes make mistakes—that for all sorts of reasons, we can misperceive—in general we tend to trust our senses.

But *if we are wise*, we also look to other people to confirm that we are perceiving reality correctly. Did you see that? Did you hear that? Am I understanding things in the right way? And this is of course one major respect in which much of the prevailing culture is *not* very wise. For its emphasis lies *heavily* on "sticking firmly to your own personal convictions." It displays massive confidence, in fact, in individual introspection and intuition as virtually infallible guides to what is true. This is a huge mistake. Humility is required in pursuit of truth—a reasonable balance between self-confidence and self-doubt. If we are wise, we do not entirely trust ourselves. We also look to others, and we trust *them*.

In fact, most of what we think we know as true derives from other people. It does not derive from our own perceptions and experience. The book *Testimony* by the Australian philosopher Tony Coady makes this point wonderfully well.[15] Coady demonstrates that "our trust in the word of others is fundamental to the very idea of serious cognitive activity."[16] He argues that "an extensive commitment to trusting the reports of others [is in fact] a precondition of understanding their speech at all."[17] We depend extensively on testimony for our knowledge, not only as children, but also as adults—and not only in obvious ways (for instance, in legal processes), but *generally*, in everyday life. For example: when we rely on a map to guide us around a foreign city as tourists, we are depending on the testimony of those who have walked before us. When psychologists accept what their clients say about their perceptions of reality, or when scientists more generally rely on what their colleagues claim about their research results, they too depend on testimony. In short, when it comes to what we call knowledge we are intellectually reliant, to a very great extent, on what other people tell us. And this is true, whether we consciously recognize it or not.

We know the truth, to the extent that we know it at all, primarily through the *testimony* of other people. And this makes trust the *central* question for truth-seekers. Whom should we trust, and why? Which persons are we going to admit to our circle of trust, and for what reasons? And which ones are we going to shut *out* of this circle?

Some of the most obvious candidates for inclusion, in the first instance, are our parents and other close family members. Each of us already believes quite a lot to be true primarily because of what people in our close family have told us about it. Our very survival as young children once depended, in fact, on trusting absolutely what our parents told us (such as the negative effects of sticking one of our fingers in an electric socket). It's perfectly sensible to continue, as we grow up, to take seriously what our close family members say—if we remain convinced that they are generally truthful people who have our best interests at heart.

This does not mean, of course, that they will always be correct, or even honest. This is why, as we grow up, we also need to engage in measured critical reflection. For many of us this reflective process begins when we encounter teachers we trust in the school setting, and at college or university. It's on the basis of what they tell us that we begin to develop the larger context in which our parents' teachings can be assessed and re-assessed. It is in this wider educational environment that we first begin to suspect that, whereas our parents know quite a bit about some subjects (e.g., which kinds of people are dangerous), they may not be the most reliable guides when it comes to other matters (e.g., nuclear physics). To the extent that our teachers are well-educated and competent people in their subject matter, we certainly learn truth from them—truth that we may never have encountered before.

But this brings up the important question of *expertise*. It is always a good idea in asking questions about truth to consider this point: is there good reason to think that the person now communicating with me knows what he or she is talking about? For example, have our teachers studied their subjects at a good school or university that has testified to their expertise? Or are there reasons to think that in at least some respects their own education has been quite poor—narrow, doctrinaire, limited? Of course, *character* also comes into the question, because a teacher might well be well-educated but more interested in indoctrinating than in educating pupils. We might have proper confidence in a teacher's *education*, but not in their *educating*.

Expertise and character matter hugely when it comes to the question of trust. They matter in relation to family members and teachers, and also when it comes to what our various media have to tell us. Do journalists possess high standards of personal integrity, for example, and do they aim for a fair and appropriately balanced account of their subject matter? Do they work under the supervision of editors who challenge them about their blind spots, prejudices, and agendas? If so, then they are worthy of admission to our circle of trust. A free and responsible press is an invaluable means of discovering truth about the world. Of course, in a post-truth society it may not be easy in practice to find a free and responsible press.

Summing up so far on this question of how we gain secure knowledge about reality—the question of epistemology: we know the truth primarily through the *testimony* of other people. Some of these people are parents, teachers, and journalists, and some of them, as we'll discuss in the next chapter, are scientists.

4

Trusting in Science

*"The heavens declare the glory of God, and the sky above
proclaims his handiwork." (Psalm 19:1)*

IN MODERN SOCIETY PEOPLE generally invest a great amount of trust in scientists as a body of people, and in the totality of what they have to say (the abstraction "science").[18] This trust is evident, for example, in the way that governments in the midst of the COVID-19 outbreak often exhorted their populations to "follow the science." For many people nowadays, it is science that actually provides the largest context within which we should assess the claims of other authorities—parents, teachers, and so on. It is science that must measure what they have to say. This is because science is widely regarded as providing us with precisely the kind of objective truth that enables us to cut through human ignorance, prejudice, limitation, and ideology. Therefore, it is said, we should invest enormous trust in those with this kind of expertise—whether in physical science, medical or social science, or whatever.

This is not bad advice. Suppose that a scientist's findings have been confirmed by other scientists, passing successfully through the "peer-review" process. Suppose that these findings have become widely acknowledged as truth among people who possess expertise in the area in question. In such a case, we would be wise to listen carefully to what scientists have to say. We typically *do* listen to them carefully, *even in* a post-truth society. For example, if science suggests that in stepping off a high cliff I shall almost certainly fall speedily to my death in the water below, but old Aunt Agnes who left school aged fifteen insists that I will float and survive, if only I will drink her magic potion, most people will not listen to Aunt Agnes.

Of course, individual scientists can make mistakes, and even tell lies. However, science itself will usually find this out reasonably quickly. An entire group of scientists may lie, or fail to see the whole truth, because of financial or political pressure—but typically science itself will also eventually catch *these* people out. This is in part because scientists quite enjoy demonstrating how other scientists have failed, and how their own scientific theories are much better. It's part of the internal dynamic of the profession, whereby we all get beyond error (and even wickedness) and deeper into the truth of things.

This is why we should generally be skeptical about large-scale global conspiracy theories concerning "science." Science may not be perfect, and some scientists may not be very competent or honest. Sometimes there are issues like climate change or virus transmission that are just incredibly complicated, and respectable groups of scientists can legitimately disagree on these, at least for the time being. But if we start to distrust science *as such*, then we turn our back on a body of knowledge that is very likely largely true, and which helps us (among other things) to know how to respond to old Aunt Agnes and to save ourselves from almost-certain death. If we start to distrust science *as such*, there is then no larger and generally reliable measuring stick against which to measure a whole range of particular types of truth claim.

Science deserves our trust within the realms of our existence about which it can legitimately inform us. It certainly deserves to be given more weight in these zones than other sources of information. Is Professor Richard Dawkins generally going to be more reliable on biology than Wikipedia, for example? For sure he is—unless the Wikipedia page is of a very high caliber, drawing Dawkins' work (for example) into a larger discussion among biologists on a given topic. Should a university graduate with a degree in nutrition be trusted in that area more than a blogger with no comprehensive education in the subject? Of course! Should we in principle trust peer-reviewed books and essays on science broadly speaking (including subjects like history, for example) much more than anything we read on the internet or come across on social media? We *should*—unless the person writing or posting on the internet is *also* working meaningfully under the constraints of a peer-review process that remains uncorrupted. In sum, scientists deserve a place within the circle of trust.

We are not quite done yet in discussing this crucial question of testimony and trust, but I want to pause here for a moment to consider what I think are the merits of the approach to truth-seeking that I've been advocating. It seems to me that this approach gives us our best chance of finding ourselves in possession of all kinds of truth and at the same time devoid of falsehood. For within an intelligently constructed circle of trust, we should be able to arrive at sound judgments concerning such important matters as character, competence, and expertise. Either we ourselves will know the people who are making the truth claims, or they will have been "recommended" to us by others whom we have good reason to trust (through processes like peer-review), or we will be satisfied that there are other meaningful constraints upon them that are likely to limit their incompetence, mendacity, and so on.

All of this provides us with a firm foundation for dealing with everyone else whom we encounter making truth-claims—especially people on social media and on the internet more generally. I'm not referring here to the vast areas of this virtual world that are merely impersonal, algorithmically constructed echo chambers engineered by mega-corporations seeking to maintain eyes-on-screens and to monopolize our attention for their profit.[19] I'm referring to actual persons interested in communicating truth. Whatever their intentions, however, the problem is that, when you pay full attention to their claims, it often becomes clear that they lack any kind of expertise to pronounce on the subject at hand. There is often no good reason to think that they know what they are talking about. There is often no evidence that the claims they are making are grounded in primary sources that have been sifted carefully prior to judicious decisions being reached about them. There is often no evidence that they are even *reporting* things firsthand and thoughtfully, rather than simply passing on rumors and innuendo. So we are wise to approach with a healthy degree of skepticism this chaotic, virtual world full of strangers who possess limited knowledge and expertise. We are wise to measure these truth-claims against the truth that, for good reasons, we believe we already securely know. We should *not* admit people in this chaotic, virtual world too easily to our circle of trust.

And so, knowing and believing the science that tells me that the world is spherical in nature, I am going hesitate before embracing any claims on the internet that the world is in fact flat, no matter how many sports personalities tell me that this is true. And when I come across the idea on social media that a certain politician's emails connect various restaurants to human trafficking and child sex rings, I'm going to try and get firsthand access to those emails, I'm going to consult serious newspapers and magazines as secondary sources to see what they are saying about this topic, and I'm going to check out my thinking with trustworthy family members and friends. And I'm going to do all of this, and think really hard about it all, before jumping in my truck with my gun and driving to Washington.

5

Beyond Science

*"I said, 'I will be wise,' but it was far from me. That which
has been is far off, and deep, very deep; who can find it out?"
(Ecclesiastes 7:23–24)*

As WE CONTINUE TO think about attaining secure knowledge—and before we even get to the question of Christian anthropology as such—there is something more to be said about science.[20] It is this: that science can only tell us *certain kinds* of truths. This is important, and it ought to affect the kind of trust we invest in it.[21] It is one thing to trust Richard Dawkins as a biologist, for example, and quite another to trust him as a philosopher—an area in which he has no expertise. This crucial point is not well understood, so it's worth spending some time on it.

I once heard Denis Alexander, at that time the director of the Faraday Institute for Science and Religion in Cambridge, helpfully define modern science as follows: "Science is an organised endeavour to explain the properties of the physical world by means of empirically testable theories constructed by a research community trained in specialized techniques." We notice here that science has its own domain: "the physical world." It also has its own particular focus of interest: "the properties of the physical world." And it has its own method: "empirically testable theories." Science aims at formulating generalizations about the properties of the physical world by way of testable hypotheses in the world of public discourse. Its interest lies in what is publicly observable and repeatable, and publishable in peer-reviewed journals. As such, science is a truth-seeking enterprise, seeking to dispel misapprehension and to correct mistakes on the way to an accurate grasp of various kinds of physical reality. However, it is set up to discover *only certain kinds of truth*: those which relate to "the properties of the physical world." Strictly as science, it's not designed to speak (and is not capable of speaking) to other important questions. It certainly cannot properly address questions of ultimate purpose, value, and significance. These realities do not form part of its domain.

An illustration may help to clarify the point. Consider the various ways in which it's possible to map a country like France. We might produce a political map that identifies its various regions. Or we might draw a map that emphasizes topographical features like mountains, hills, valleys, and lakes, and provides their height in relation to sea level. Or we might prioritize transport networks like roads and railways. Each of these maps, with its own language, symbols, metaphors, and indeed colors, would tell us some of the truth about France. But which map we might use on any particular occasion would depend on the kind of wisdom we were looking to gain from the exercise. Each map provides useful information—but not the same *kind* of information as the others.

To return to science, and what is beyond science: consider in outline what modern science tells us about the physical origins of the world in which we live, and about the physical origins of human beings themselves. It proposes that the universe in which we live is very old, originating in a Big Bang about 13.75 billion years ago, after which galaxies began to form. About 4.57 billion years ago our own sun came into being, and the earth shortly afterwards. As our planet cooled, clouds formed and rain created the oceans, and the stage was set for life to emerge and to evolve. By around 2 million years ago the first creatures classified in the genus *Homo* had appeared. Archaic *Homo sapiens* is then believed to have originated somewhere around 500,000 years ago in Africa, evolving into anatomically modern humans (*Homo sapiens sapiens*) around 200,000 years ago. By 11,000 years ago *Homo sapiens sapiens* had journeyed to the southern tip of South America, the last of the uninhabited continents (except for Antarctica). And then, somewhere between 8500 and 7000 BC, humans in the Fertile Crescent in the Middle East began the systematic husbandry of plants and animals: agriculture and livestock-farming. Surplus food allowed a priestly or governing class to arise, followed by increasing divisions of labor across society. This led to the planet's first civilization, in Sumer in the Middle East, between 4000 and 3000 BC. Additional civilizations quickly arose in ancient Egypt, in the Indus River valley, and in China.

Concerning how we came to live on this planet, this is the standard narrative that forms the bedrock of mainstream science at the present time. It does so precisely because it accounts well for all the evidence that we currently possess about our planetary history *within the domain of science*. But notice the important human questions that are not answered in this narrative. Scientists can tell us that there was a Big Bang, and they can also tell us a terrific amount about the moments just after it occurred. But they cannot, as scientists, tell us anything about where the universe came from, or indeed what happened before the Big Bang, for the simple reason that space and time themselves did not yet exist prior to the Big Bang, and without space, there is no "where," and without time, there is no "before." Did someone intend it? Scientists also cannot tell us, as scientists, why there was a beginning at all (which was not the prevailing scientific view until quite recently). Did this involve a *decision*? And when it comes to the mechanics of how life on this planet (including human life) emerged, slowly and over a long period of time, through a process of genetic variation and natural selection, science is informative. But it cannot tell us what it all *means*. It cannot, as science, tell us everything about who we are, and certainly little about how we should live, and how we should treat other creatures on the planet, and what we should hope for, and so on. In other words, science is not able to help us with a whole host of human questions to which we desperately need answers if we are to live our lives well.

This reality has been well understood by intelligent people for some time. The father of modern sociology, Max Weber, was already talking about it in a university lecture in 1918:

> Who . . . still believes today that a knowledge of astronomy or biology or physics or chemistry could teach us anything at all about the *meaning* of the world? Tolstoy gave us the simplest answer to the only important question: "What should we do? How should we live?" The fact that science does not give us this answer is completely undeniable.[22]

This is not at all to "blame science" for inadequacy. That would be as foolish as blaming a topographical map of France for failing to help us complete our journey from Paris to Bordeaux on the French railway system. It's just that in fully pursuing the question of knowledge via trust, we must necessarily look beyond science and into the domain of "metaphysics." This language derives from the title of some of the edited works of the Greek philosopher Aristotle. It refers to matters "beyond the physical" (meta-physical), over against Aristotle's other books about the natural world (his *Physics*).

But how are we to gain reliable knowledge about this metaphysical domain beyond "nature"? The philosophers and religious teachers who have claimed to speak the truth about this realm are of course many and various, and they by no means agree on what the truth is. I have written another book, *Seriously Dangerous Religion*, that outlines the main options in this marketplace of philosophical/religious ideas, and I'm not going to repeat that exercise in the present volume. The point that I need to emphasize *here* is simply that, once again, knowledge is bound up necessarily and fundamentally with trust. Of all the people who have claimed to speak truth about the metaphysical realm, whom shall I trust, and why? That is the question that faces each one of us. It's a very important question—which makes it all the more surprising that many modern people seem to think they can get along well enough without asking it.

6

Personal Matters

Jesus said to him, "I am the way, and the truth, and the life."
(John 14:6)

I BEGAN IN CHAPTER 1 by suggesting that the stakes are high when it comes to the question, "What is a human being?"[23] The answer that we give to this disputed question *matters*, I proposed, and we need to ensure as best we can that we have a *good* answer. This led us in chapters 2 through 5 to some general reflections on what is involved in the serious pursuit of truth, and how we can ensure, as far as possible, that we are avoiding error. The critical issue here, I suggested, is "whom shall I trust, and why?" Whom shall I admit to my circle of trust, and on what grounds? Hitherto I have asked this question largely of the *physical* realm, considering the ways in which parents, teachers, journalists, and scientists "tell us the truth" about it (or do not). But the question is just as important when it comes to the *metaphysical* realm—the realm "beyond the physical." Of all the people who have claimed to speak truth about that metaphysical realm, whom shall I trust, and why?

All of this brings us now to the nature of the argument that I want to develop in this book, which is grounded in a specifically *Christian* set of metaphysical convictions. For me, it is these convictions—and not the truth that science certainly does deliver to us (chapter 4)—that inevitably set the larger frame for everything else. It is these convictions that provide the larger context in which I engage in all the smaller acts of trust that are bound up with my understanding of who I am. And I must now tell you why I possess these convictions.

I want to begin by returning to the words of Pilate's conversation-partner in John 18—Jesus of Nazareth. "Everyone who is of the truth listens to my voice." This is startling enough, but not as astonishing as what he says just a few chapters previously: "I am the way, and the truth, and the life."[24] I am the truth! This is in fact only one of several statements in John's Gospel that make it clear that Jesus regarded himself as God. Consider this other one, for example: "Truly, truly, I say to you, before Abraham was, I am."[25] This is the culminating point of a section of the Gospel that begins with Jesus's claim to be the light of the world, leading on to a long reflection on who Jesus's father is, and who the father of his conversation partners might be.[26] Jesus disputes their claims that their father is Abraham (since they do not behave as Abraham behaved) and that God is their father (since if this were true, they would love Jesus).[27] He then presents himself as the person who can give others eternal life.[28] The "before Abraham" statement that follows this alludes to the revelation of God to Moses: "I AM WHO I AM."[29] It's not surprising that his Jewish audience "picked up stones to throw at him."[30] These are crazy, blasphemous words—unless Jesus is telling the truth.

And herein lies the paradox with which many Bible-readers across the ages have had to wrestle. Jesus, when we first encounter him, appears in so many ways to be extraordinary, admirable, and worthy of imitation—and at the same time, to be quite mad. Yet some of the people who were the least likely in the ancient world to accept that he really was God incarnate came to believe it. I'm referring here to some Jews of the first century AD. These were people deeply rooted in the worship of the one God, and therefore fiercely hostile to the surrounding polytheism of the Roman world. But in spite of this, they came routinely to use the language of "Father," "Son," and "Holy Spirit" in speaking about God. They spoke and wrote in this way to express their belief that God, although one, is also three Persons. And it is because of this belief that Christians then came to be baptized in the name of "Father, Son, and Holy Spirit."[31] How exactly to *say* that God is one and yet three without falling back into polytheism, on the one hand, or "simple" oneness, on the other, then became a matter of considerable discussion in the early church, before the matter was finally settled in the Christian "creeds" of the fourth and fifth centuries AD.

Just as these first-century Jews, and later many non-Jews ("gentiles"), came to believe in Christ's divinity, so too have millions of other people throughout history—for it's impossible to explain Jesus in any other plausible way. If Jesus was not God, but nevertheless claimed to be, then (as C. S. Lewis once put it) he must have been mad (deluded), or bad (deceiving). He certainly could not have been good, and at the same time sane. As I read the Gospels, however, I encounter someone who is supremely good and supremely sane. Therefore, I am obliged to take Jesus's astonishing claims about himself deeply seriously—to accept him, along with doubting Thomas, as "my Lord and my God!"[32]

When it comes to my metaphysical convictions, then—the answers that I give to a whole host of important questions that I cannot finally answer through what we might call "ordinary means" such as science—I fundamentally trust the Lord Jesus Christ. I do not fundamentally trust (for example) the Buddha, the prophet Mohammed, or anyone else who claims to speak truth about the world "beyond science." It is inevitable, in fact, that the teaching of Jesus will be the very touchstone by which I respectfully assess how near or far these other thinkers are from the truth.

This includes Jesus's teaching about the literature that I should fundamentally consult in pursuit of the truth—that is, the Scriptures of the NT *and* the Old Testament (OT). It has been a popular idea in some quarters throughout church history that somehow we can have Jesus as our Lord without taking seriously his reading suggestions. As I have argued in numerous books, this is entirely wrong.[33] Christians are obliged by the terms of their discipleship to receive all Holy Scripture as "breathed out by God and profitable for teaching, for reproof, for correction, and for training in righteousness, that the man of God may be complete, equipped for every good work."[34] From a genuinely Christian point of view, it's the entire story thus narrated from Genesis to Revelation, and centered on Jesus Christ, that provides us with our fundamental orientation to what is true. This is the case when it comes to who God is, and what his world is—and it is, of course, also the case when we're thinking about what it means to be a human being.

It follows, then, that the particular argument about the nature of our humanity that I want to develop in this book will be a Christian, biblically grounded argument, rather than some other kind. That is where I shall be "coming from" as I fully engage at the same time with the kinds of truth about our humanness that can be safely and genuinely derived from other sources (such as science).

We begin in Part II with some Fundamentals, and it may help you to have, in advance, a summary of what I'm going to propose in this section of the book. I shall argue that we human beings are "personal matter." We share in common with other creatures that we are created with intentionality in an ordered cosmos by a personal God as irreducibly *material* creatures into whom God breathes the breath of life. We are "like them" in this way. We are at the same time radically different from these other creatures in being divinely animated *personal* matter—"like God," in momentously important ways. As such we are highly exalted, beautiful creatures capable (among other things) of appreciating beauty in ways that other creatures cannot. As image-bearers of the living God, innately dimorphic in nature (male and female), we are called to a particular vocation: to rule over and to look after God's sacred, beautiful creation, in right relationship with God, with each other, and with other creatures. As fallen creatures who are compromised by evil we often fail in these tasks, and all creation suffers as a result; but

God is committed to saving his creation and has acted decisively in Christ to do so. Human beings ought to be hopeful creatures, therefore—not least because in Christ they are promised bodily resurrection and immortality. Personal matter has a glorious future.

Part II is about "personal matter," then. And I propose that all who truly follow Jesus will also make its content "a personal matter," accepting Holy Scripture's teaching about who they are.

This brief description of the biblical idea of humanity may well be quite familiar to you. If so, consider Part II to be "revision" of some important biblical themes in advance of considering their "implications" in Part III. I have written for a broad readership, however, and such a readership will inevitably include those with limited or no previous exposure to these themes. My pre-publication "trials" of my material suggest that such readers may well find it a little challenging, because of the level of biblical detail I'm asking them to absorb, chapter after chapter, in Part II. If you discover, as you proceed, that this describes *you*, I urge you in the words of *The Hitchhiker's Guide to the Galaxy*: "Don't Panic!"[35] Slow and steady is the way to go. And "going" with a group of friends may well be wiser than "going it alone," so that you can help each other with the problems and questions that you may have. Above all, *keep* going. Don't stop because you can't work something out, but park the problem on a mental shelf in a mental cupboard with a label on it saying, "To be picked up later"—and come back to it down the road. Not everything in the following chapters is going to be simple to grasp—but it is *all* important biblical truth that we need to drive deep into our hearts, for our own and others' good. So stick with it! You'll be glad that you did.

PART II

Fundamentals

7

In the Beginning

"In the beginning, God created the heavens and the earth."
(Genesis 1:1)

WE BEGIN AT THE beginning, which Christian theology understands in terms of a creation.[36] In Genesis 1, a person—as it first appears—*creates* the world. The emphasis lies on the *one* living God over against the many gods of the ancient world who are manufactured out of "wood and stone"—"the work of human hands, that neither see, nor hear, nor eat, nor smell."[37] Of course, as the biblical story progresses—and we saw this in the previous chapter—we discover that this one God is at the same time three Persons (Father, Son, and Spirit). So it's problematic to use the word "person" also for God in his oneness. It is better simply to write of "the personal God." To begin again, then: a personal God once created the world. In fact, he still does so in an ongoing way and with our own involvement. For example, he causes "the grass to grow for the livestock and plants for man to cultivate, that he may bring forth food from the earth and wine to gladden the heart of man, oil to make his face shine and bread to strengthen man's heart."[38] We have become increasingly sophisticated in our ability to analyze through science the processes involved in the material aspects of this reality, both historically and in our present world. But how are these processes to be understood?

If we were to ask this question of many of our contemporaries, they would affirm that the processes in question have developed and continue merely "naturally." Moreover, they have developed and continue to do so as a matter of chance, with no guiding hand involved in the whole business. The outcomes of these processes, however, tell strongly against such beliefs. We live in what scientists themselves sometimes refer to as a "finely tuned" universe. It exists as a complicated matrix of what they describe as fundamental physical constants. And if even one of these constants—just one!—were even slightly different than it is, life on earth would be impossible. I suppose that such fine-tuning *could be* the product simply of chance—but this is not a very *plausible* explanation for the way things are. It requires a huge amount of faith in "luck"—the elevation of Luck (now capitalized, in honor of its promotion) almost to status of a god. And it is indeed this kind of almost religious awe that one routinely hears in the voices of scientists struck by the sheer beauty and wonder of the finely tuned cosmos but appealing to chance to account for it. Consider, for example, the following comments made by a cosmologist speaking on the BBC in 2010:

> There are many, many flukey things about the architecture of our solar system. The earth, for example, has a moon which is a comparable size . . . and the effect of that double planet is to stabilize the earth in its spin and make a very stable platform in which things are sort of constant for literally billions of years over the timescales for evolution. So you have a flukey thing that happened early on in the history of the solar system—a particular kind of collision that produced a particular kind of double planet in exactly the right place . . . and there are other examples of similar sorts of things.[39]

There are indeed *many* "examples of similar sorts of things." There are so many of them, in fact, that the universe certainly *looks* as if it has come about by design, with life on earth being its central focus—including human beings. It is hugely improbable that all of this has occurred by chance.

Wishing to avoid "design" as the conclusion that must be drawn from these empirical realities, some people then attempt to deal with the probability issue by positing the existence of multiple universes (a multiverse). Our universe does *look* as if it is designed (they concede), but if we possessed a sufficient number of universes generated over a sufficient amount of time, sooner or later the right kind of universe would naturally "emerge." This is a variant of what is called "infinite monkey theorem," which states that a monkey hitting keys on a keyboard at random for an infinite amount of time will eventually produce (say) the complete works of Shakespeare. These works will *appear* to be "designed," but this will not be true. There is no *evidence*, of course, to support these speculations about a multiverse.[40]

Our biblical authors do not trade in the language of flukes or multiverses. Nor do they agree with those who, conceding that we are indeed living in a cosmos that is truly (and not merely *apparently*) designed, attribute its origins to aliens.[41] "Someone" must have been responsible for creating our world (they agree), but it was most likely ET and his friends. Holy Scripture concurs with the idea that there is a "Someone"—but it does not encourage us to identify this "Someone" with aliens. Whatever the physical processes involved in *how* our cosmos came to be as it is, our biblical authors tell us that we are to understand the outcome as representing the plan of the good God who has made all things (including aliens, if they exist at all). It was this personal God who (among other things) *put* the sun and the moon (and so on) exactly where they are in order to allow life to flourish on the earth. And when we get down to the individual, human level, specifically, this is the Big Idea: that whatever the physical processes involved in bringing a human being into existence, these too are not a matter of chance. We are *created*, each of us, by God. Psalm 139:13 puts it beautifully, taking us where science of itself (via an ultrasound, for example) cannot finally take us: "For you formed my inward parts; you knitted me together in my mother's womb." There *is* natural process, but it is all part of a grand design.

What is a human being? A human being is a creature of the one living God—one of his many creatures, it turns out, each of which finds its own important place in God's world within its own domain. The differing domains are defined in Genesis 1 using the recurring language of "according to their kinds."[42] This is an ancient way of referring to what modern science would call "speciation." Here again we must reckon with both natural process and grand design. However we think about the processes by which the separate species in the world came into existence, there *is* now obviously an order to this world in which such species exist. As Leon Kass puts it:

> In reproduction, like still mates with like, and the progeny are, for the most part, always like their parents in kind. Genealogy may explain lines of descent or kinship of genotypes, but existent organisms behave largely true to their type. . . . Species, however mutable, still make sense.[43]

In Genesis this givenness of "kinds" is all part of the goodness of things. It implies a God-given usefulness and dignity in the case of each member of the various families of creation—including plants and trees—that is not dependent on human beings. All creatures are God's creatures, of whatever "kind" they may be. We see the same "democratic" emphasis emerging in Holy Scripture in other ways as well. For example, in Genesis 1 humans do not have a day of creation to themselves but share the sixth day with the other land creatures, with whom they have a considerable amount in common. Moreover, the seven days of creation do not end with the creation of human beings, but with Sabbath. This day of rest was later observed weekly in ancient Israel, and it is again the *commonality* of all creatures that is emphasized when we read about it, not the usefulness of some for others.[44]

Genesis 2 later goes on to underline this reality, when it portrays humans as being formed from the earth in the same way as the other animals.[45]

So what is a human being? The first of the Christian answers offered to this question is that a human being is one of many creatures intentionally created in an ordered cosmos by a personal God. This creative work is later described in explicitly *Triune*, personal terms by John:

> In the beginning was the Word, and the Word was with God, and the Word was God. He was in the beginning with God. All things were made through him, and without him was not any thing made that was made. In him was life, and the life was the light of men. The light shines in the darkness, and the darkness has not overcome it.[46]

This "Word," at a certain point in history, "became flesh and dwelt among us"—whose glory people saw, "glory as of the only Son from the Father, full of grace and truth."[47] God himself became a human being. We shall return in chapter 18 to the significance of this mind-blowing truth. For the moment, we are thinking about creation as a whole, which is also the emphasis of the apostle Paul in writing about Christ to the church in Colossae: "For by him [Jesus] all things were created, in heaven and on earth, visible and invisible, whether thrones or dominions or rulers or authorities—all things were created through him and for him."[48]

8

Animated Bodies

"The Lord God formed the man of dust from the ground
and breathed into his nostrils the breath of life, and the man
became a living creature." (Genesis 2:7)

THE SECOND CHRISTIAN ANSWER to our core question about humanness also stresses the *connectedness* between humanity and the remainder of God's creation. But at the same time, it begins to make some important *distinctions* among the creatures of the earth.[49] What are human beings? They are intrinsically physical creatures, given life by God, who breathes into each one the breath of life. They are, in a particular way, divinely animated matter.

The key text early in the biblical narrative that addresses this issue is Genesis 2:7. The human being is formed, first, from the dust of the ground, which speaks to the physical nature that we have in common with other creatures. We derive from the same ground as the vegetation ("let the earth sprout vegetation"), the livestock and other animals ("let the earth bring forth . . . livestock and creeping things and beasts of the earth according to their kinds"), and the birds ("now out of the ground the Lord God had formed every beast of the field and every bird of the heavens").[50] Humans are irreducibly *material* beings inhabiting a *material* creation. This was the Creator's purpose.

At the same time, a human is a particular *kind* of physical creature. We belong to that group of creatures into whose nostrils God has "breathed . . . the breath of life," with the result that each one has become "a living creature." Genesis 1:20 uses the same term, "living creature," for sea life, and Genesis 2:19 uses it for land animals and birds. Genesis 7:21–22 speaks of a great flood destroying "everything on the dry land in whose nostrils was the breath of life." This includes "birds, livestock, beasts, [and] all swarming creatures that swarm on the earth," as well as humans. We are like all such creatures in being "animated" in a particular way. All living creatures depend on this ongoing gift of God's breath, and when it is taken away, all of them cease to live. Psalm 104:27–30 tells us about this:

> These [creatures] all look to you, to give them their food in due season. When you give it to them, they gather it up; when you open your hand, they are filled with good things. When you hide your face, they are dismayed; when you take away their breath, they die and return to the dust. When you send forth your breath [my own translation], they are created, and you renew the face of the ground.[51]

We are also like these other physical creatures in being fragile—always right on the edge of "returning to the dust" from which we came. We depend upon our Creator, like them, for *every* breath.

It is especially important to observe what Genesis 2:7 does and does not say about the outcome of this animating process when it comes to human beings in particular—the focus of our concern in this book. As a consequence of the divine inbreathing, the human "became a living creature," or a living "soul" (the Hebrew word *nepeš*).[52] Notice that the human being was not *given* "a soul." This is important because of a longstanding tendency among Christians to think wrongly about our human nature. In this wrong way of thinking, human beings comprise a conglomeration of "bits" (as it were)—most importantly "a body," "a soul," and perhaps also "a spirit." These "bits" are then often assigned different levels of importance in a hierarchy. The body typically fares badly in this ranking process, ending up at the bottom of the hierarchy. So it is that we commonly hear people in Christian circles speaking about the body merely as a temporary home for the eternal soul. The soul, in this narrative, is the important, transcendental "bit" that survives our physical death and flies off to heaven (in the best-case scenario) to be with God.

The U2 song "Yahweh" appears to reflect this view, for example, when it pictures the human soul as a castaway stranded on an island of flesh and bone.[53] The soul is "stranded" in the world of matter and it is, apparently, in need of rescue from it. Beyond this, a considerable number of contemporary worship songs in our churches focus on human souls, as well as spirits and hearts, without ever mentioning the body. The content of these songs often corresponds to the apparent purpose in singing them, which is somehow to transcend our physicality and thus (supposedly) to come closer to God. That is: they frequently appear not only to *celebrate* disembodiment but to be sung *in pursuit of* disembodiment. We'll return in chapters 21 and 46 to this question of worship, and what a genuine Christian anthropology has to say about its nature, purpose, and form.

This negativity towards physical matter in the church, in favor of a more "spiritual" approach to reality, is not a new phenomenon. The apostle Paul was already dealing with the problem in his own time. Writing to Timothy, for example, he finds it necessary to confront those "who forbid marriage and require abstinence from foods that God created to be received with thanksgiving by those who believe and know the truth," reminding his young friend that "everything created by God is good."[54] I'll say more in chapter 41 about the origins of the wrong view of "spirituality" that Paul is opposing here. For the moment let me illustrate a much more biblical perspective, specifically regarding "abstinence from foods," by quoting Robert Farrar Capon's advice to his calorie-watching friend Harry:

> Let him fast until he is free to eat like a true son of Adam, . . . real eating will restore his sense of the festivity of being. Food does not exist merely for the sake of its nutritional value. To see it so is only to knuckle under still further to the desubstantialization of man, to regard not what things are, but what they mean to us—to become in short solemn idolaters spiritualizing what should be loved as matter. A man's daily meal ought to be an exultation over the smack of desirability which lies at the roots of creation. To break real bread is to break the loveless hold of hell upon the world, and, by just that much, to set the secular free.[55]

I repeat and underline: Genesis 2:7 does *not* tell us that a human being is a (spiritual) soul inserted into a (material) body. It does *not* tell us that humanness involves the combination of "a (material) body" and "a (spiritual) soul." Instead, Genesis 2:7 teaches us that, as a result of divine animation, a body *becomes* a living soul. A soul is an animated body—an "alive human," rather than a lifeless corpse. So it is that the term *nepeš* is often used in the OT to refer simply to "the human self/person"—just as the term "soul" is still used in contemporary English to refer to the same. For example, when a 2021 newspaper report described the drowning of many migrants attempting to cross the Mediterranean Sea from Libya, the headline was: "130 Souls Lost at Sea."[56] That is, numerous persons died tragically.

Biblically, we encounter this use of *nepeš*, for instance, in Leviticus 17:10 and 23:30, where God says: "I shall set my face against any 'soul' [person] who eats blood" (my own translation) and "whoever does any work on that very day, that person ['soul'] I will destroy from among his people." We see the same kind of use of the word when the authors of the Psalms engage in "soul-talk." For example:

> Bless the LORD, O my soul, and all that is within me, bless his
> holy name! Bless the LORD, O my soul, and forget not all his
> benefits, who forgives all your iniquity, who heals all your dis-
> eases, who redeems your life from the pit, who crowns you with
> steadfast love and mercy, who satisfies you with good so that
> your youth is renewed like the eagle's.[57]

Here the writer exhorts *himself* to praise God for everything he has received from God, including *bodily* benefits such as healing from disease
and relief from hunger. Indeed, it is of the entire human being possessing
such *needs* that the term *nepeš* is most often used in the OT—for example,
the "soul" who is hungry or thirsty.[58] Hans Walter Wolff summarizes the
situation in this way:

> If we survey the wide context in which the *nepeš* of man and
> man as *nepeš* can be observed, we see above all man marked out
> as the individual living being who has neither acquired, nor can
> preserve, life by himself, but is eager for life, spurred on by vital
> desire[;] . . . *nepeš* shows man primarily in his need and desire.[59]

This is only one aspect of an important general truth about OT anthropology: that although various dimensions of the human being can be
differentiated for particular purposes in Hebrew thinking, these are only
"aspects" of an entire, integrated organism. This is such a crucial matter
when it comes to accurate Bible-reading that I'm going to spend the entirety of the next chapter talking about it. If you don't need further convincing
on this point, and you don't like word studies, feel free to fast-forward to
chapter 10. Otherwise, proceed in the normal manner to chapter 9. In fact,
I recommend that you do, because chapter 9 concludes with resurrection,
which is a truly happy ending.

9

Whole Persons

"The afflicted shall eat and be satisfied; those who seek him shall praise the LORD! May your hearts live forever!" (Psalm 22:26)

A SUPERFICIAL READING OF the OT—which all true Christians receive as "breathed out by God and profitable for teaching, for reproof, for correction, and for training in righteousness"—might well lead us astray in our thinking about the "composition" of a human being. It might cause us to think that a human comprises various independent "parts," such as "body" and "soul."[60] In reality, this is not what the OT teaches at all. The reality is that our biblical authors thought of the various "parts" of the human being only as aspects of one entire, integrated organism. In the previous chapter we established that the word "soul," for example, often characterizes the entire human being from the perspective of need and desire. In the present chapter I want to introduce you to other examples of a similar kind.

We begin with the Hebrew term *bāśār*.[61] This word *can* refer simply to the "flesh" on animal and human bones.[62] Consider, however, Psalm 56:

> In God, whose word I praise, in God I trust; I shall not be afraid.
> What can flesh do to me? All day long they injure my cause; all
> their thoughts are against me for evil. They stir up strife, they
> lurk; they watch my steps. . . . This I know, that God is for me.
> In God, whose word I praise, in the LORD, whose word I praise,
> in God I trust; I shall not be afraid. What can man do to me?[63]

The poet commits to trusting in God and not being afraid of his enemies, first of all asking the question, "What can flesh do to me?" Later he returns to his commitment, but he asks the question differently: "What can man [a human being] do to me?" In this psalm, "flesh" refers to humanness. It does so in terms of what Wolff calls "man in his infirmity."[64] Animated bodies humans may be, but we are weak and frail when compared to God, who is

39

worthy of our "trust." Jeremiah 17:5 equates "flesh" with humanness in the same way in making a similar point:

> Cursed is the man who trusts in man and makes flesh his strength, whose heart turns away from the LORD. He is like a shrub in the desert, and shall not see any good come. He shall dwell in the parched places of the wilderness, in an uninhabited salt land. Blessed is the man who trusts in the LORD, whose trust is the LORD.[65]

This weakness in human beings extends to the moral life, for which we must all sooner or later account before God, who once "determined to make an end of all flesh, for the earth is filled with violence through them."[66] The fact is that we are prone to being overcome by evil, which necessitates (once again) trust in God rather than ourselves: "O you who hear prayer, to you shall all flesh come. When iniquities prevail against me, you atone for our transgressions."[67]

Assuredly these texts do *not* intend to suggest that it's our bodies *rather than* our souls that indulge in evildoing. It is, rather, entire persons in their weakness (their "flesh"). In the same way, it's as whole persons in Genesis 2 that a male and a female human in their individual fragility come together in strengthening marriage to be "one flesh."[68] Their "souls" are not omitted from this union just because only flesh is explicitly mentioned in the text. Nor indeed are the bones discounted that are mentioned immediately beforehand.[69] Rather, in Wolff's words, "different parts of the body enclose with their essential functions" the one, entire human organism that is being described.[70]

We encounter the same phenomenon when we turn to the Hebrew *rûaḥ*, which is often translated into English as "spirit." Here is an example: "in the morning [Pharaoh's] spirit was troubled."[71] But it's important to know that this word refers more broadly in the OT to moving air—often to the wind. And the "wind" or "moving air" in a human being is, of course, her breath. Consider Isaiah 42, where God "gives breath [*nǝšāmâ*] to the people on [the earth] and *rûaḥ* to those who walk in it."[72] Just as in the case of "soul," this language is about animation. In Job 12:10, in fact, it is *nepeš* rather than *nǝšāmâ* that is used in parallel with *ruach*. In God's hand lies "the life ('soul') of every living thing and the breath of all mankind." As we saw in our previous chapter, it is when God provides this breath that his creatures are created, and they die when it's taken away.[73] And then God is also envisaged in many texts as breathing still more of this vitality into human beings or stirring up what is already present. In this way, God endows them, at least for a time, with various kinds of notable power, including great determination of will.[74] Conversely, "breath" can be thought of as diminishing temporarily, as when the Queen of Sheba is rendered "breathless" in the face of Solomon's splendor, or when King Ahab retires to his bed in a bad mood.[75]

The third Hebrew term we need to consider is *lēb* (or *ləbab*), often translated "heart." The heart's "essential activities" (in the words of Wolff) "are in the Bible mental and spiritual in kind."[76] This may come as a surprise if you are accustomed to associate the heart primarily with feelings and desires. The OT *can* also employ the language of "heart" to describe the human being as an emotional, desiring creature, experiencing (for example) joy and grief. As such, *lēb* is closely related to "soul" and "breath," as in the following example: "A joyful heart is good medicine, but a crushed spirit dries up the bones."[77] But predominantly the focus of heart-language is the human as an intellectual, rational being. The task of the heart is to know and to understand: "the heart of him who has understanding seeks knowledge."[78] It is King Solomon's "breadth of mind"—in Hebrew, his "breadth of heart"—that allows him to write all the proverbs and songs mentioned in 1 Kings 4, and to engage in the astonishing scholarship described therein.[79] Conversely, the person without "heart" is a stupid person: "I passed by the field of a sluggard, by the vineyard of a man lacking sense"—that is, a person lacking *lēb*.[80] In other words, "heart" in the OT "includes everything that we ascribe to the head and the brain—power of perception, reason, understanding, insight, consciousness, memory, knowledge, reflection, judgment, sense of direction, discernment."[81] These are the *aspects* of our humanity that are in view when *lēb* is deployed. For here, too, we are not dealing with a discrete "part" of the human. We are dealing with a window onto the whole self. This is why Psalm 22 can express the hope that the "hearts" of the afflicted may "live forever"—which is simply to hope that *those people* will live forever.[82]

Much more could be said about the significance of OT references to various aspects of the human person, but for our present purposes no more is needed. All that I must add here is that the NT approaches the matter similarly.[83] The Greek word *soma* refers in the NT not only to the physical body but to the whole human self. The word *sarx*, meaning "flesh," is sometimes synonymous with *soma*, and speaks of human transience and sinfulness. The term *psyche*, often translated as "soul," has in mind the human as a living being. The word *pneuma* ("spirit") sometimes overlaps with *psyche* in referring to the inner self. The term *kardia* ("heart") can be used of emotion and volition, although *nous* is the Greek term that more commonly focuses attention on the human as a conscious, rational being. All in all (in the words of J. Stafford Wright), "man is seen [in the NT] as a whole being, and whatever touches one part affects the whole."[84] Biblically, we are—in the terminology of modern science—"psychosomatic entities."

All of this explains why a truly Christian faith cannot possibly regard the body as a merely temporary home for the eternal soul—the transcendental "bit" that survives our physical death and flies off to heaven. Holy Scripture does of course envisage an "in-between" phase in our existence, between physical death and the consummation of all things, in which our "selves" are temporarily "away from the body and at home with the Lord," having "fallen asleep in Christ."[85] But orthodox Christian faith expects as our *final* consummation a *bodily* resurrection—the resurrection of the whole person. We shall return to this important "matter" (in both senses) in chapter 19. For the moment let's just remind ourselves of how the apostle Paul articulates our Christian hope in writing to his fellow-Christians in Rome:

> If the Spirit of him who raised Jesus from the dead dwells in you, he who raised Christ Jesus from the dead will also give life to your mortal bodies through his Spirit who dwells in you. . . . For we know that the whole creation has been groaning together in the pains of childbirth until now. And not only the creation, but we ourselves, who have the firstfruits of the Spirit, groan inwardly as we wait eagerly for adoption as sons, the redemption of our bodies.[86]

10

Image Bearers

*"So God created man in his own image, in the
image of God he created him; male and female
he created them." (Genesis 1:27)*

So what is a human being?[87] The first Christian answer is: one of many creatures created with intentionality in an ordered cosmos by a personal God. The
second is: an irreducibly physical creature given life by God who breathes into
each one the breath of life. Human beings are, in a particular way, divinely
animated matter. Together these two answers emphasize what *connects* humanity with the remainder of God's creation, while also beginning to make
some important *distinctions* among the creatures of the earth. Our third answer now adds a further, *radical distinction* between humanity and *all* other
creatures. Human beings are divinely animated *personal* matter.

The biblical language that first introduces this idea is found in Genesis
1:26–27. "Then God said, 'Let us make man in our image, after our likeness. . . .' So God created man in his own image, in the image of God he
created him; male and female he created them." What does this mean?

In order to understand this language, we must reckon first with the
numerous temples that dotted the landscape of the ancient Near East—the
world in which our biblical texts were first written. These were sanctuaries
built on what their builders considered to be sacred space, and from them
flowed (it was imagined) the very waters of life that nourished society at
large. As such these temples "mirrored" the larger cosmic reality that people
believed in; they gave architectural expression to their builders' beliefs about
the nature of the cosmos as a whole. That was a cosmos inhabited, of course,
by many gods, some of whom were particularly important to this or that
set of worshippers. They viewed temples as the palaces of the particularly
important gods who had taken up residence in them.

And now we come to "images." The presence of divinity in each temple was expressed by way of a manufactured statue or "image" of a god. Long-established rituals invested such images with divine "life." In this process, the deity magically came to inhabit the temple-image. The image would then be led out by the priests to a garden by a river to enjoy its new power. The idea was that by such means a particular god would come to find "rest" in a particular temple, in a particular city-state. Through his "image" each god's person and presence would be mediated to the city-state, expressing in this local way the divinity's overall participation in the governance of the cosmos, with its outcomes in peace and security.[88]

Obviously, biblical faith turns its face resolutely against this way of understanding the cosmos. It disputes the real existence of the many gods of the ancient Near East, characterizing their images as merely human artifacts of wood and stone (chapter 7).[89] These images, our biblical authors assure us, are as dead as the gods they allegedly embody. This is why the OT forbids the worship of the many gods, including their imaged forms. True divinity cannot (usually) be represented in any created thing. This is also why the ancient Israelites were instructed not to "make for yourself a carved image, or any likeness of anything that is in heaven above, or that is in the earth beneath, or that is in the water under the earth."[90] Consequently, Israelite temples built and furnished in conformity with God's commands were "aniconic." They did not contain any "icon" (artifact) designed to "image" even the one, living, creator God. Therefore, no image sat on the cherubim-throne in the Holy of Holies in the Jerusalem temple. God's presence there was "image-less."

To sum up so far: in biblical thinking, what is created cannot image the one, true, living God—generally speaking. And now we return to what we can now perceive clearly, for the first time, as the astonishing exception. There *are* "gods" in the world, in a way. There *are* legitimate, true images of God in the cosmos. They are human beings!

These images, too, inhabit a "temple," metaphorically speaking—for that is how our biblical authors invite us in Genesis 1 and 2 to view creation itself. Creation is, for example, a sanctuary lit by "lights," just like the Israelite tabernacle (the portable temple prior to Solomon's time).[91] After its construction God "rests" in it. It is a garden-like sanctuary (Genesis 2) with its entrance on the east side, just like the Jerusalem temple. This entrance is guarded by the "cherubim" who appear elsewhere in the OT only in connection *with* the Jerusalem temple and the tabernacle.[92] The tree of life in this garden is represented in the tabernacle by the branched lampstand with its floral motifs—and so on.[93] Creation is sacred space—a temple-cosmos.

It is into this cosmic "temple" that God, in Genesis 1–2, places his image, male and female in nature. Having fashioned it from the clay of the
ground, he has animated it with divine breath, just like ancient temple images in general. But it is this human creature alone who, in biblical thinking,
can be said to be "like" God. In the words of one author:

> Against the canopy of space and the topography of earth—beat-
> ing, swarming and lumbering with fertile and fantastic life—
> Adam stands in unique relationship with God. . . . No stone or
> wood chiseled into a godling's image, "the Adam" in two . . .
> is an animated, walking, talking and relating mediation of the
> essence, will and work of the sovereign creator God. As living
> image of the living God, Adam bears a relationship to God like
> that of child to parent.[94]

Whereas creatures in general—animated or not—cannot image the living
God at all, God *can* be imaged by humans. Insofar as there are any "gods"
in the world, then, human beings are those "gods." In one movement Genesis thereby elevates humanity to an extraordinarily high position in the
hierarchy of creation. We are no longer *caretakers* of a divine image in a
temple (as ancient priests would have been). We are *ourselves* divine images in a temple.

Psalm 8 speaks about this same reality without explicitly using the
language of "image." "What is man [a human being] that you are mindful
of him," the Psalmist asks, "and the son of man that you care for him?"[95]
He is looking up at the heavens, which an ancient contemporary from
Babylon would have understood as the home of the mightiest gods—especially the sun and the moon. The Psalmist does not hold this opinion.
Nevertheless, the heavens are still to him a wondrous sight, and as such
they raise questions about human significance. But then he remembers
that "you have made him a little lower than God, and crowned him with
glory and honor."[96] That is, the human being is a king crowned with two of
the attributes of God himself.[97] Each and every human person possesses
the status of *divinity and royalty* in creation.

So although it's quite correct that as "biblical people" we should stress
the ways in which human beings are "like" other creatures—creatures in
general, and animated creatures in particular—we need to do much more.
If we are to begin to tell the whole story about our humanness, we also
need to stress quite different realities. And here metaphysics goes where
physics cannot take us. Theology goes where biological science cannot
go—even though the latter reveals a substantial amount about all kinds of
human uniqueness. Human beings are "like God" as no other creature is,

Holy Scripture teaches us. We are not only *animated* matter, but *personal* matter—and as such, we are highly exalted creatures. That is what a Christian anthropology compels us to say.

It is this same image of God that is fractured, but not destroyed, in our present human experience (as we shall see in chapter 17). It is now in the process of being restored in Christ, who is himself the very image of God (chapter 18).[98] Christians in becoming saved are "predestined to be conformed to the image of [God's] Son, in order that he might be the first-born among many brothers"—exchanging "the image of the man of dust" for "the image of the man of heaven."[99] In putting on this "new self," we find ourselves "being renewed in knowledge after the image of its creator."[100] We were created as highly exalted creatures, and we remain so now. In the mercy of God, we shall also be exalted creatures in the future.

11

Beautiful

*"And out of the ground the LORD God made to
spring up every tree that is pleasant to the sight
and good for food." (Genesis 2:9)*

A CONSIDERABLE AMOUNT OF ink has been spilled over the centuries pressing further into the question of how, exactly, human beings are, and are not, "like" God.[101] Like the personal God, the human person possesses the capacity to reason and imagine, for example. We are able to make moral choices through free will, rather than simply being driven by instinct and environment. And so on. Other animals are not so endowed. But according to Holy Scripture, humans are also very *unlike* God in all kinds of ways. Significantly, many of these are precisely the ways in which ancient peoples believed, to the contrary, that the gap between humanity and divinity is small. Not at all, Scripture teaches us; it is *large*.

For example, like human beings these ancient gods possessed an anatomy that allowed for sexual intercourse and childbearing. They possessed human-like inclinations, desires, and needs, as well as limitations, and they followed similar daily routines. They were certainly not morally superior to human beings. In short, human beings were "like" these ancient gods on quite a grand scale. So it was believed.

In biblical faith, conversely, humans are like God in a number of highly significant and consequential ways, but they are also radically *unlike* God in many *other* ways. For example, the living God does not engage in sexual activity, procreate, or give birth. He neither slumbers nor sleeps. He knows neither shame nor fear. He *is* morally superior to human beings; for example, "God is not a man, that he should lie."[102] The gulf thus fixed between God and the gods in Holy Scripture is vast. God is incomparably God: "O LORD, God of Israel, there is no God like you in heaven above or on earth below."[103] An enormous gulf separates God from the gods, and a similarly enormous gulf separates the divine from the human, even though we bear God's image.

At least one aspect of our image-bearing nature has been under-emphasized in a considerable amount of Christian theology throughout the ages, and it's worth pausing to consider it here. It is our human capacity for comprehending beauty. We encountered this already in the previous chapter when considering Psalm 8. Here the author contemplates in wonderment "your heavens, the work of your fingers, the moon and the stars, which you have set in place." But well before that, in Genesis 1 and 2, it's already clear that among other things the biblical story of creation is a narrative about emergent beauty.

God speaks into being the wondrous world that we inhabit, and it is in every respect "good."[104] What does "good" mean? Genesis 2, in particular, helps us to see that this is not simply a matter of pragmatics, but also of aesthetics. For in its ninth verse we learn that the trees in God's glorious garden are "pleasant to the sight" *as well as* "good for food." Jesus later proclaims that "man shall not live by bread alone, but by every word that comes from the mouth of God."[105] But it's already true in Genesis that human beings need other things beyond food (however wonderful and beyond-pragmatic food itself may be). We are created for beauty, and indeed we are formed *as* beautiful. We are fashioned in the image of God and we reflect, therefore, the divine beauty and glory. From the beginning we have been beautiful, and we have always needed beauty as well as bread. There is therefore no embarrassment among our biblical authors in drawing attention to beauty, which they do frequently.[106] This is only one aspect of the marvelousness of creation upon which Psalm 8 reflects.

It is the beauty of creation that is also the driving theme of an entire chapter like Song of Songs 2.[107] Here the beauty of springtime, specifically, is the theme, as life bursts afresh from the ground and all of God's creatures become newly active. The poet sees it all—flowers and fruit trees, mountains and hills, deer and doves—and he invites us to join him in marvelling at it all. The two human lovers at the heart of his description identify themselves with this wider creation. They affirm each other using images drawn from the flora and the fauna that they see around them, each competing with the other to find ways of praising the other's beauty:

> The voice of my beloved! Behold, he comes, leaping over the mountains, bounding over the hills. My beloved is like a gazelle or a young stag. Behold, there he stands behind our wall, gazing through the windows, looking through the lattice. My beloved speaks and says to me: "Arise, my love, my beautiful one, and

come away, for behold, the winter is past; the rain is over and gone. The flowers appear on the earth, the time of singing has come, and the voice of the turtledove is heard in our land."

There is in all of this no "unease" with beauty of the kind that has marked certain strands of Christian thinking throughout the ages. Unsurprisingly, these are the very strands that have tended to denigrate matter in relation to "spirit" in general. Our biblical authors themselves recognize, of course, that physical beauty is transient and vulnerable to destruction, like everything that is created. Beauty should not blind us to our mortality, such that we live foolish lives.[108] In particular, it's entirely possible to be beautiful but to lack important qualities of character. It's possible even to neglect the *development* of character because of an attachment only to the outward appearance of things.[109] Beauty is not to be valued above godliness. It is indeed not to be valued above those many other attributes or gifts that make up the human person.[110]

With all of that said, however, we are created beautiful and *for* beauty. We should certainly not divinize it, allowing it to become more important to us than it should. Beauty should not become an idol. Yet at the same time we should not despise nor dismiss it. Received as a gift from God and set in the context of all that is good in God's creation, beauty enhances our lives and becomes itself a signpost directing us to the God whose own personhood it reflects.

So the image-bearing human in a Christian anthropology is not only someone who possesses the capacity to reason and imagine, or to make moral choices through free will. She is also one possessing a capacity for the recognition and enjoyment of beauty and aesthetic experience. We shall not find any tiger, beautiful in itself, reflecting on the beauty of tigers. We shall not find a killer whale gazing in awe at the glory of the most recent sunset, or pondering the majesty of the music of Johann Sebastian Bach. Our human capacity to enjoy and experience beauty is something that belongs to image-bearers alone. In the words of C. S. Lewis—although he was distinguishing between humans and angels, rather than humans and animals, when he wrote this: "Yet here, within this tiny, charmed interior, this parlour of the brain, their Maker shares with living men some secrets in a privacy forever ours, not theirs."[111]

Unsurprisingly, then, the destination toward which our journey with God is taking us is also stunningly beautiful:

Then I saw a new heaven and a new earth, for the first heaven and the first earth had passed away, and the sea was no more. And I saw the holy city, new Jerusalem, coming down out of

heaven from God, prepared as a bride adorned for her husband. And I heard a loud voice from the throne saying, "Behold, the dwelling place of God is with man. He will dwell with
them, and they will be his people, and God himself will be with
them as their God." . . . And he carried me away in the Spirit
to a great, high mountain, and showed me the holy city Jerusalem coming down out of heaven from God, having the glory
of God, its radiance like a most rare jewel, like a jasper, clear
as crystal. . . . The wall was built of jasper, while the city was
pure gold, like clear glass. The foundations of the wall of the
city were adorned with every kind of jewel. . . . Then the angel
showed me the river of the water of life, bright as crystal, . . .
also, on either side of the river, the tree of life with its twelve
kinds of fruit, yielding its fruit each month.[112]

Beauty is here to stay. It is a permanent aspect of the cosmos that God has
made, and that he will make again at the end of time. It's just that there will
be a lot *more* beauty in the future—for "glory" has differing degrees.[113]

12

Rulers

"Be fruitful and multiply and fill the earth and subdue
it, and have dominion over the fish of the sea and over
the birds of the heavens and over every living thing
that moves on the earth." (Genesis 1:28)

THE CLARIFICATIONS IN THE two previous chapters concerning what it means, and does not mean, that human beings are divine image-bearers are important.[114] It is arguable, however, that this interest in delving deeply into the "composition" of image-bearers has sometimes distracted attention from the immediate interest of our biblical authors in describing their creation. Their immediate interest, in Genesis 1 and 2, is to tell us what image-bearers are created to *do*. Genesis 1:26 and 1:28 are the first verses to address this question—the question of human vocation. It is not surprising, in view of the reference in Psalm 8 to humans being "crowned," that this vocation is described in Genesis 1 in terms of "dominion," as well as "subduing": "Be fruitful and multiply and fill the earth and subdue it, and have dominion over the fish of the sea and over the birds of the heavens and over every living thing that moves on the earth."

These key words echo language elsewhere in the OT concerning kingship. "Dominion" is the language of government—of kings ruling their subjects, and of other kinds of ruling as well.[115] "Subdue" is the language of conquest—something in which ancient kings were typically deeply interested.[116] So human beings are to do in creation what kings generally do in their own domains: to rule and to subdue.

We must be careful here, however, not to read this language as legitimating an aggressive and exploitative human approach to the remainder of creation. What did the vocation of kings in the ancient world actually involve? Among other things, the job description included this: it was above all the king who was tasked with ensuring the well-being of his subjects and with delivering justice to all of them.[117] Therefore, to picture all human beings as "kings" over the earth in Genesis 1 is not to imply that humanity has permission to exploit and plunder the earth. After all, the kings in question are ruling and subduing *as image-bearing representatives of* God. This is the personal God who is alone truly King, but who then delegates this rule to his image-bearers. Genesis does not have in view, then, absolute, unrestrained power, with no moral boundaries, that can be used just as human beings want. Humanity's responsibility is instead to exercise "dominion" on behalf of the God who created the world in which they live. The character of such dominion is described in Psalm 72, whose opening verses express the following hope for Davidic kingship:

> May he judge your people with righteousness, and your poor with justice! Let the mountains bear prosperity for the people, and the hills, in righteousness! May he defend the cause of the poor of the people, give deliverance to the children of the needy, and crush the oppressor![118]

The broader context of this kind of ruling is this: "The earth is the LORD's and the fullness thereof, the world and those who dwell therein."[119]

This human "rule," then, must necessarily take account of the nature of creation at large as we have encountered it in our earlier chapters. All creatures, whatever "kind" they may be, are the creatures of *God*. Each one possesses its own God-given usefulness and dignity, independently of human beings—even though the latter have their own important role to play in the cosmos. Consider further along these lines Psalm 104, which begins with a vision of the ongoing kingship of God who is "clothed with splendor and majesty [Hebrew *hādār*]" (verse 1):[120]

> O LORD my God, you are very great! You are clothed with splendor and majesty, covering yourself with light as with a garment, stretching out the heavens like a tent. He lays the beams of his chambers on the waters; he makes the clouds his chariot; he rides on the wings of the wind; he makes his messengers winds, his ministers a flaming fire.[121]

This is the rule under which all image-bearers rule. This is the divine "majesty" that is merely reflected in the "honor" (also Hebrew *hādār*) of the human creatures who are made in God's image in Psalm 8.[122] After all, merely-image-bearing kings do not have cloud, wind, and lightning as their servants. They have never stretched out "the heavens like a tent," nor built a palace for themselves above the celestial waters.

Verses 5–13 go on then to describe God's sovereign control over the waters, without which the earth could not exist at all. The next section (verses 14–23) develops the idea that God looks after the needs of all his animal creation. Both kinds of animal—human and non-human—are important; each one finds its own place in God's creation. The "places" are various, and each is suitable for its own inhabitants. God not only provides a suitable environment for *humans* on the earth, but he looks after *all* his creatures in this way. And all *earthbound* creatures also benefit from his arrangements in the *heavens*, where he has "made the moon to mark the seasons, and the sun knows when to go down."[123] It is in the consequent cycles of light and darkness, both of them good in their own ways, that all of God's creatures flourish. Human beings do their work in the full light of day, but the evening and the nighttime are important for other creatures.[124] This is not a world that has been designed, either in space or in time, with only the interests of human beings in mind. God looks after *all* his creatures, including the sea-creatures.[125]

It is of course not *only* that each creature possesses God-given useful-ness and dignity, independently of human beings. It is also that—and here we are circling back to our previous chapter—creation at large reflects, like human beings, the splendor and majesty (the *beauty*) of its Creator. This is something that clear-sighted image-bearers well understand, and it leads them to praise—as in Psalm 147. Here the poet exhorts his readers to "sing to the LORD with thanksgiving; make melody to our God on the lyre!" Why is that? "He covers the heavens with clouds; he prepares rain for the earth; he makes grass grow on the hills. He gives to the beasts their food, and to the young ravens that cry."[126] God also "gives snow like wool; he scatters frost like ashes. He hurls down his crystals of ice like crumbs."[127] The cosmos that the human king is to "rule" is something of extraordinary beauty, reflecting who God himself is. Remember Psalm 19: "The heavens declare the glory of God, and the sky above proclaims his handiwork."[128] The kingdom's in-habitants are all of them, in their own way, worshippers of the Creator, as Psalm 148 make clear. They are worshippers *alongside* kings, princes, and rulers of all kinds.[129] These worshippers include "great sea creatures and all deeps, fire and hail, snow and mist, stormy wind. . . . Mountains and all hills, fruit trees and all cedars! Beasts and all livestock, creeping things and flying birds!" It stands to reason that the character of any person's rule will be (or ought to be) dictated by his understanding of the nature of his subjects. In the present case, the subjects are co-worshippers ("let them praise the name of the LORD") of a God whose "name alone is exalted."[130]

It is just such an understanding of "dominion" that followers of Christ are obliged to embrace—those who take Jesus as their supreme example when it comes to what kingship looks like:

> Have this mind among yourselves, which is yours in Christ Jesus, who, though he was in the form of God, did not count equality with God a thing to be grasped, but emptied himself, by taking the form of a servant, being born in the likeness of men. And being found in human form, he humbled himself by becoming obedient to the point of death, even death on a cross. Therefore God has highly exalted him and bestowed on him the name that is above every name, so that at the name of Jesus every knee should bow, in heaven and on earth and under the earth, and every tongue confess that Jesus Christ is Lord, to the glory of God the Father.[131]

Here is a king who willingly lays down his prerogatives in order to save his subjects from evil. He is a servant-king, "obedient to the point of death" in suffering *with* his creation rather than coolly observing it from a distance. Our own calling as his followers is to "suffer with him in order that we may also be glorified with him."[132] We are explicitly not to imitate "the rulers of the gentiles" in lording it over any of our subjects. In fact, "whoever would be great among you must be your servant, and whoever would be first among you must be your slave, even as the Son of Man came not to be served but to serve, and to give his life as a ransom for many."[133]

Our cosmos is sacred, created, beautiful space for whose wellbeing our Creator holds its image-bearing rulers accountable—servant-kings who are co-worshippers in creation. That is what biblical "dominion" entails.

13

Priests

"The LORD God took the man and put him in the garden of Eden
to work it and keep it." (Genesis 2:15)

IF YOU STILL HARBOUR any doubts about my reading of Genesis 1's "dominion" in the previous chapter, then what Genesis 2 adds to the biblical understanding of the human vocation should dispel them.[134] For whereas Genesis 1 presents the image-bearer as a ruler, Genesis 2 uses a quite different metaphor. The key text here is the fifteenth verse, and we'll get to it in a moment. But it's worth pausing first to notice something important about all of Genesis 2:4–25 when compared to Genesis 1:1—2:3.

Genesis 1:1—2:3 emphasizes the importance of human beings in the cosmos by placing them last in a narrative sequence that ends prior to the final day of rest. This sequence ends with their particularly astonishing creation: they are unparalleled in their nature upon the earth. That is, Genesis 1:1—2:3 describe creation as a number of creative steps that rise to a high-point (an *apex*) in the creation of humanity. Everything else prepares the way for human beings.

Genesis 2:4–25, on the other hand, describe creation as something that cannot function properly without human beings at the *center*. It is only when a gardener exists, placed by God in his garden, that there can be other created realities such as shrubs and "plants" (Genesis 2:5). This second word, "plants," refers to edible plants or to those that provide food. Genesis 2 helps us to see in a particularly clear way, then, that humanity is created *for* the rest of creation—to facilitate its optimal functioning. Our special, created nature brings with it important responsibilities in respect of the remainder of creation.

So what exactly is the human being created to do? Here we must get a hold of the idea of a "priest" in OT thinking—a person called to serve God and to pass on his blessings to others, as in Numbers 6: "The LORD bless you

55

and keep you; the LORD make his face to shine upon you and be gracious to you; the LORD lift up his countenance upon you and give you peace."[135] A central aspect of this priestly role was to look after the tabernacle, where the Lord had made himself especially "present" in Israel's midst. The priest was to "guard" (or "keep") various things (Hebrew *šāmar*) and to "minister" (or "serve," Hebrew *ʿābad*) at this sacred site.[136] This is precisely the language of Genesis 2:15 concerning *all human beings* in relation to God's *cosmic* temple. This Genesis verse tells us that God made humans and put them in his garden in order "to work it and keep it ['take care of it']" (*ʿābad* and *šāmar*).[137] In Genesis 2, then, the language of kings gives way to the language of priests, who are called to protect the earth as they "work" it (*ʿābad*). This verb *ʿābad* can also mean to "serve" a ruler, or indeed to serve God.[138] So in Genesis 2 the ruler of Genesis 1 serves the earth that he rules, as he fulfils a sacred task—like a priest in a temple. He is indeed a servant-king, passing on God's blessing to his kingdom.

It is even clearer now that the dominion granted to human beings in Genesis 1 is certainly not about *lording it over* the remainder of creation. It is about *looking after* creation—imitating God in his providential care for the earth and its creatures. In the Genesis story itself Noah provides our earliest extensive picture of this care. He is the righteous conservationist who preserves all kinds of life from destruction in a great flood. And he does this, of course, at the command of the God who cares for his entire creation:

> Of every living thing of all flesh you shall bring two of every sort into the ark to keep them alive with you. They shall be male and female. Of the birds according to their kinds, and of the animals according to their kinds, of every creeping thing of the ground, according to its kind, two of every sort shall come in to you to keep them alive.[139]

So it is unsurprising that when we later turn to the NT we discover that the entirety of creation still belongs to God: "From him and through him and to him are all things, the earth . . . and everything in it."[140] Into this world for which God still cares comes the person (Jesus Christ) in whom human image-bearing reaches its highest point—"the image of the invisible God," in whom "all things hold together."[141] The redemption that this image-bearer initiates is naturally creation-wide in its scope: "God was pleased . . . through him to reconcile to himself *all things* [my emphasis], whether on earth or in heaven, making peace by the blood of his cross."[142] And the entire non-human creation now awaits "in eager expectation" this cosmic redemption.[143] There's nothing in any of this material to suggest that God has now ceased (in NT times) to care for all of creation. We should not expect there to be. There's also nothing here that implies that God's image-bearers have now been relieved of their duty to look after the whole of creation on God's behalf.

It is in this context that we must now return to the idea of "subduing" in Genesis 1. For now it's possible to understand what this language does and does not signify. It does not signify a human approach to the remainder of creation that is antithetical to serving and conserving. However, it *does* underline an important reality: that the creation described in Genesis 1–2 is not viewed, biblically, as a "finished product." It's not understood as a kind of spa utopia complete with sunbeds for its inhabitants, in which the only human work that needs to be done involves lifting one's gin and tonic from the table to one's mouth. Biblically, creation is not "perfect," as self-indulgent humans might measure perfection. It is instead "good," as measured by God. And this "good" creation is dynamic, rather than static.

In fact, it is a garden that requires for its flourishing considerable, on-going gardening work, carried out by the human gardener who has been delegated that task. This work necessarily includes "subduing" of various kinds, as humans go about their God-ordained business—the business of being fruitful, multiplying, and spreading out over the entire planet.[144] To some extent, jungle and forest must be cleared, and then contained, in order for human settlement to occur. Ground must also be cleared for agriculture—for the farming that emerges in the biblical story under the blessing of God, who guarantees "seedtime and harvest."[145] Farmers must then pay ongoing attention to their fields, since planting alone, without weeding ("subduing"), will not bring success. And "protecting" domestic livestock naturally requires the "subduing" of wild carnivores such as lions and bears.

In sum, there is work to be done in pursuit of what is good for creation (including for human beings). And this work brings *change*. It is part of our createdness in God's image that we should imitate him *both* in his providential care for creatures *and* in his ordering creativity. So it is that, in the aftermath of God's guarantee of seedtime and harvest, the conservationist Noah becomes a successful "man of the soil"—albeit that he does not handle his success very well.[146]

Subduing is necessarily *part* of what the human governance of the planet requires. However, only a reader who is not paying attention to the overall Genesis context, or indeed to the Psalms, could possibly imagine (as some have done) that this makes biblical faith "anthropocentric" in nature (see further chapter 49). Biblical faith decidedly does *not* encourage anthropocentricism. But neither does it diminish the importance of the human being in maintaining on the earth what the Bible calls "shalom" (Hebrew *šālôm*)—"flourishing."[147]

This sets our biblical tradition at odds, of course, with some contemporary ways of thinking about what is "good" for our planet—ways of thinking that hold that the removal of the human would solve "the problem with the planet." Yet at all the Earth Summits ever convened the delegates have been members of only one species. For among all of God's creatures, it's only human beings who are capable of drastically changing the world for good or for ill. It's also only human beings who might be anxious about doing so. And here science and Christian theology once again converge. "Dominion" is not only a theological category, but also a biological reality. The only question is, how are human beings going to exercise dominion, and why? Will it be exercised in line with the unbiblical views of the seventeenth-century natural philosopher (scientist) Francis Bacon, "who hijacked the Genesis text to authorize the project of scientific knowledge and technological exploitation whose excesses have given us the ecological crisis"?[148] Or will it be exercised in line with the considerably more truly Christian thinking of someone like the sixteenth-century French theologian John Calvin, who understood that human "dominion" is not an excuse for plundering the earth, and who taught that every human being must "regard himself as the steward of God in all things that he possesses."[149]

14

Community with God

"And they heard the sound of the LORD God walking in the garden in the cool of the day. . . . The LORD God called to the man . . . ." (Genesis 3:8–9)

IT'S ALREADY CLEAR FROM our earlier chapters that, biblically, "no man is an island"—that human beings are created as social creatures, wired for relationship, rather than as isolated individuals.[150] In the next three chapters we'll press more deeply into this reality. We'll begin with our relationship with God (the present chapter) before moving on to our relationship with neighbors in general (chapter 15), and then to the male-female relationship in particular (chapter 16).

In biblical faith a personal God, Triune in nature (and therefore "relational" in himself) has created human persons *for* relationship—first of all with *him*. It's not a relationship of equals, since God is God, and we are not. But it's a *real* relationship, already pictured in Genesis 1–3 as involving (for example) conversation. At its heart, this relationship involves trust—trust in the goodness of the Creator. We see this trust expressed on many occasions in Holy Scripture, as people praise God in acknowledgement of his goodness. Consider, for example, "you, O LORD, are good and forgiving, abounding in steadfast love to all who call upon you"; and "the LORD is good; his steadfast love endures forever, and his faithfulness to all generations."[151]

Here already we encounter various specific aspects of God's goodness. There is God's steadfast love, for example, which is not only "abounding" but also unceasing: "The steadfast love of the LORD never ceases; his mercies never come to an end."[152] Also "abounding" is God's faithfulness, which reaches to the skies.[153] And then there is God's forgiveness. There is no one like God, "pardoning iniquity and passing over transgression for the remnant of his inheritance. . . . He does not retain his anger forever, because he delights in steadfast love."[154] God may be rightly angry when confronted with evil—as any good person would be. God may well be (thankfully) a "God of vengeance" who brings retribution on "the wicked" when they assault and oppress the weak.[155] But as determined as God may be to confront such people robustly, he is at the same time "a God merciful and gracious, slow to anger, and abounding in steadfast love and faithfulness."[156] The other persons in the cosmos ought to worship and adore such a wonderful God—the One upon whom we each depend (remember!) for our every breath.

It is this trust in God that our biblical authors regard as the essence of genuine *faith* in God. Faith is not merely *believing* certain truths about God, but instead *trusting* oneself to God. It's this kind of faith that is illustrated, for example, in the story of Abraham, who "believed the LORD, and he counted it to him as righteousness."[157] In this particular case a human being trusted that God's good intention to bless him with descendants would not be frustrated. But Abraham also trusted himself and his family in other ways to the God whom he believed to be good, and he lived his life accordingly. This is why he is presented in the Bible as such an important model for all believers.[158]

It is out of this seedbed of trust that God is truly *for* us that there grows and blossoms our love for God—our affection for, care for, delight in, and admiration for another person.[159] As God has loved his people "with an everlasting love," so we are responsively to love God with the entirety of our being: "Hear, O Israel: The LORD our God, the LORD is one. You shall love the LORD your God with all your heart and with all your soul and with all your might."[160] Remembering our earlier reflections on the "composition" of the human being, we are not going to make the mistake here of reading "heart" and "soul" (Hebrew *nepeš* and *ləbab*) as limiting our love for God only to some "bits" of our life, and not to others. Rather, *the whole person* is to put everything into responding in love—physically, emotionally, intellectually, morally—to the personal God.

Out of this trust in and love for God emerges, next, joyful obedience. The human being is not envisaged in our biblical tradition as morally autonomous. We are created for obedience to Another Person. So it is that Deuteronomy 6 follows its love-command with these words:

> And these words that I command you today shall be on your heart. You shall teach them diligently to your children, and shall talk of them when you sit in your house, and when you walk by the way, and when you lie down, and when you rise. You shall bind them as a sign on your hand, and they shall be as frontlets between your eyes. You shall write them on the doorposts of your house and on your gates.[161]

God's ancient people were not rescued from Egypt so that they could live in any way that they chose. They were saved for a life that is bounded by God's commandments—in NT language, "the law of Christ."[162] But since these commandments are good, it's a joyful matter to obey them. We are not called to obedience out of fear of reprisal if we fail (as a slave might obey a master), but out of love and trust. We *know*, when we're thinking straight, that it's only sensible to "delight . . . in the law of the LORD" and to meditate on it "day and night."[163] This is the reason:

> The law of the LORD is perfect, reviving the soul; the testimony of the LORD is sure, making wise the simple; the precepts of the LORD are right, rejoicing the heart; the commandment of the LORD is pure, enlightening the eyes; the fear of the LORD is clean, enduring forever; the rules of the LORD are true, and righteous altogether.[164]

It is obedience to these wonderful commandments that actually brings the human being true freedom, as she finds herself "in a wide place": "I will keep your law continually, forever and ever, and I shall walk in a wide place, for I have sought your precepts. . . . I find my delight in your commandments, which I love."[165]

Trust, love, obedience—and prayer. We are created to walk this path along *with* God, and this certainly involves conversation with God (prayer) as we journey. All kinds of prayer are modelled for us in Holy Scripture, providing us with resources for all kinds of life-circumstances. Some of these prayers focus on praise or thanksgiving, grounded in God's actions in his people's history, perhaps, or in aspects of God's character: "Oh give thanks to the LORD; call upon his name; make known his deeds among the peoples! Sing to him, sing praises to him; tell of all his wondrous works!"[166] Sometimes we find praise for a specific act of deliverance experienced by a worshipper: "O LORD my God, I cried to you for help, and you have healed me. O LORD, you have brought up my soul from Sheol; you restored me to life from among those who go down to the pit." [167] Sometimes the praise relates to God's creation of the world, as we have already seen in Psalm 8.

And then we find, also, many lament psalms, in which individuals or groups speak to God out of a situation of distress (e.g., illness; attacks by enemies). Psalm 88 is the darkest of these: "Your wrath has swept over me; your dreadful assaults destroy me. They surround me like a flood all day long; they close in on me together. You have caused my beloved and my friend to shun me; my companions have become darkness."[168] Psalm 22 is probably the most famous of them: "My God, my God, why have you forsaken me? Why are you so far from saving me, from the words of my groaning? O my God, I cry by day, but you do not answer, and by night, but I find no rest."[169] And there are many more types of prayer besides.[170]

Our NT authors build on and develop these prayer-models in various ways. For example, they write out "recollection" prayers, praising God for his mighty works, or more general thanksgiving prayers, such as those often used in Paul's letters to introduce petitions and intercessions.[171] Before prayer is anything else, in both Testaments it is about *remembering who God is*. That is the foundation for everything else, including remembering who *we* are.

For God does not change in character somewhere around AD 1, and nor do the fundamentals of a right relationship with him. Therefore, we are still exhorted in the NT to *trust* in God's steadfast love for us. But since it is clear by this point in the biblical narrative that the *Son* is God as well as the *Father*, we are now to trust not only in the steadfast love of the Father, but also in "the love of Christ."[172] In the same way, we are to trust not only in the *faithfulness* of the Father, but also in that of the Son.[173] Likewise, the *mercy* of God is in the NT the mercy of Jesus Christ.[174] And we are still to *love* God in NT times.[175] But this love for God is love for the Son as well as for the Father.[176] In the same way, *obedience* remains at the heart of right-relating to God in the NT—but it is offered to both Father and Son.[177] In other words, trust, love, obedience, and prayer remain at the heart of right relating to God in the NT, but inevitably everything is impacted in some way by the convictions that the NT authors held about Jesus—who he is, and what he has done.

15

Community with Our Neighbors

"It is not good that the man should be alone."
(Genesis 2:18)

IN BIBLICAL FAITH, a personal God has created human persons *for* relationship—first of all with the Triune God, but also with *each other*.[178]
Unlike our relationship with God, these human relationships *are* fundamentally between equals—between creatures who are, all of them, image-
bearers of the same living God.

The fundamentally social nature of the human being—and the human
need specifically for society with other humans—is addressed in the biblical
narrative early on. In Genesis 2:18 we encounter something in creation that is
not yet "good"—despite the frequent comment in Genesis 1 on the goodness
of each day's work, and the "very good" nature of the final product.[179] We
immediately realize that we are dealing in Genesis 2:18 with a "flashback."
We are back at a point in creation before there was human community, "male
and female."[180] At this point in the story there is only a single "earth-creature"
(Hebrew ' *ādām*) who has been created from "the ground" (' *ădāmâ*)—an
important, meaningful play on words.[181] And we are in a situation of non-
good: "It is not good that the man (' *ādām*) should be alone."

The Genesis 2 narrative proceeds to focus on the female nature of the
solution to this problem, and we'll return to the male-female relationship,
specifically, in the next chapter. But we should not fail to notice at this point
the more general truth that is expressed here. The singular earth-creature is
already one that is in relationship with God—but this is not enough.[182] He
is almost immediately, next, surrounded by other creatures with whom he
also forms relationships.[183] By "naming" them, in fact, he finds each one its
appropriate place in the world:

> Now out of the ground the LORD God had formed every beast
> of the field and every bird of the heavens and brought them to
> the man to see what he would call them. And whatever the man
> called every living creature, that was its name. The man gave
> names to all livestock and to the birds of the heavens and to
> every beast of the field.[184]

Throughout the ancient Near East, "naming" was part of the way in which something came into existence and was assigned a function in the cosmos—as is the case in Genesis 2.[185] But having completed the naming process on this occasion, the naming creature discovers that none of *these* relationships is enough for him either. The creature remains "alone" even though he is in relationship with both God and a multitude of other creatures. Only *human* society can resolve the problem. Only human society can turn "not good" into "good." The "good" human being is intrinsically a being-in-human-society.

What is the nature of this society, when it is functioning properly? Again, we shall leave the specifically male-female dimensions of this question until later. The first thing we discover at a more general level is that human beings are supposed to look after each other. We learn this by way of its opposite in Genesis 4:

> In the course of time Cain brought to the LORD an offering of
> the fruit of the ground, and Abel also brought of the firstborn
> of his flock and of their fat portions. And the LORD had regard
> for Abel and his offering, but for Cain and his offering he had no
> regard. So Cain was very angry, and his face fell. . . . And when
> they were in the field, Cain rose up against his brother Abel and
> killed him. Then the LORD said to Cain, "Where is Abel your
> brother?" He said, "I do not know; am I my brother's keeper?"[186]

Abel responds to God's good provision by bringing him in sacrifice a tithe of the best cuts of "the firstborn of his flock." Conversely, his brother Cain brings only some "of the fruit of the ground." Cain is not in a right relationship with God; his sacrifice is not whole-hearted. Things go from bad to worse when he first responds badly to God's unfavorable reaction to this sacrifice, and then murders his brother. This powerfully illustrates the common biblical view, that turning away from the one true God inevitably leads to injustice, and indeed to bloodshed, in human society. Conversely, how a *righteous* person would respond to a brother is revealed in the dialogue between God and Cain that follows. We see this above all in Cain's question: "Am I my brother's keeper?"

This question is never explicitly answered in the narrative, and it does not need to be, because to biblical faith the answer is obvious. *Of course* you who have been created to "keep" the garden and its inhabitants in general (Hebrew *šāmar* in Genesis 2:15), should also "keep" your brother (*šāmar* in Genesis 4:9). The righteous God "keeps" his worshippers from all harm; so too a righteous worshipper will watch over the life of fellow image-bearers, each of whom is a "neighbor."[187] The Hebrew word behind the translation "neighbor" here is *rēaʿ*. It can refer to a friend, a lover, or a husband, but also simply to another person within one's proximity.[188] Most strikingly, the neighbor includes the *enemy* who exists within one's proximity. He, too, must be treated properly as an image-bearer. So it is that the book of Proverbs teaches us that "if your enemy is hungry, give him bread to eat, and if he is thirsty, give him water to drink."[189] It is for God, not humans, to bring vengeance on an enemy if he persists in his hostility.[190] Outside of a properly sanctioned legal framework, this is not something in which human beings should indulge. And so the righteous Job claims that he has not even "rejoiced at the ruin of him who hated me, or exulted when evil overtook him," nor has he let his mouth sin "by asking for his life with a curse."[191] Biblically, this kind of "keeping" lies at the heart of all right-relating to my various human "brothers" or "neighbors" on the planet. To fail in this duty is a dreadful fault, and to murder someone is especially so. Therefore, "whoever sheds the blood of man, by man shall his blood be [legitimately] shed, for God made man in his own image."[192] In creation, image-bearing life is especially precious.

Other parts of Holy Scripture unpack further what this "keeping" of our neighbor entails. The latter part of Exodus 20:1–17, describing "the Ten Commandments," is especially important here. The first three commandments concern our right relationship with God. The Sabbath is then described as the central symbol of the difference between God's good society and oppressive ones like Pharaoh's Egypt (where it is "work, work, work"). On this Sabbath day space is cleared in which all creatures can remember that life is *more* than work. And then we encounter numerous injunctions urging the rejection of neighbor-destroying, and the embrace of neighbor-keeping. These include honoring one's parents and avoiding (in addition to murder), adultery, stealing, and giving false testimony against a neighbor. The last of the injunctions is perhaps the most fundamental of them all, underlying all the others: we should not "covet" (that is, yearn for something that belongs to someone else).

These are important commandments—but from a biblical perspective they do not exhaust our human duty toward our fellow human beings. We need other texts to help fill out the picture. Taken together, all of these

Scriptures demand generosity toward our human neighbors, whoever they may be. They demand the kind of openheartedness in seeking our neighbor's good that Leviticus 19:18 describes as love: "Love your neighbor as yourself." That is, we are not to put our own interests ahead of those of our neighbor. Instead, we are to consider them at the same time as, and alongside, our own interests. The apostle Paul puts it in exactly this way in writing to the Christians in Philippi: "Let each of you look not only to his own interests, but also to the interests of others."[193] Earlier, Jesus had explicitly referenced the Leviticus text in summing up God's law. "Teacher," someone asked him, "which is the great commandment in the Law?"

> And he said to him, "'You shall love the Lord your God with all your heart and with all your soul and with all your mind.' This is the great and first commandment. And a second is like it: 'You shall love your neighbor as yourself.' On these two commandments depend all the Law and the Prophets."[194]

The question of who my neighbor *is* comes up explicitly for discussion in Luke 10:

> A lawyer stood up to put [Jesus] to the test, saying, "Teacher, what shall I do to inherit eternal life?" He said to him, "What is written in the Law? How do you read it?" And he answered, "You shall love the Lord your God with all your heart and with all your soul and with all your strength and with all your mind, and your neighbor as yourself." And he said to him, "You have answered correctly; do this, and you will live." But he, desiring to justify himself, said to Jesus, "And who is my neighbor?"

Jesus's answer is, unsurprisingly, "anyone in your proximity who needs you to be merciful"—including your traditional enemies.[195] That our neighbors include our enemies is also confirmed in the NT in Matthew 5.[196]

God has created human beings for relationship—not only with himself and with non-human creatures, but also with each other. This is part of what *makes* us human.

16

Male and Female

"Male and female he created them."
(Genesis 1:27)

ONE ASPECT OF OUR social nature as image-bearers of God is that we are designed, not just for community in general, but for family in particular.[197] At the heart of this institution of the family stand a man and a woman—a binary (dimorphic) distinction within the class of image-bearers. "So God created man in his own image, in the image of God he created him; male and female he created them." They are both "like God" in this binary state.

They are, therefore, substantially "like" each other in a way that neither is like the other creatures. And now we are burrowing down into the specifically male-female dimensions of the subject matter that we looked at in the previous chapter. The "good" human being is intrinsically a being in *human* society, not merely *other kinds of* society. So "aloneness" cannot be solved, for example, by way of animal society. Accordingly, examination of the non-human animals and birds in Genesis 2, in order to see whether any might be suitable as a partner for the earth-creature, results in failure. Even though every such creature is somewhat "like" ' *ādām* in being a "living creature" formed from "the ground" (' *ădāmâ*),[198] none is *sufficiently* like him. The special place that human beings occupy in the cosmos is in this way underlined.

This examination completed, God turns aside from animal creation and proceeds to use the raw human material at his disposal to create two finally fully formed human beings:

> So the LORD God caused a deep sleep to fall upon the man, and while he slept took one of his ribs and closed up its place with flesh. And the rib that the LORD God had taken from the man he made into a woman and brought her to the man. Then the man said, "This at last is bone of my bones and flesh of my flesh;

she shall be called Woman, because she was taken out of Man."
Therefore a man shall leave his father and his mother and hold
fast to his wife, and they shall become one flesh.[199]

The ESV translator here, along with many interpreters historically, understands this process as involving the extraction of a "rib" from the earthling.
But this is unlikely to represent the best understanding of the Hebrew.
More likely the idea is that the earth-creature is cut in half, resulting in
two "sides"—one of which becomes male, and the other female.[200] These
are now two separate beings, but of course they exist in the closest possible
relationship. She is, as the male affirms, "bone of my bones and flesh of my
flesh"—a combination that refers elsewhere to a member of one's family.[201]
In Genesis 2 the language has an even more intimate significance, for the
male and the female are destined to become again "one flesh" in marriage.
They are destined to "return," as it were, to their original condition, as the
inhabitants of one body.[202]

　　The birds and the animals have found their own places in the cosmos,
in their communities, and now the human beings have also done so—all
of them properly "named." Everything is "good," and the image-bearers
can now proceed with their joint task of "ruling and subduing" the earth
together as God's royal and priestly gardeners. For now, together, they are
properly equipped for this task. This was not true beforehand, when the
earth-creature still needed "help"—a word used most often in the OT to
refer to divine assistance provided to human beings.[203] So this is a word
that suggests an insufficiency in the "earthling" by itself. Alone, he is not
ready for the important tasks that have been assigned to humanity. The
human vocation in the cosmos can only be fulfilled in community, not
individually. And the family stands as the core human community at the
heart of the entire operation.

　　The two kinds of human are substantially "like" each other. Yet they are
also significantly *unlike* each other. Genesis 2:18 tries to capture the tension
in its curious Hebrew term kᵊnegdô, which is sometimes translated as "fit
for him."[204] But this does not capture the essence of the word, which really
means "like opposite him." It is an unusual use of language by an author
attempting to communicate both similarity and difference. The female who
solves the problem of the earth-creature's "aloneness" must be a helper who
is like him. But she must also be "opposite, over against, at a distance from
him"—perhaps even "boldly in front" of him or "in his face."[205]

　　How exactly are male and female different? Biology is of course an
important part of the answer to this question. Men and women are different biologically—and this, too, contributes to their ability to fulfil their

God-given vocation. For that vocation is not only to rule and subdue, but also to "be fruitful and multiply and fill the earth."[206] In doing all this together they will inevitably need to decide in specific circumstances which roles and tasks each must fulfil in order to be successful—which will in part depend on their gifting. For individual men and women are different from each other in ways that go well beyond biology. How they "help" each other will be influenced by this reality.

It is in this "family zone," created when a man and a woman leave their original families to begin a new community (Genesis 2:24), that sexual activity finds its rightful place in human society, biblically speaking. Sexual intimacy is designed for the marriage relationship between a man and a woman who are tasked by God with being fruitful and multiplying. Sex is a marital matter, pure and simple. Biblical faith therefore sets its face against sexual activity outside of this kind of relationship—not because Holy Scripture is prudish, but because it keeps the question of purpose front and center. In this, as in all matters, the NT stands in massive continuity with the OT, assuming the creation vision of Genesis 1–2 as the basis for its own teaching on sexual expression. The Genesis union of a man and a woman in marriage is, in fact, compared explicitly in Paul's letter to the Ephesians to Christ's relationship with the church:

> "Therefore a man shall leave his father and mother and hold fast to his wife, and the two shall become one flesh." This mystery is profound, and I am saying that it refers to Christ and the church. However, let each one of you love his wife as himself, and let the wife see that she respects her husband.[207]

Such a human marriage, mirroring Christ's marriage to the church, is necessarily a covenantal bond that must not be violated in any way. Therefore, in urging the Christians in Corinth to "glorify God" in their bodies, the apostle Paul expresses his horror at the thought that any of them might get into a sexual relationship with a prostitute: "Or do you not know that he who is joined to a prostitute becomes one body with her? For, as it is written, 'The two will become one flesh.' . . . Flee from sexual immorality."[208] In the Gospel of Matthew, even *thinking* sexually about a woman to whom one is not married is a problem: "I say to you that everyone who looks at a woman with lustful intent has already committed adultery with her in his heart."[209] All forms of sexual practice outside a marital relationship between one man and one woman are wrong, including same-sex practices:

> Do you not know that the unrighteous will not inherit the kingdom of God? Do not be deceived: neither the sexually immoral,

> nor idolaters, nor adulterers, nor men who practice homosexu-
> ality, nor thieves, nor the greedy, nor drunkards, nor revilers,
> nor swindlers will inherit the kingdom of God.[210]

All such forms of sexual practice represent an abandonment of the created order of things, as people make up their own sexual rules rather than conforming themselves to the will of the Creator. Along with other kinds of practices common to humanity, these illegitimate sexual practices represent a departure from the "sound doctrine" that followers of Jesus Christ, and especially Christian leaders, are tasked with upholding and following:

> The law is not laid down for the just but for the lawless and
> disobedient, for the ungodly and sinners, for the unholy and
> profane, for those who strike their fathers and mothers, for
> murderers, the sexually immoral, men who practice homosexu-
> ality, enslavers, liars, perjurers, and whatever else is contrary to
> sound doctrine, in accordance with the gospel of the glory of the
> blessed God with which I have been entrusted.[211]

In biblical thinking, we note, "sound doctrine" is right belief *and* practice. It is not just a way of *thinking*, but also a way of *living*.[212]

The clarity of Holy Scripture on these matters has led the church to an equal clarity in its traditional teaching about them, such that Christian Scripture and tradition have until relatively recently times spoken with one voice in such matters. But that, of course, was before our current anthropological crisis had yet revealed its full depths.

As male and female image-bearers of the living God, we are designed not just for community in general but for family in particular—for family life that has a particular, God-given shape to it in pursuit of God's grand design for the cosmos.

17

Fallen

*"She took of its fruit and ate, and she also gave some to her
husband who was with her, and he ate." (Genesis 3:6)*

MY COMMENTS IN THE previous chapter about image-bearers abandoning
the created order of things bring me naturally now to another important
aspect of the biblical idea of the human being.[213] In all kinds of ways, and
with terrible consequences, humanity has given itself over to evil.

The evil in question enters our human story almost at the beginning,
in Genesis 3, by way of personal but non-human creatures. Its first foothold
is human doubt concerning the goodness of God:

> "Did God actually say, 'You shall not eat of any tree in the
> garden'?" And the woman said to the serpent, "We may eat of
> the fruit of the trees in the garden, but God said, 'You shall not
> eat of the fruit of the tree that is in the midst of the garden,
> neither shall you touch it, lest you die.'" But the serpent said to
> the woman, "You will not surely die. For God knows that when
> you eat of it your eyes will be opened, and you will be like God,
> knowing good and evil."[214]

This was a God who had told humanity that "you may surely eat of [almost]
every tree of the garden."[215] But the crafty serpent represents him as saying
the opposite: "You shall not eat of any tree in the garden." So is God really
"for us," after all? Is he "for us" in his commandments, and specifically the
one concerning the tree of the knowledge of good and evil? The temptation is to answer "no"—to adopt a suspicious attitude toward God—and this
turns out, in fact, to be the human response. Although these image-bearers
are already, legitimately, "like" God in various ways, they cannot resist the
temptation to become "like God" more extensively in "knowing good and
evil"—that is, in becoming "wise" (Genesis 3:5–6). Other OT texts help us

to understand that this is the language of adult independence from a parent. Notice for example these words from Deuteronomy 1: "And as for your little ones, who you said would become a prey, and your children, who today have no knowledge of good or evil, they shall go in there."[216] The wisdom in question in Genesis 3 is the kind that allows "grown-ups" to make autonomous judgments. Humanity is not content with the knowledge that God has already given them so that they can fulfill their vocation as image-bearers. They want more. In fact, they want to *be* gods.

Skepticism about the goodness of God is allied in Genesis 3, then, with idolatry—the worship of some created thing as a god. The Bible identifies such worship as typifying humanity in its fallen state. This idolatry takes many forms. It includes, for example, inappropriate human devotion to, or dependence upon, other human beings.[217] So idolatry is not only a matter of "religion," narrowly defined. Biblically speaking, idolatry marks all aspects of human social, economic, and political life. But certainly it is also explicitly religious in nature. Humans characteristically blur the distinction between Creator and creation in their worship of the kinds of "images" of the gods that were widely found in the temples of the ancient world (and still exist all over the world nowadays). These are the "gods" associated with natural phenomena like planets, weather systems, and fertility. It is this naturalistic polytheism that the Bible so often (and unsurprisingly) attacks, forbidding God's own people from even attempting to represent the unseen God by any created thing.[218] Holy Scripture's determination to distance itself from this way of thinking about "the gods" is evident even in what we are told in 1 Kings about God's "living" in the Jerusalem temple. "Will God indeed dwell on the earth?" Solomon asks. "Behold, heaven and the highest heaven cannot contain you; how much less this house that I have built!"[219] We *should* worship God as the Creator—but we do not:

> What can be known about God is plain to them, because God has shown it to them. For his invisible attributes, namely, his eternal power and divine nature, have been clearly perceived, ever since the creation of the world, in the things that have been made. So they are without excuse. For although they knew God, they did not honor him as God or give thanks to him, but they became futile in their thinking, and their foolish hearts were darkened. Claiming to be wise, they became fools, and exchanged the glory of the immortal God for images resembling mortal man and birds and animals and creeping things.[220]

In this NT text we hear very clearly the echoes of Genesis 3. In our pursuit of wisdom we have become fools, substituting idols for the living God.

Idolatry takes many forms. At its heart, however, is the worship of the human *self* as god. It is the worship of the image of God in *us*. And then, as we turn inwards on ourselves as autonomous selves in this way, we generate our other idolatries. For in reality we are quite incapable of supplying our own need for divinity. Wearying of looking inwards, therefore, we look elsewhere. We become, inevitably, polytheists, recruiting multiple gods to feed our spiritual hunger. It is this polytheism, rather than atheism, that our biblical authors identify as the outcome of our abandonment of the one living God. In this they are much more clear-sighted than most modern people.

The consequences of idolatry are very serious, and Genesis 3 begins immediately to explore them. It draws attention centrally to a series of relational breakdowns:

> [God] said, "Who told you that you were naked? Have you eaten of the tree of which I commanded you not to eat?" The man said, "The woman whom you gave to be with me, she gave me fruit of the tree, and I ate." Then the LORD God said to the woman, "What is this that you have done?" The woman said, "The serpent deceived me, and I ate."[221]

This conversation makes it clear that the man blames both the woman and God for the trouble, while the woman blames the serpent. Genesis 3:14–19 then unpacks for all these participants some further dimensions of the problem. The woman's creation-calling included conceiving and giving birth to children; that calling now becomes more problematic. The man's creation-calling included working the land, and this labor now becomes marked by a new level of struggle. The "pain" that both will now experience partially arises because they no longer face the world in an uncomplicated way as "one flesh."[222] The dynamics of their own relationship have changed. They were created to work in partnership, jointly ruling and subduing the earth.[223] But now the future of the woman lies in being a subject "ruled" by her husband (the Hebrew verb *māšal*). This is the very word used in Psalm 8 to describe the human "ruling" over the other creatures.[224] The man now relates to the woman as if she were *part of* creation, rather than a co-ruler *over* creation. In turn, she tries to control and even to "consume" the man.[225] Intended for partnership in dominion, the human pair now find themselves embroiled in a struggle for dominance, each of the other. They become incapable, therefore, of fulfilling their roles as gardeners. The close connection in terms of consequences between these three now-dysfunctional relationships is powerfully illustrated in Hosea 4:1–3:

> There is no faithfulness or steadfast love, and no knowledge of
> God in the land; there is swearing, lying, murder, stealing, and
> committing adultery; they break all bounds, and bloodshed fol-
> lows bloodshed. Therefore, the land mourns, and all who dwell
> in it languish, and also the beasts of the field and the birds of the
> heavens, and even the fish of the sea are taken away.

Humans turn away from the living God. All kinds of human dysfunction
follow. But there are also, inevitably, dreadful consequences for non-human
creation. Creation is in all respects "fallen"—compromised by evil from very
near the beginning of the human story.

Our NT Scriptures underline the extent of the problem, as people
with "an evil, unbelieving heart" turn away from "the living God."[226]
Thereby they come under the sway of the dark power of the cosmos referred to now as "the ruler" or "the god" of their world. This is the central
deity (Satan) of those who reject the true God.[227] To the extent that they
choose to listen to his voice, "the whole world lies in the power of the evil
one."[228] And out of the fallen human heart possessing such an allegiance
come "evil thoughts, murder, adultery, sexual immorality, theft, false witness, slander."[229] We find ourselves

> filled with all manner of unrighteousness, evil, covetousness,
> malice, . . . full of envy, murder, strife, deceit, maliciousness,
> . . . gossips, slanderers, haters of God, insolent, haughty, boast-
> ful, inventors of evil, disobedient to parents, foolish, faithless,
> heartless, ruthless.[230]

There is no end to the catalogue of suffering that arises from the human embrace of evil. "Your passions are at war within you," James tells his
readers; "You desire and do not have, so you murder. You covet and cannot
obtain, so you fight and quarrel."[231] The whole of God's law "is fulfilled in
one word," Paul writes to the Galatians: "You shall love your neighbor as
yourself." But they prefer to "bite and devour one another," opening up the
possibility that they will be "consumed by one another."[232]

We recognize this world that Christian anthropology presents to us—
and we recognize ourselves in it, too. What is to be done about it all?

18

Saved

"Take heart, my son; your sins are forgiven."
(Matthew 9:2)

ALTHOUGH IT'S TRUE, BIBLICALLY, that humans are *fallen* beings living in dysfunctional societies, it's equally the case that they remain *image-bearing* beings, whose lives are precious to God.[233] Genesis 9 makes this clear.[234] And although it's also true that non-human creation at large is impacted by human fallenness, it's equally the case that God's interest in and commitment to these creatures, too, remains undiminished.[235] Genesis 9 also makes *this* clear: "Then God said to Noah and to his sons with him, 'Behold, I establish my covenant with you and your offspring after you, and *with every living creature that is with you* [my emphasis]; . . . never again . . . shall there be a flood to destroy the earth."[236] God is in fact out to *save* his fallen creation. And at the heart of this saving process, in the biblical narrative, lies his establishing of "covenants."

The term "covenant" (Hebrew *bərît*) indicates an agreement between two parties in which a relationship is formed. It involves moral obligations on each side.[237] Here in Genesis 9, importantly, the covenant is between God and "every living creature." God has not given up on his plan to bless *all* creation, despite the fall into sin. He is firmly committed to proceeding with this plan. This includes the part that involves human fruitfulness, increasing numbers, and filling the earth.[238] The last of these commitments is particularly clearly expressed in Genesis 11, where God frustrates human plans to settle down in Mesopotamia and instead scatters them "over the face of all the earth."[239] So God makes a covenant with the whole of creation in Genesis 9—the creation that he has just saved (with Noah's help) from a great flood. God saves fallen creation in order to bless it. This is a central theme of the biblical narrative that ensues, and covenant lies at the heart of it all.

We next encounter it in the story of Abraham and his family. Here we read about a covenant, not with every living creature, but more specifically with Abraham, and thereby with *all human beings*. The promise associated with this covenant in Genesis makes this clear:

> Now the LORD said to Abram, "Go from your country and your kindred and your father's house to the land that I will show you. And I will make of you a great nation, and I will bless you and make your name great, so that you will be a blessing. I will bless those who bless you, and him who dishonors you I will curse, and in you all the families of the earth shall be blessed."[240]

It is through Abraham that "all the families of the earth shall be blessed." It is in pursuit of this promise that God calls out this one fragment of the human race—Abraham's family—for a mission that is still cosmic in its implications. This family is by no means perfect; it is actually quite dysfunctional. But the promise survives because it is the promise of a covenant God who is determined to see his creation flourish.

In due course the descendants of Abraham and Sarah end up in Egypt. It is in this context that God remembers his covenant with Abraham.[241] This leads on to the great escape from Egypt known as the exodus—another mighty act of God in saving his people. And as in Genesis 9, so also in Exodus through Deuteronomy, salvation leads on to covenant. On this occasion the covenant is associated with the gathering of the post-exodus people of God at Mount Sinai. If the Noahic covenant is about all living creatures, and the Abraham covenant is about all nations, the Sinai covenant is focused much more closely on *one* nation, Israel. But in this covenant Israel is still called to fulfil a much larger role, as Exodus 19 makes clear:

> You yourselves have seen what I did to the Egyptians, and how I bore you on eagles' wings and brought you to myself. Now therefore, if you will indeed obey my voice and keep my covenant, you shall be my treasured possession among all peoples, for all the earth is mine; and you shall be to me a kingdom of priests and a holy nation.[242]

If the whole earth remains God's domain (which it does), then the task of God's people, as a "kingdom of priests," is to mediate God's blessing to it (chapter 13). Thereby they will continue to do in some measure what all human beings, as priests, are called to do throughout the garden of God (Genesis 2).

In some sense, then, covenant may have narrowed down in the book of Exodus, but God's eye is still on the larger agenda, which is the blessing of all creation. In pursuit of this outcome, he promulgates laws that are designed not only to help the Israelites to be "a holy nation," but also to deal with the reality that they are not. A sacrificial system is instituted, whose most important idea involves atonement. In the spilling of the blood of a sacrificial victim, peace is made between God and human beings. The central principle here is the principle of substitution, which is found throughout the biblical texts that touch on sacrifice and is illustrated in narrative form in Exodus 12.[243] When God's justice falls on the land of Egypt, it is the blood of the sacrificial lamb on the doors and lintels of the Israelite homes that causes him to "pass over" them: "I am the LORD. The blood shall be a sign for you, on the houses where you are. And when I see the blood, I will pass over you, and no plague will befall you to destroy you, when I strike the land of Egypt."[244] God does not just *demand* holiness, but also institutes measures to deal with its *absence*. He engages, at the individual level, in voluminous, daily "saving acts."

In the biblical narrative that follows—even in the absence of holiness—God works actively in the world to pursue his good ends. With one of his flawed people—King David—he makes a still further covenant, in 2 Samuel 7.[245] Here an individual Israelite is promised an everlasting royal house: "Your house and your kingdom shall be made sure forever before me. Your throne shall be established forever."[246] Salvation has now come to involve a royal line—a son of David—within Israel. Once again, covenant has in a sense "narrowed down"—from the whole of creation, to all humans, to one nation Israel, and now, finally, to one Israelite. But it has always narrowed down in the context of a larger plan.

The most important descendant of David in this biblical story of salvation is of course Jesus of Nazareth, the "Son of David" and the "King of the Jews."[247] Crucified by the Romans, Jesus nevertheless rises from the dead as "the Lion of the tribe of Judah, the Root of David."[248] Thereby "the kingdom of the world has become the kingdom of our Lord and of his Christ, and he shall reign forever and ever."[249] Jesus is the fulfillment of the promise to David—and also of all the other covenantal promises of the OT. In addressing a Jewish audience in the book of Acts, for example, Peter explicitly connects the coming of Christ to the promise to Abraham:

> You are the sons of the prophets and of the covenant that God made with your fathers, saying to Abraham, "And in your offspring shall all the families of the earth be blessed." God, having raised up his servant, sent him to you first, to bless you by turning every one of you from your wickedness.[250]

Then Paul, in writing to the Christians in Galatia, connects this same promise to the non-Jewish world: "in Christ Jesus the blessing of Abraham" has come "to the gentiles."[251] In line with such covenant promises God has engaged in his most decisive and supreme saving act, ensuring that Christ has become "the source of eternal salvation to all who obey him."[252] This is possible, in line with biblical thinking more generally, only through atoning sacrifice. As Paul writes to the church in Corinth: "Christ died for our sins in accordance with the Scriptures."[253] The language of covenant in fact re-emerges in this context in the NT, when at a meal with his disciples Jesus says of the cup that he is holding that it is "the new covenant in my blood."[254] It is precisely because of this saving action, still in his future, that Jesus is already able in his present moment to say (controversially) to a paralyzed man in Matthew 9: "Take heart, my son; your sins are forgiven."[255]

So it is true that human beings are fallen. But God is in the ongoing business of saving what is fallen. And this includes non-human creation, which "waits with eager longing for the revealing of the sons of God."[256] Why does it wait? It waits because it's only when the image-bearers are finally saved, experiencing "the redemption of our bodies," that the rest of creation can finally be "set free from its [own] bondage to corruption."[257] It is only when the "royal priesthood" of all believers is finally sanctified that it can mediate God's blessing properly to other creatures in the temple of creation.[258] That is just the way things are. That is how God has designed the cosmos.

19

Hopeful

"If God is for us, who can be against us?"
(Romans 8:31)

IT SHOULD BE CLEAR by this point in the book that our biblical story is an *optimistic* story.[259] It is not a tragedy, but a comedy, in the old-fashioned, Shakespearean sense of that word. There may be lots of tragedy *within* it—but it has an inevitably happy ending. I do not mean by this anything like the forced cheerfulness of the ending to *Life of Brian* (1979)—a movie in which the crucified "hero" with no hope of resurrection (Brian) begins to sing the song, "Always look on the bright side of life." This is in fact a parody of true comedy. In true comedy, the story *actually* ends happily. And all such true comedy is grounded in the ultimate (biblical) Comedy, in which there is, in fact, resurrection. Happy endings are possible because a Happy Ending is already scripted, in which (as the medieval mystic Julian of Norwich put it), "All shall be well, and all shall be well, and all manner of things shall be well." This Final Ending is *inevitably* happy because the only living, good God is determined to get us there, and he has no serious rivals who can stop him. The apostle Paul wonderfully proclaims the implications of this truth in Romans 8:

> If God is for us, who can be against us? He who did not spare his own Son but gave him up for us all, how will he not also with him graciously give us all things? . . . I am sure that neither death nor life, nor angels nor rulers, nor things present nor things to come, nor powers, nor height nor depth, nor anything else in all creation, will be able to separate us from the love of God in Christ Jesus our Lord.[260]

One of the implications of this is that we should not allow ourselves to become solely defined by the truth that the world and we ourselves are fallen—as if this were the most important thing that could be said about reality. Some strands of Christian theology have succumbed to this temptation, historically. Negativity about the present world has therefore been their predominant note—not least when it comes to our own human condition. They have indulged in what I call "worm theology." I'm borrowing this language from Psalm 22: "I am a worm and not a man."[261] The reality is, however, that the speaker *is* a man, and not a worm. It's just that he feels dehumanized by his suffering—persecuted by other humans who are behaving like beasts, and cut off both from God and from human community.[262] The entire psalm is designed to help persons similarly afflicted to recover a true perspective on their situation. It celebrates the saving God who reintegrates the suffering soul into a worshipping community that includes "all the families of the nations"—those who have died, and those who have yet to be born.[263] In reality the worshipper has always been an image-bearer of the one living God, living under his care in a good (but fallen) world and destined for a glorious future. It's just that he has temporarily lost the plot of his narrative, indwelling the Middle of the story while forgetting (in this case) *both* the Beginning and the End.

The fall does not *define* the human person, biblically-speaking. Even though the fallenness of the world represents a constant challenge to image-bearers, we must remain focused on the larger truths about our situation, including our future. It is therefore an important aspect of the biblical view of human beings that, when they are thinking rightly, they are optimistic, hopeful creatures. The contours of this hope are first drawn in an extensive way by the OT prophets. They are later provided with more precision by the authors of the NT, who describe how various aspects of the prophetic vision have already "touched down," in our present time, in Jesus Christ. All these visionaries know about the currently somewhat broken state of creation that is graphically represented elsewhere in Holy Scripture. They themselves describe it at great length. However, they do this in the context of envisioning the future transformation of the three broken relationships described in Genesis 3. These are the human relationship with God; the human relationship with other human beings; and the human relationship with the rest of creation. They look ahead to a time when all these relationships will be completely healed. And then they look *beyond* all that, to an entirely new order of things in the cosmos—sometimes described as "the new heavens and the new earth."[264]

When the OT prophets write about our relationship with *God*, they announce first that God will entirely cleanse his own people from sin, giving them a new heart and a new spirit that result in renewed obedience.[265] There will not only be *forgiveness*, but also *transformation*.[266] However, the reconciliation that the prophets envisage doesn't only involve God's own people Israel. It is universal in nature, including nations that have previously been Israel's most bitter enemies: "Egypt my people, and Assyria the work of my hands."[267] It is altogether a *radical* transformation. As we saw in the previous chapter, it's this "eschatological" forgiveness (the forgiveness of "the end times") that in the present time God already offers to everyone, both Jew and gentile, in Jesus Christ. The apostle Paul also writes about this in Colossians 2: "You, who were dead in your trespasses . . . God made alive together with him, having forgiven us all our trespasses."[268]

When the prophets write about *human society* in the future, secondly, they picture it as completely redeemed and reconciled. Their near horizon is a restored community of Israel, governed by a righteous king. Ezekiel, for example, envisages a time in which God the Shepherd will gather his lost sheep together and set over them another shepherd, who is "my servant David."[269] This transformation of human society inevitably involves forcing the enemies of God to submit to godly rule. The righteous king will first deliver from these enemies those who are oppressed by them.[270] The long-term goal, nevertheless, is that all the nations will live in harmony with one another, worshipping the only living God.[271] They already do so in the community of the King, Jesus Christ—for in this community (the church)

> you who once were far off [the gentiles] have been brought near
> by the blood of Christ. For he himself is our peace, who has
> made us both one and has broken down in his flesh the dividing
> wall of hostility . . . that he might . . . reconcile us both to God in
> one body through the cross.[272]

The biblical prophets hope, thirdly, for the transformation of creation itself. Any present alienation of humans from the animal and the natural world will be completely overcome in this transformation.[273] We see this in Isaiah 11, for example, where the Davidic king's deliverance of *people* from oppressors is immediately followed by *cosmic* peace.[274] Colossians 1 later tells us that it was to bring about this cosmic redemption that Christ died: "For in him all the fullness of God was pleased to dwell, and through him to reconcile to himself *all things*, whether on earth or in heaven, making peace by the blood of his cross."[275]

It is in this context of future transformation that we must return finally to the question of individual "afterlife" that we left hanging in chapter 9. It seemed at first, in Genesis 3, that any human hope of life beyond this present reality had died with the expulsion of Adam and Eve from the garden and its tree of life. Yet the prophets envision a future in which "many of those who sleep in the dust of the earth shall awake, some to everlasting life."[276] "Your dead shall live," proclaims the book of Isaiah, "their bodies shall rise"—encouraging those who "dwell in the dust," therefore, to "awake and sing for joy."[277] Immortality is not impossible after all, and Paul writes to his readers in Rome about those who rightly "seek" it.[278] He also describes to the Corinthians a point at the end of time when "this perishable body must put on the imperishable, and this mortal body must put on immortality." This will mean that "death is swallowed up" in a victory gifted us "through our Lord Jesus Christ." He it is who has "abolished death and brought life and immortality to light through the gospel."[279] Christ is in fact the first human to *experience* the bodily resurrection—*not* the escape of a "soul" from a body, we notice—that such texts foresee. His body is missing from the tomb on Easter morning, and after the resurrection it still bears the scars that he received on the cross.[280] Those who follow Christ look for a similar bodily resurrection, leading on to eternal life.[281]

What is the human being to hope for, in biblical faith? We are to hope for all the things that the OT prophets hoped for—with the exception of what has already happened because Jesus has come. And it's in that mighty hope that we should *live*, "more than conquerors through him who loved us."[282] This is one of the key aspects of a properly Christian anthropology.

20

Confessing

"Everyone then who hears these words of mine
and does them will be like a wise man who built
his house on the rock." (Matthew 7:24)

AS WE LOOK BACK on chapters 7 to 19, let me repeat the forward-looking summary of their content that I provided in chapter 6. We human beings are "personal matter." We share in common with other creatures that we are created with intentionality in an ordered cosmos by a personal God as irreducibly *material* creatures into whom God breathes the breath of life. We are "like them" in this way. We are at the same time radically different from them in being divinely animated *personal* matter—"like God," in momentously important ways. As such we are highly exalted, beautiful creatures capable (among other things) of appreciating beauty in ways that other creatures cannot. As image-bearers of the living God, innately dimorphic in nature (male and female), we are called to a particular vocation. It is to rule over and to look after God's sacred, beautiful creation, in right relationship with God, with each other, and with other creatures. As fallen beings who are compromised by evil we often fail in these tasks, and all creation suffers as a result. Mercifully, God is committed to saving his creation, and he has acted decisively in Christ to do so. Human beings ought to be hopeful creatures, therefore—not least because, in Christ, they are promised bodily resurrection and immortality. Personal matter has a glorious future.

If this represents a true account of the fundamentals of "humanness" as presented in Holy Scripture, what does it mean? Well, followers of Jesus Christ are obliged to make it their own—to make it "a personal matter." For it represents the rock-solid truth about our humanity that will endure long after the waves of culture that seek to overwhelm and drown it have done their worst and have retreated whence they came.

If this is indeed what Holy Scripture teaches us, then we are obliged (first of all) to embrace it *as a whole*, and not in part. It will not do to pick and mix. We cannot have the high view of the human person as an image-bearer without the responsibilities assigned to that image-bearer in creation—just because we like the one idea, but not the other. We cannot have dominion without priesthood, just because we prefer ruling to caring. We cannot have the resurrection of the body in the next life without the commandments about honoring God with our bodies in the current one—just because we like the notion of living forever, but not of living under God's rule. In all such cases and others what we are really doing, in picking and choosing, is installing in a primary position in our lives authorities other than the authority of Scripture, and therefore the authority of Jesus Christ. We have become autonomous actors, who get to dictate which parts of Scripture we shall live by and which we shall ignore. It's important to say this especially at the present time, precisely because of the prevalence of such "pick and mix" Christianity in our culture—and the apparent, widespread lack of understanding concerning its desperately problematic nature. But it *is* desperately problematic—*deeply incompatible* with living under the lordship of Christ.

We are obliged to embrace Christian truth *as a whole*, and not in part, and (secondly) we are also obliged to embrace it *as whole persons*, and not in part. Biblical Christianity is not about what is happening in our hearts rather than our heads, in our souls rather than our bodies, in our spirits rather than our imaginations. God has created us as whole persons, and it as whole persons that we are called to love him.[283] Biblical faith knows nothing, then, of having Jesus "in my heart" but not in my head (for example). It utterly rejects the idea that true faith is a matter of feeling rather than intellect. All such dichotomies must be rejected. Biblical faith presents itself to the whole person, and it's the whole person who is summoned to respond appropriately to its proclamation.

Biblical faith demands right *thinking*, then—accepting *what* is proclaimed as the truth of our humanity, regardless of what we might initially "feel" about it. It also demands, in consequence, right *living*—a commitment to living our entire embodied lives in the light of biblical truth, once again irrespective of what our feelings might be about it. And biblical faith then assumes that, on the journey with Christ, our feelings will be transformed, our imaginations purified, and so on, such that we "grow up in every way into him who is the head, into Christ."[284] Biblical faith is absolutely not, then, the "faith" that is presented as "Christian faith" in many of our contemporary churches. For in *that* faith, it's entirely possible to have Jesus "in your heart" but possess little to no idea of the importance of having sound doctrine in your head. It's also possible to have some right ideas in your head, but at the same time to reserve the right to do exactly what you want with the remainder of your body. And it's entirely possible that those around you will think that none of this is a big deal.

To the contrary, biblical faith envisages as *integral* to our Christian journey the need for (not just an initial but also an) ongoing *conversion* from wrong ways to right ways of thinking *and* living in all aspects of life. Every Christian is a recovering heretic. That is, every convert to Christ, having first embraced the truth of Christ and trusted himself or herself to him, is in the process (hopefully) of moving deeper into "sound doctrine" (both beliefs and actions), and of rejecting ideas and practices that hitherto they considered unproblematic. So it is that the apostle Paul appeals to the Roman Christians "to present your bodies as a living sacrifice, holy and acceptable to God. . . . Do not be conformed to this world, but be transformed by the renewal of your mind, that by testing you may discern what is the will of God, what is good and acceptable and perfect."[285] They are Christ-followers—but they still need to be transformed.

Their minds, specifically, are still marked by the fallenness described by Paul in Romans 1.[286] They are clouded, and they need to be renewed. Only then will these Roman Christians be able to make right moral judgments—to discern "what is good and acceptable and perfect." The goal in it all is to be "conformed," not to cultural norms, but to "the will of God." Paul's exhortation in this letter is aimed at ensuring, then, that these Roman Christians become still "more Christian" in thought and life than they already are.

The thought and the life are of course reciprocally related. What we believe to be true necessarily leads us to behave in certain ways, and not in others. And how we *live* is the only sure way of discerning what we actually *believe* to be true. It's the only sure way of testing whether our claims about what is happening in our often-deceitful hearts/minds are deluded. In biblical faith, belief and action are two sides of the same coin. As C. K. Barrett puts it, "The Christian finds out the will of God not to contemplate it but to do it."[287] Renewal of the mind, if it's real, leads on to a certain way of living our lives. "Even the renewed mind needs a good deal of instruction" to that end; "hence the detailed advice and exhortation of the following paragraphs [after Romans 12:1–2]."[288]

To bring Part II to a conclusion, then: we are obligated by the terms of our Christian discipleship to embrace biblical truth about our humanity *as a whole* and as *whole persons*, rather than in part. This is not about being "conservative" or "progressive"—labels that themselves indicate the extent to which idolatrous commitments have currently taken hold of our hearts and minds. For it should be no part of the ambition of the true Christian to be conservative or progressive, and consequently to be a member of one or other of these two defining "groups." A true Christian seeks only to be a faithful member of the community that is gathered around Christ. This will sometimes require us to be conservative, and sometimes not, in relation to the surrounding culture. Such faithfulness may well require considerable effort on each of our parts—a daily commitment to transformation by way of the renewing of our minds through reading, reflection, prayer, and so on. For many of us live in cultural environments deeply shaped by ideas about humanness that are antithetical to the gospel. Many of us actually inhabit *churches* that are now deeply shaped in the same ways. And it is never easy for individuals to think and act "outside the group"—to withstand peer pressure. But it wasn't at all easy for the first Christians either. We need to make our truly Christian confession regardless, in the clear understanding that true Christian faith has never been about slightly adjusting our worldview to find a place for a Jesus who is confined to "our hearts." And then we need to continue to explore the implications of that confession.

Part III is devoted to some of that continuing exploration. It will consider further the implications of a properly Christian anthropology, first of all for our worship of God and for our understanding of his creatures' rights (chapters 21–22). We shall consider next the human life "chronologically," as it moves through time from the beginning to the end (chapters 23–24). Then we'll think about it more "geographically" (as it were), in terms of a male or a female life (chapter 25) that is bound up with different communities. We'll consider in turn family (chapters 26–27), church (chapters 28–29), work (chapters 30–32), and society at large (chapters 33–34). We'll conclude with some exhortations in relation to all of this (chapter 35). What does a Christian anthropology imply about how we ought to approach these various, important areas of our lives?

As in Part II, many readers will encounter ideas in Part III that are new to them, and which perhaps they will initially find troubling or confusing. Maybe they will occasionally even be offended. If it turns out that this describes *you*, "Don't Panic!" For if these chapters are grounded in the truth of God, you will eventually discern that this is the case, and you will work out how it applies to you. And if these chapters turn out *not* to be grounded in the truth of God—well, in that case you don't need to concern yourself with them at all. But we should each remember, on the other hand, that sometimes being offended (in particular) is the first step on the journey toward exchanging bad ideas for good ones, and wrong ways of living for right ones. Christ himself offended plenty of people.

PART III

Furthermore

21

Worship

*"Present your bodies as a living sacrifice, holy and acceptable
to God, which is your spiritual worship." (Romans 12:1)*

WE LEARNED IN CHAPTER 9 that God has created human beings as "psychosomatic entities." And we briefly followed the implications of what this
means when it comes to *loving* God. We are to love God with the entirety
of "heart," "soul," and "might"—with all of our being, and not just some of
the "bits."[289] We are to love God physically, emotionally, intellectually, and
morally. I want to follow the same line now in considering the *worship* of
God. Clearly Holy Scripture teaches us that in relating rightly to God we are
to worship him.[290] But what *is* Christian worship?

The apostle Paul unsurprisingly describes "worship" in Romans 12
in much the same way that the OT earlier described "love." He writes, "I
appeal to you . . . brothers, by the mercies of God, to present your bodies
as a living sacrifice, holy and acceptable to God, which is your spiritual
worship." Worship is not, for Paul, something that we do in a special area of
life, separate from the rest of it. It is not first and foremost something that
we *do* at all—at least, if we have in mind specific religious actions or rituals.
Worship is fundamentally the offering of the entire self to God. That is
what Paul describes in Romans 12 as "your spiritual worship."

The Greek word behind the translation "spiritual" here is *logikós*,
meaning "reasonable." It is related to our English word "logical." Back in
Paul's time it was a favorite expression of Greek philosophical (and particularly Stoic) thought.[291] It refers to what is appropriate to human beings, in distinction from other creatures, and what relates us specifically
to God. In the Stoic worldview, what relates human beings to divinity is
our rationality. In using this same word, the Christian writer Paul does
not of course mean to refer to worship offered *only* by the mind. But he is

certainly advocating worship that *includes* the mind as part of the bodily reality of everyday living.

So for the Christian, worship is a way of life. Everything we do, in our home and in our family relationships, in our broader social relationships, in our work and our play, in our intellectual engagement, our music, our art, and so on—everything ought to be regarded as worship. And if something cannot be regarded as worship, then we should be asking why we're engaging in it at all. There is, in this important sense, no distinction in the Christian worldview between a "secular" and a "sacred" sphere. As the Dutch theologian Abraham Kuyper once put it, "There is not a square inch in the whole domain of our human existence over which Christ, who is Sovereign over all, does not cry: 'Mine!'"[292] Correspondingly, as we saw in chapter 13, there is already in the OT "service" in the tabernacle, but also "service" in the wider world (in both cases, the Hebrew word *'abad*).[293] It is *all* part of what it means to worship the Creator who made it all, and to do his will. Eugene Peterson manages nicely to capture the connection between these two allegedly separate "sacred" and "secular" spheres in *The Message*, when he paraphrases one line in the Letter to the Hebrews as follows "God takes particular pleasure in acts of worship—a different kind of 'sacrifice'—that take place in kitchen and workplace and on the streets."[294] It's *all* worship. That's the point. Worship is fundamentally the offering of your whole life, at all of its moments, to God.

It's important that we then to try to understand everything that we often *call* worship in this much larger biblical context. For we often *use* the term, and *think* about the topic of, "worship" in an incredibly narrow way. To focus on just one context, we say things in church meetings like, "Let's begin our worship service now." But what about our activities prior to getting to the church gathering? Do they belong to a different category called "non-worship"? And then one often hears in the same gathering-context, at a particular point in the meeting, that "we're moving now into a time of worship"—as if what happened earlier in the gathering was something else entirely. In both cases, what we actually mean by this language is only that we are about to start playing music and singing. Well, these are undoubtedly *some* of the wonderful ways in which we can worship God. But they *must* be understood, biblically, as forming only *part* of Christian worship. They form part of the general Christian worship that is the giving of our whole selves to God. If we're thinking biblically, playing music and singing are no *more* worship than doing our jobs excellently or raising our children strenuously to the glory of God. Music and song are in fact best understood as designed to support and strengthen this broader life of worship in various ways. And if they do *not* support and strengthen our life-worship in such ways, then they are frankly not of much use to us. Worse, they may actually become *obstacles* to us as Christ-followers. This will certainly be the case if they get us thinking in the wrong way about God, ourselves, and the world, rather than helping us to think in the right way. If our music and songs are theologically superficial, or just plain wrong, then they will make it harder, rather than easier, for us to worship God truly and completely in our everyday lives.

This is why it's essential that we always strive to keep clearly in mind, as we decide how to "handle" what we routinely call "worship services," what we are aiming for in our Christian lives more generally. It is crucial that we always measure our particular "worship activities" against the rule (or "canon") provided by the larger understanding of worship that Holy Scripture presses upon us. Otherwise we shall not even be able to *ask* whether our worship-activities-in-particular are consistent with, and helping us towards, a truer worship in general. In the end we shall perhaps not even *think* of asking this question. Our "worship activities" will become simply ends-in-themselves, unrelated to the rest of life. And what we do in our "worship services" will be governed by tradition (including contemporary tradition), rather than by Holy Scripture and a truly Christian theology.

As the early Christians gathered together for worship services with all this in mind, they certainly sang songs.[295] It is important to notice, however, what Augustine tells us (in his *Confessions*) about this sung worship, at least in fourth-century Milan. Its purpose, he writes, was "mutual comfort and exhortation."[296] The songs were designed to impart true teaching about the Christian faith. They were, therefore, packed full of Christian doctrine. The singing drove this doctrine deep into people's hearts and minds. The songs functioned, then, much like the recitation of the early creeds and confessions that developed out of rudimentary confessional formulas already found in the NT, such as "Jesus is Lord!" In this respect, early Christian songs were somewhat like the comprehensive, serious sermons that Christian leaders typically preached back then. These offered both high-level theological instruction and pastoral exhortation. The context for these serious sermons was, in turn, the considerable time that gathered Christians spent beforehand reading Scripture together, in line with Paul's injunction to Timothy: "Devote yourself to the public reading of Scripture, to exhortation, to teaching."[297] The second-century writer Justin Martyr, in our earliest full account of a Christian worship-gathering (in his *First Apology*), refers to a regular practice of reading, early in each worship service, "the memoirs of the apostles or the writings of the prophets . . . for as long as possible."[298] For as long as possible! We cannot *live* in the biblical story if we do not *know* it and hear it explained. We cannot *live* in it if we do not confess it in word and song as ways of remembering it. And everything in the early Christian worship-service, including prayer and Eucharist, was designed with these goals in mind, engaging the whole person in worship.

The holistic nature of Christian worship, which we shall spend all of Part III unpacking further in its various aspects, is well captured (again) by Eugene Peterson in *The Message*—this time in his rendering of Romans 12:1–2. The connection between right worship and right living comes out particularly clearly:

> So here's what I want you to do, God helping you: Take your everyday, ordinary life—your sleeping, eating, going-to-work, and walking-around life—and place it before God as an offering. Embracing what God does for you is the best thing you can do for him. Don't become so well-adjusted to your culture that you fit into it without even thinking. Instead, fix your attention on God. You'll be changed from the inside out. Readily recognize what he wants from you, and quickly respond to it. Unlike the culture around you, always dragging you down to its level of immaturity, God brings the best out of you, develops well-formed maturity in you.

The first implication of a truly Christian anthropology, then, is that Christians should worship the one true and living God with their entire, integrated being and across the entirety of their lived experience. We'll return especially in chapter 46 to the "worship activities" best designed to support this life of worship, and those that are not.

22

Rights

"Are the trees in the field human, that they should be
besieged by you?" (Deuteronomy 20:19)

As WE TURN NOW from our relationship with God to begin to consider
further our relationships with other creatures, I want to begin by recalling
one of the answers I provided in Part II to the question, "What is a human being?"[299] I proposed that a human being is one of many creatures of
the one living God, each of which finds its own important place in God's
world within its own domain. All creatures are God's creatures, and all are
important to God.

As such, all creatures are endowed, biblically, with "rights." Human beings cannot simply treat non-human creatures, first of all, in any way that
they like. Trees have rights, for example, when they are caught up through
no fault of their own (obviously) in human warfare. Fruit-trees, in particular,
have the right to be left alone.[300] And animals have rights, too. Even in a
world in which animals of all kinds—domestic and wild—have become human food-items, they are still described in Genesis 9 (significantly) as "every
moving thing that lives."[301] We are reminded at exactly this point in the story
that non-human creatures are like humans in precisely this way: they are not
merely "produce," but living beings. This leads on immediately in Genesis 9
to instructions concerning how to treat animals properly—even while turning them into food. An animal must be completely dead before it is eaten.[302]
A similarly rule-governed approach is evident later, in Leviticus and Deuteronomy. Here we discover that a person who is "lawless" in such matters "shall
be considered guilty of bloodshed."[303] The killing of animals should never be
done casually. It is a serious business.

Trees and animals have rights, and so (secondly) do human beings.
For example, they have a right to share in the goods of their Creator's world,
rather than be shut out of that bounty by powerful people who want it all

for themselves. We see this idea reflected in 1 Samuel 8, where the prophet Samuel warns his contemporaries what it will mean to have a typical ancient Near Eastern monarch ruling over them. The recurring drumbeat of Samuel's rhetoric is that this king will "take." He will, for instance,

> take your daughters to be perfumers and cooks and bakers. He will take the best of your fields and vineyards and olive orchards and give them to his servants. He will take the tenth of your grain and of your vineyards and give it to his officers and to his servants. He will take your male servants and female servants and the best of your young men and your donkeys, and put them to his work. He will take the tenth of your flocks, and you shall be his slaves.[304]

Speaking of slaves in this fallen world: they also have rights. An owner cannot simply treat a slave in any way he likes. Slaves of Hebrew descent in the OT are "contracted," for example, to serve for only a limited period of time. At the end of their service, unless they choose to stay with their master, they must be released.[305] While they are enslaved they should share in the Sabbath rest and take part in sacrificial meals.[306] Furthermore, an escaping slave who has found refuge somewhere should not be handed back. And if a slave is blinded by his owner, or his tooth is broken, he must be set free in compensation.[307]

In short, in biblical thinking there are various, God-given human rights. The most fundamental of these is the right to life. No human being can take another human life without just cause, because that life (just like animal life) belongs to *God*—and not to any creature of God. The connection—but also the difference—between these animal and human rights to life is evident in Genesis 9, which deals with them together. When the passage speaks of the rights of animals, these rights are grounded generally in the animals being "living creatures" of God. But the human right to life is grounded specifically in the image-bearing nature of humanity: "From his fellow man I will require a reckoning for the life of man. Whoever sheds the blood of man, by man shall his blood be shed, for God made man in his own image."[308]

Each and every image-bearing human life, male and female, is deeply significant, and each one is inviolable. It is a dreadful thing to snuff out such a life in a murder, and this heinous act will certainly bring a "reckoning" on its perpetrator from God. For even if no one else notices the murder, God will always hear "the voice" of human blood "crying to me from the ground."[309] The Father hears it and so does the Son, as he addresses in Matthew's Gospel the "sons of those who murdered the prophets." He anticipates a time when there will be a reckoning for "all the righteous blood shed on earth, from the blood of righteous Abel to the blood of Zechariah . . . whom you murdered between the sanctuary and the altar."[310]

So it is that ancient religious rituals involving human sacrifice, for example, were outlawed in the OT.[311] Human life was not to be regarded as "product" to be wasted on "the gods." This is also why the biblical prophets would attack kings who viewed human life as a dispensable commodity on the way to the fulfillment of their desires. One of most striking narratives about this common ancient reality concerns King Ahab (1 Kings 21), who desires a vineyard belonging to someone else, a man called Naboth. Naboth refuses to give it to the king, since it is "the inheritance of my fathers."[312] In short order Ahab's wife Jezebel organizes a conspiracy involving "two worthless men," who are tasked with falsely accusing Naboth of a crime. He is stoned to death, and Ahab takes possession of the vineyard. To whom could anyone possibly turn for redress when faced with such a corrupt government and legal system? Well, God sends Elijah to deal with the situation, promising to bring disaster upon Ahab: "I will utterly burn you up, and will cut off from Ahab every male, bond or free, in Israel."[313] If human institutions will not protect image-bearers, then God will step in directly to do so. There will be a reckoning.

Of course, the reality is that everyone who embraces a biblical vision of the human person should, in fact, already be committed to recognizing and protecting the equal image-bearing status, dignity, and rights of each human person, including the right to life. This is especially true when it comes to the weakest members of society, who cannot easily look after their own interests. Biblical people are necessarily "pro-life" people right across the spectrum of what God-given life *is*. And this commitment requires of us not only the protection of our fellow image-bearers from murder, but their rescuing from hunger (for example), as implied generally by this specific commandment in Deuteronomy:

> At the end of every three years you shall bring out all the tithe of your produce in the same year and lay it up within your towns. And the Levite, because he has no portion or inheritance with you, and the sojourner, the fatherless, and the widow, who are within your towns, shall come and eat and be filled.[314]

The human failure to engage in exactly *this kind of* pro-life activity is a serious matter in the book of Job, as this particular passage reveals:

> You have given no water to the weary to drink, and you have withheld bread from the hungry. The man with power possessed the land, and the favored man lived in it. You have sent widows away empty, and the arms of the fatherless were

crushed. Therefore snares are all around you, and sudden terror overwhelms you.[315]

Serious biblical people have always behaved otherwise—imperfectly,
but substantially. And the consequence is that the world has gradually
become an immeasurably better place, on the whole, than it once was. It is
indeed a world now clearly shaped in many significant ways by these biblical ideas about the intrinsic value of human beings and their rights. This
is simply a fact—even though for some time now many people devoted
to these *ideas* have seemed quite determined to forget their true point of
origin in the Bible.[316]

For example, when "the peoples of the United Nations," having reaf-
firmed in their Charter their "*faith* [my italics] in fundamental human
rights," wanted to make a public declaration about this, they published
in 1948 the Universal Declaration of Human Rights.[317] It's a document
steeped in biblical thinking—but you would never guess this from how its
content is communicated.[318] The corporate "faith" mentioned is startlingly
left entirely without definition. And this is precisely because the people
responsible for the Declaration could not arrive at a consensus—in the
absence of divine revelation—on what a defensible theoretical basis for
human rights might be. As the French philosopher Jacques Maritain said
at the time: "Yes, we agree on the rights, but on condition that no one asks
us why."[319] We'll return to this significant problem in all modern thinking
about justice in chapter 47.

The second implication of a Christian anthropology, then, is that
Christians should contend for biblically grounded human rights, and they
should have no difficulty in saying why they do so—and why they will not
involve themselves in abrogating any of them.

23

Life

*"For you formed my inward parts; you knitted me together
in my mother's womb." (Psalm 139:13)*

IN THIS CHAPTER AND the next we'll think further about the Christian idea of the human right to *life* in particular.[320] Our focus will be on how it relates to Christian views about both "beginning of life" and "end of life" questions.

First of all: if biblical people are necessarily "pro-life" in general, then this certainly includes human life in the womb in particular. These emerging image-bearers are without doubt some of the vulnerable persons—like the foreigners, the fatherless, and the widows of our biblical texts—whom we must "keep." As we saw in Part II, all life comes from God as a gift. As Psalm 100 puts it: "Know that the LORD, he is God! It is he who made us, and we are his."[321] He formed us from the clay of the ground as a potter forms an artifact: "But now, O LORD, you are our Father; we are the clay, and you are our potter; we are all the work of your hand."[322] We did not form ourselves. It's God who gives life, and it's God who takes it away again, in his good time. This is why—as we saw in the previous chapter—no human being can take another human life without just cause, and before God has ordained it.

But when, in biblical faith, does the individual life that is hedged around with such protection *begin*? It begins in the womb. Job addresses this reality: "Did you not pour me out like milk and curdle me like cheese? You clothed me with skin and flesh, and knit me together with bones and sinews."[323] Here the human being is pictured, first of all, in terms of "milk" (semen) being poured into a churn (the womb), in which it will over the course of time become something solid ("cheese"). And then, secondly, this entity is "clothed" with flesh, bones, and sinews. Jeremiah also speaks about God forming him in the womb in this way, reporting this word that came to him from God: "Before I formed you in the womb I knew you."[324] But perhaps the most famous passage along these same lines derives not from Job or Jeremiah, but from the Psalms. It is found in Psalm 139, which uses the same verb as in Job for "the knitting together" of the child in the womb (Hebrew *sākak*):

> For you formed my inward parts; you knitted me together in my
> mother's womb. . . . I am fearfully and wonderfully made. . . .
> My frame was not hidden from you, when I was being made in
> secret, intricately woven in the depths of the earth. . . . [I]n your
> book were written, every one of them, the days that were formed
> for me, when as yet there was none of them.[325]

What is especially striking here is that this person's days were actually *numbered* while he was still in the womb. This is the beginning point from which the life of the unborn child is "counted out" on the way ahead. And then we must add one more biblical text that also captures the mystery at the heart of this hidden, creative process in the womb. As in Psalm 139, Ecclesiastes 11 ascribes this process to God, as one aspect of his making of everything: "As you do not know the way the spirit [better, 'breath'] comes to the bones in the womb of a woman with child, so you do not know the work of God who makes everything."[326]

God-given human life begins in the womb. And this means that people of biblical faith are obliged to regard life inside the womb as just as sacrosanct as life outside it. It means that we are obliged to regard the illegitimate destruction of this pre-natal human life as morally wrong. It is a violation of the God-ordained human right to life that we discussed in the previous chapter. Babies in the womb have an intrinsic right to life.

This right is not *earned*. It derives merely from the fact that the life of the child in the womb belongs to God, and to no one else. It is important to say this plainly. Often in contemporary debate about the pre-natal rights of children, people argue that babies only begin to "accumulate" rights as they develop in the womb. They begin to gain what one author has called a child's "developmentally acquired capacities," such as "reasoning ability, language, and self-consciousness."[327] It is these "acquired capacities" that ultimately makes a child "a person" worthy of our protection.

But from a Christian point of view, this is entirely wrong-headed. Children in the womb possess the right to life because their lives belong to God and to no creature of God. So all the many contemporary arguments about when (if ever) we should consider life in the womb to be worthy of protection from being terminated are beside the point. They are just as much beside the point as other, similar arguments concerning whether this or that *already-born* human being has "sufficient personhood yet" or "sufficient personhood remaining" to "deserve" our protection.

For example, what about healthy but very young children with limited-to-non-existent "reasoning ability, language, and self-consciousness"? In a well-known academic paper written in 2013, Alberto Giubilini and Francesca Minerva shared with the rest of us their own views on this topic. They maintained that "there are no morally significant differences between a newborn and a fetal human being in utero."[328] Neither one is a "person," they proposed. Consequently, if abortion is ethically permissible, then so too is post-birth killing. This would presumably be true until a child is around two years of age, since that is the point at which children typically become aware of their own existence, and they can take an interest in its continuing.

This is a horrific enough idea in itself, and one that is probably still without broad support, even in a post-Christian society—although infanticide as such, at least for infants with disabilities, is certainly an idea that is gaining traction in some contemporary political and legal environments.[329] But let us press on further. On this "functional" view of "personhood," does the killing necessarily stop at age two? What about intellectually or physically challenged, older minors? Are they "sufficiently personal" to have their right to life maintained? What about impaired adults of various kinds? What about elderly adults? Where does this process of categorizing humans as persons or non-persons in terms of their "capacities" end? And where do the *consequential actions* end—given the "nasty feature of human social psychology" that we should all know about by this point in history. That is, "the tendency to divide people into in-groups and out-groups, and to treat the out-groups as less than human."[330] We've seen this before—on many, many occasions.

The value of human beings, in biblical faith, categorically does not lie in "developmentally acquired capacities." It does not lie in *anything* that we might believe makes other humans more similar to the ones already in "our group," or more useful to our society. The value of human beings lies in the simple but wonderful fact that we are all image-bearers of God. We are all creatures in the care of the Creator, from the womb and until the end of life. And this guarantees everyone their rights for the whole of their lives, no matter what happens to their various "functions" or "capacities" along the way.

From the very beginning of the Jesus movement, true Christians have understood and wholeheartedly embraced this truth. This is why the early Jesus-followers took such a radically different view from their own contemporaries, the Stoic philosophers, concerning both abortion and infanticide. The Stoics happily endorsed both practices. Prior to birth the mother could do anything she wished to her baby.[331] She had the right to choose. This was because—the Stoics held—a baby was part of the mother's body until birth.

After birth, they believed, babies with mental or physical abnormalities could and *should* be discarded.[332] Lacking the appropriate "developmentally acquired capacities," they were useless.

The early Christian document the *Didache*, on the other hand, robustly forbids both procuring abortion and committing infanticide.[333] The *Epistle of Barnabas* says something very similar. This second document makes it explicitly clear, indeed, that a baby in the womb is *not* part of its mother, but is already a "neighbor" who requires "keeping."[334] There is no "right of choice" that a mother (or indeed a father) possesses over the life of a child in the womb—no "right to choose" that trumps the right to life. So it was that the early Christians frequently visited the garbage pits of Rome to rescue children left there by their parents to die. They knew that each one was a precious image-bearer and must be saved.

The contemporary church, likewise—as a third implication of its Christian anthropology—is called to be a place of refuge, safety, and support for young and yet-unborn children. We are further called to care for their parents, who are also our neighbors, and who are often in need of very significant support in walking the right path in this area of their lives in our contemporary culture. In particular, a mother has as much of a right to life as anyone else. So if she elects to have necessary surgery (for example) that will lead, as a consequence (but not as a goal), to the death of her unborn child, this is tragic but morally unproblematic. In this case no one is participating in infringing a God-given right to life. The sad and complicated reality is that two "rights to life" find themselves in conflict.[335]

24

Death

"You are not your own, for you were bought with a price."
(1 Corinthians 6:19–20)

IN THE PREVIOUS CHAPTER, in relation to a "functional" view of "personhood," I asked about the question of "sufficient personhood" when it came to impaired or elderly adults.[336] This leads us directly from the implications of a Christian anthropology for "beginning of life" issues to its implications for "end of life" questions.

We live in a time when many people believe that it's morally defensible, or even "right," actively to cause another person's death, especially in advanced years, if that person requests it. This "voluntary euthanasia" can be accomplished, for example, by administering a lethal substance, thereby achieving "a gentle and easy death" (the meaning of "euthanasia" in the Greek language). If people already think in this way, they will also likely believe that "assisted suicide"—a less active form of enabling someone to die—is unproblematic. This involves giving assistance to another person in taking his or her own life when they wish to do so. This might be achieved, for example, by placing drugs within a person's reach who is physically unable to fetch them for himself or herself. Both euthanasia and assisted suicide have become much more common throughout the world in the past several decades than they were beforehand. How does a biblical anthropology shape our thinking and living when it comes to such matters?

The fundamental Christian assumptions here are exactly the same as in the case of abortion. Human life is a gift from God, and it is only God (or those authorized by God) who can take it away. At this point "the dust returns to the earth as it was, and the spirit [breath] returns to God who gave it."[337] God has determined that this part of our existence is over. "We are stewards, not owners, of the life God has entrusted to us," as the Catechism of the Roman Catholic Church puts it; "it is not ours to dispose of."[338] We are only the "keepers" of this life—our own life—just as we are only the keepers of life in God's good creation in general. We don't "own" any of it.

It is far from surprising, then, that we find no grounds at all in Holy Scripture for thinking that taking one's own life might be morally acceptable. Consider the narratives where suicide is described. In each case the people concerned are characterized as disreputable. In no case are their actions praised by anyone.

In Judges 9, for example, the murderous king Abimelek commits suicide with the help of his servant after a millstone is dropped on his head and cracks his skull. He is dying, but he chooses to go more quickly, in case anyone should be able to report that a *woman* killed him.[339] In 1 Samuel 31 King Saul, desperately clinging to power in spite of God's rejection of him and his dynasty, kills himself in order to avoid the judgment of God that is soon to fall at the hands of the Philistines.[340] In 2 Samuel 17 the royal counsellor Ahithophel—a traitor who wants to see King David dead—kills himself because Absalom does not take his advice.[341] In 1 Kings 16 the famously ephemeral King Zimri, who reigned for seven days over northern Israel, kills himself to avoid being captured by his enemies. He, too, is under the judgment of God at this point in the story, because he did "evil in the sight of the LORD, walking in the way of Jeroboam."[342] And in Matthew 27 Judas, overcome with remorse for betraying Jesus, hangs himself.[343]

This is a rogue's gallery of suicides. All these stories associate the action with other, negative realities. At the same time, there is nothing at all in our biblical narrative tradition the least bit like the case of the Greek philosopher Socrates (469–399 BC), whose suicide is portrayed by Plato's character Phaedo as noble and right.[344] Conversely, we find at least one suicide prevented in the NT, as a Philippian jailor is dissuaded from killing himself because of a failure of duty.[345] We also encounter explicit Christian teaching that strongly presses against any such practice.

Paul tells the Roman Christians, for example, that "none of us lives to himself, and none of us dies to himself."[346] Of the Christians in Corinth he asks, "Do you not know that your body is a temple of the Holy Spirit within you, whom you have from God? You are not your own, for you were bought with a price."[347] When it comes to suffering, specifically—which is very much to the point in respect of voluntary euthanasia and assisted suicide—Holy Scripture does not advocate fleeing life to avoid pain. It urges us to endure it for the sake of "the bigger picture." Paul writes in Romans 5, for example, that we Christians "rejoice in our sufferings, knowing that suffering produces endurance, and endurance produces character, and character produces hope, and hope does not put us to shame."[348] We "hope" that even in suffering God is working out all things to good ends.

The early post-apostolic church took the same position. They did so even though Christian lives in the Roman Empire could be *extremely* difficult. Life could come to an *end*, in particular, in very painful circumstances. Nevertheless, the Christian author of the *Shepherd of Hermas* (an early-second-century text) clearly thinks that suicide "owing to distress" is a serious sin. He also considers anyone failing to help the sufferer travel a *different* path to be "guilty of his blood." Later in the same century Tertullian, discussing the idea that a Christian should give to anyone who asks, is careful to set limits around this duty. It certainly does not mean, for example, giving "poison or a sword to him who longs for death."[349]

So Christian Scripture and tradition lead us to consider suicide to be morally wrong. It follows that assisting others in achieving it, or acting as their agent in making it happen, is also wrong. "Voluntary co-operation in suicide is contrary to the moral law."[350] It has long been regarded in this way in the Christianized world—and not only because of specifically Christian thinking. The question is also explicitly addressed in the Hippocratic Oath. This is the best known of the ancient Greek medical texts, and it is still used nowadays in the graduation ceremonies of many medical schools. The relevant line is this: "I will neither give a deadly drug to anybody if asked for it, nor will I make a suggestion to this effect." As Leon Kass notes, "The Hippocratic physician rejects the view that the patient's choice for death can make killing the patient—or assisting the patient in suicide—right."[351] He also claims that "medicine has never, under anyone's interpretation, been charged with *producing or achieving death itself*. Physicians cannot be serving their art or helping their patients . . . by making them disappear."[352] Medical doctors have for a long time, then, resisted any involvement in such practices.

The pressure is now on, however, to make them change their minds and their practice. No doubt many will do so, in the absence of strong, metaphysically grounded convictions to the contrary that would lead them to risk their careers and their livelihoods for a point of principle. It is very important, then, to underscore Christian teaching on this point. A Christian healthcare professional (or indeed any other Christian) cannot rightly involve himself or herself in assisted suicide. It is equally wrong for that professional or any other Christian to engage in any kind of voluntary euthanasia. There are many other better ways—and more traditional ways—in which we can practice compassion toward the suffering. We can seek to ensure excellent palliative healthcare for the dying, for example. Here the goal of intervention is not to kill or to facilitate self-killing, but "the optimization of quality of life until death ensues, and the provision of comfort in death."[353]

But what true Christians cannot do is agree to participate in curing one evil (suffering) with another (premature death).

At all costs, then, we must stay away from the burgeoning death-industry that is now arising in many parts of the world, in which it's not even suffering that lies at the heart of the argument, but "choice." It is the individual *right* to death that is emphasized—one of those various "rights" that has been conjured out of nowhere in post-Christian times simply by asserting that it exists. Just because someone wants death, or thinks that she does—so the story goes—she should have it, for an ever-increasing number of reasons, including mental illness. In my own country, as things stand even at present, "Canadians who suffer from mental illness, poverty, or chronic pain frequently cannot get help—but they can get killed."[354] This kind of "service" is of course something *else* that doctors have traditionally refused. They have been resolutely unwilling "to do what patients want solely because they want it."[355] But the pressure is now on, and the language of rights is designed to intensify it.

Margaret Somerville has linked together the topics discussed in our last two chapters by noting that the cultural question has quickly evolved from "should the baby live?" to "should the grandparents die?"—or indeed anyone else who "wants to" die, or can be pressurized into thinking that they do.[356] There is an inevitability about this. When an endowment view of human personhood begins to be replaced by another, and belief in the absolutely sacrosanct, inviolable nature of the human life begins to get eroded, it necessarily affects right-to-life issues all across the spectrum of human existence. The fourth implication of holding a Christian anthropology is that, for everyone's good, we must strenuously promote a different vision of human existence, at the end of life as well as at its inception, from the societal visions currently beginning to prevail.

25

Gender

"Do you not know that your body is a temple of the
Holy Spirit within you, whom you have from God?"
(1 Corinthians 6:19)

As WE NOW BEGIN to consider some of the implications of a Christian anthropology for human relationships in the period *between* conception and
our last days, we turn first to the question of male and female.[357] One aspect of our social nature as image-bearers of God is that we are designed,
not just for community in general, but for family in particular (chapter
16). And at the heart of this institution stand a man and a woman: "God
created man in his own image, in the image of God he created him; male
and female he created them." Humanity is male *and* female. Individual human beings are male *or* female. There is a binary (dimorphic) distinction
within the class of image-bearers.

Modern science can tell us a considerable amount about this binary
differentiation at the biological level. Of course, scientists recognize that
very rarely babies can be born with unusual anatomical features. But even
in the most unusual cases "they usually fall within the female/male binary,
and . . . no one clearly falls beyond it."[358] The point is that these tiny image-
bearers are still designed to produce entirely different "gametes" from each
other—the reproductive cells capable of uniting with those of the opposite sex in sexual reproduction.[359] This leads evolutionary biologist Colin
Wright to state categorically that "sex in humans is functionally binary . . .
the final result of sex development in humans are unambiguously male or
female over 99.98 percent of the time."[360]

The science here is merely describing in a granular, analytical way
what ordinary persons perceive more broadly as they go about their business in the world. It's a world still populated—for the moment, anyway—by
generally easily distinguishable males and females. So it's surprising that the

very notion of a male-female binary has recently become contentious across the globe. We must try to account for it.

The doorway to our new situation was opened initially by way of a novel redeployment in modern academic circles of the word "gender." For most of its history, "gender" had previously functioned as a synonym for "biological sex." It then became entangled with the word "identity," referring to the person that one "really is." The compound term, "gender identity," correspondingly now refers to the person that one "really is." As *Merriam Webster* puts it, gender identity is "a person's internal sense of being male, female, some combination of male and female, or neither male nor female."[361] Your "sex" might well be "biological woman." But what is your true "gender identity"? And so we arrive at the idea of the "transgender" person: one "whose gender identity differs from the sex the person had or was identified as having at birth."[362] On this view, who I really am may or may not have something to do with my physical body. Perhaps I'll discover that I'm actually resident in completely the wrong body, and I'll need to take steps by way of drugs and surgery to correct that fault.

To be clear, it's not discomfort with one's given body, or even a sense of being trapped in the wrong body, that is new to human experience. Medical professionals have long recognized the condition nowadays known as "gender dysphoria." It used to appear relatively rarely in mainly younger children, and it would disappear in most cases by the onset of puberty.[363] What is new in very recent times is, first of all, the explosion of cases of gender dysphoria among people of all ages, and especially young teenage girls. Secondly, there has been a notable change of public mood when it comes to dealing with the issue. Whereas a person's intuitions about his or her "real identity" used to be regarded as a reason for seeking professional help, now they are regarded (even in the case of very young children) as indicating "the very truth of the matter." The "treatment" that quite often follows is inevitably designed to make a given body look, in due course, more like a man's or a woman's (depending on choice). In pre-pubescent minors this begins with puberty-blocking drugs. Later, there is hormone therapy and surgery. Some aspects of the treatment are reversible only with difficulty, and some (like double mastectomies) not at all. Matching the astonishing speed with which an entirely new order of things has arisen in this area of "gender," a vast legal framework has also quickly sprung up that is designed to suppress public debate about it, and dissent from it.

In this world of ever-multiplying "genders" (eighty-one, according to one recent count—but rising fast on a seemingly weekly basis), what does a Christian anthropology require of us?[364] Well, in none of the biblical material touching on our image-bearing nature is there any basis for the notion that any human being possesses a "gender" that is not intrinsically connected to his or her God-created biological sex. It is true that in Holy Scripture, as in life, persons of each sex express their masculinity and femininity in culturally specific ways. But Scripture gives us no reason to understand such differences in expression as entailing the existence of multiple genders dissociated from biological sex.

Nor does Scripture provide us with any ground for believing that the "true" identity of any human born with a female body is in reality male, or vice versa. Nor does it provide us with any foundation for refashioning our God-given bodies in order to make them more like those of the opposite sex. In fact, a Christian anthropology insists (remember!) that human beings are "psychosomatic entities" (chapter 9). It does not encourage belief in any kind of "body-self dualism," whereby my body is not really my "self," but the self lives instead somewhere "inside" my body, waiting to burst out into authentic existence. So any notion that a person's true identity is "internal" to them, having little or nothing to do with his or her bodily form, is *deeply problematic* from a truly Christian point of view. Our God-given bodies, as they are, are in fact temples of the Holy Spirit.

All this being so, Christians are required to reject transgender ideology, and instead to live out and teach to others our very different vision of "humanity male and female."[365] That is the fifth implication of our Christian anthropology. In doing so we need to reach out to and make common cause with groups of gender-dysphoria sufferers—not necessarily religious people—who themselves do not find an ideological approach to the problem at all helpful. They want the condition still to be treated *as* a condition for which help and support are available.[366] This is one way in which we Christians can care for our neighbors in the midst of the current chaos.

Another important aspect of our care for others will involve addressing more robustly than ever before the pernicious lies about (especially female) bodies that have created so much of the angst that currently makes transgenderism look so attractive. It's no coincidence that the explosion of "rapid onset gender dysphoria" among teenage girls should have occurred at a point in history when they possess such unrestricted access to social media. Among other things, their engagement with such media often makes them painfully self-conscious about their body type and personality, while at the same time introducing them to countless other people who have undergone different kinds of surgery precisely so that "they can be who they want to be." It's a form of social contagion, and like any contagion we must play our part—if we love our neighbors—in disrupting its transmission.[367]

We also need to care for our neighbors in other ways. We need to care for very young children whose childhoods are being ruined by

irresponsible schoolteachers who seem to think that one of a child's greatest needs is to ask questions about his or her true gender. Once the world
was populated by adults like the German designer Alma Siedhoff-Buscher
(1899–1944), who in order to "spare the child inner confusion" decided
in her toy designs to use only two basic colors (green and white). "She
wanted children to laugh when they played, to give them space and allow
their imagination to run wild"—that is, to be children.[368] Now the world
is populated by adults who believe that it is a good idea to introduce children—children!!—to a vast range of (not colors but) gender possibilities.
We need to protect young children from such madness. We also need to
care for older minors who are in the process of making catastrophic decisions about drugs and surgery under the influence of other irresponsible
adults, and for parents who don't know where to turn in the crisis. And we
need to reach out to and care for all the damaged people who have recognized too late the false promise in transgenderism, who have consequently
"de-transitioned," and who now have no community that will accept them
in their "strange," in-between condition.[369]

Perhaps we shall not need to deal with this problem for very long.
There are already signs that more and more of our neighbors are coming
to doubt the objective basis of gender ideology. When all is said and done,
why should we accept at face value (they ask)—and in the absence of any
properly scientific evidence—any claim about a "real" gender identity unrelated to a person's sex? Can't people's perceptions about themselves—especially minors—simply be *wrong*? We used to think so—and disciplines
like psychiatry, and medicine more generally, depend on this possibility.
We cannot sensibly (or morally) simply go along with other people's feelings about themselves—with their "self-diagnosis." The medieval King
Charles VI of France, for example, believed that he was made of glass, and
he is "reported to have wrapped himself in blankets to prevent his but-
tocks from breaking."[370] Was he really made of glass? Or was he mistaken
in his interpretation of reality?

26

Children

"Train up a child in the way he should go."
(Proverbs 22:6)

IN THE SOBERING CONTEXT provided by chapter 25, we must now consider further the matter of children. We are created for community, in general, and for family, in particular (chapter 16). This means among other things that we are designed to "be fruitful and multiply." So where they are able to do so—and not everyone is able—married couples should have children. This is also part of what it means to be "pro-life"—that along with other creatures, in their binary sexuality, we should *produce* life, and so fulfil God's grand cosmic design. Our biblical authors naturally recognize that, in the fallen world as we know it, producing such progeny can bring with it significant pain. Nevertheless, the predominant note struck in Scripture where children is concerned is joy. Children are a blessing from God, who "gives the barren woman a home, making her the joyous mother of children."[371] Children "are a heritage from the LORD, the fruit of the womb a reward," and grandchildren "are the crown of the aged."[372] The promise to the man who fears God is that "your wife will be like a fruitful vine within your house; your children will be like olive shoots around your table."[373]

What are we to *do* with such children? We are to treat them as image-bearers who are important to God. Jesus said, "Let the little children come to me and do not hinder them, for to such belongs the kingdom of heaven."[374] We are not to "provoke [our] children to anger," but to be gentle with them, and to avoid discouraging them.[375] We are to love them, but also keep them in line.[376] In sum, we are to "bring them up in the discipline and instruction of the LORD."[377]

Children are not born fully formed. First of all, they have a lot of physical development ahead of them, including brain development. Modern science has taught us a considerable amount about this. Brain development is a long process that begins two weeks after conception and continues into a person's twenties. In the womb it's largely driven genetically, but later much of it is influenced by our experience as social beings. Interactions with the outside world in the early years of childhood, when the brain is especially "plastic," are particularly important. These shape the "bedrock" upon which higher-level brain functions will later be built. But the brain also retains an expansive capacity to "rewire" itself in response to much later experiences.

In tandem with *physical* development children also undergo *emotional, moral, and spiritual* development. A child is not born fully formed in these respects either. And this is why we admit children to fully adult society only as they reach stages in their development when we are confident that they can handle adult responsibilities. Where I live in Canada, for example, one cannot drive a vehicle, or consent to sexual activity, until the age of sixteen, while the legal drinking age with respect to alcoholic drinks is nineteen.

The point is that children need to be actively "brought up" by the parents to whom God has gifted them. They need to be proactively "raised"—to be trained in all respects "in the way [they] should go."[378] This is hugely important; children cannot successfully raise themselves. And Holy Scripture urges them, in fact, to recognize this *for themselves*, and therefore to cooperate in the training process, which can only do them good: "Hear, my son, your father's instruction, and forsake not your mother's teaching."[379] Scripture by no means encourages young people to abandon this project in favor (for example) of looking inside themselves to discover "who they are."

In fact, at the heart of this training process, biblically, lies the *inculcation* of a true understanding of who a child *is*. Our biblical authors lay great emphasis on the importance of this aspect of a parent's task. They already know that the nature of the human being has always been a *disputed* question in the midst of "the war of myths" in which God's people are always involved (chapter 1). So they already know that children won't just "pick up" a right understanding of themselves along with the cultural air that they breathe. They need to be *taught* a right understanding, and it must be constantly *reinforced*. At the same time, they need to be perpetually reminded of what they should *not* believe about who they are, and why they should not.

This is why the OT people of God are not only instructed as adults to remember the events of the exodus (for example), actively refusing to "forget" their true identity; they are also told to make those events "known to your children and your children's children."[380] This is why children in OT times took part in the Passover ritual—so that they could ask questions about its meaning and receive the right answers.[381] This is why the Israelites taught God's commandments "diligently to your children" throughout

the course of each day and in all of its circumstances.[382] Of course, parents in ancient times instructed their children in other important areas as
well—such as how to practice a profession.[383] But it was far more important
for young persons to know who they *were* than to understand what they
should *do* for employment. They were the children of Abraham and Sarah.
They were not Egyptians or Babylonians.

The sixth implication of our Christian anthropology, then, is that we
ought to welcome children joyfully into God's world as his gift to us, and we
ought to strive with all our might to raise them in accordance with biblical
truth. This includes, fundamentally, the truth concerning their own human
nature. We must strive to inculcate in them the Christian anthropology that
we believe to be true, and we must strenuously attempt to dissuade them
from other opinions that we hold to be false. It is only natural that we shall
want to succeed in this, if indeed we believe that it's important (and good) for
our children to *embrace* what is true and to reject what is false.

So what is the content of this "curriculum" as we have laid it out so far
in this book? We must teach our children that the world into which they
have been born is in all aspects the creation of a personal God. We need
then to exhort them to worship this one true and living God with their entire, integrated being and across the entirety of their lived experience. We
must explore with them all of creation's integrity, and its beauty, and teach
them about their responsibility toward it. We must encourage them to see
themselves as integrated, beautiful, and precious image-bearers beloved by
God. We must instruct them on what this means for how they think (for
example) about sex and gender. We must teach them about human rights
under the rule of God, and about our consequent duty toward others,
from the womb until the grave. We must offer them guidance about their
fallenness and how to handle it, we must instruct them on the glorious
truth about our salvation in Christ and what it means, and we must exhort
them to live in Christian hope.

However, this curriculum cannot possibly only consist in "what." It
must also be a matter of "how." The point is to raise our children as *integrated* Christian people in line with a truly Christian understanding of the
person. We shall fall at the first hurdle, I'm afraid, if we seek to impart this
truth in a *disintegrated* way. For we always teach children what we really
believe, theologically and anthropologically, as much by *how* as by *what*
we teach. So if we seek to engage only their minds, we communicate that
their imaginations are unimportant. If we seek to teach only by image, we
tell them that pictures matter much more than words. If we emphasize only
facts, and never introduce our children to beauty; if we focus on science,

and never induct them into the wonders of art; if we teach them to present their opinions effectively, but never to pray—in all such cases we sell them short, as image-bearers of the living God.

Even if we touch all these bases but fail to help our children see how everything is organically related in God's amazing world as one glorious Truth, then we let them down. Indeed, we lead them astray about the Truth. And given that their brains are themselves being wired throughout the course of our curriculum, in making such mistakes we are all the time also making it harder and harder for our children to retrieve the situation later, when they are fully formed adults. It's not impossible, of course. Christians are not determinists, and brain science itself confirms that we should not be. Brains are not fixed entities.[384] Still, it's a general truth that if we "train up a child in the way he should go" then "even when he is old he will not depart from it."[385] This is true both for good and for ill, unfortunately. And this makes it imperative that as parents we are *very* conscious, all the way through a person's childhood and teenage years, of *where* we think he or she "should go," and how we are going to try to ensure that she or he gets there.

27

Education

"[Solomon] spoke of trees, from the cedar that is in Lebanon to the hyssop that grows out of the wall. He spoke also of beasts, and of birds, and of reptiles, and of fish." (1 Kings 4:33)

IN THE PREVIOUS CHAPTER we were thinking about the parental Christian duty to raise our children in accordance with biblical truth.[386] I want to begin the present chapter by developing this point: that it is indeed the duty of *parents* to do this noble and necessary work. Our children are gifted by God to *us*. It's *our* responsibility, and no one else's, to ensure that they are brought up "in the discipline and instruction of the Lord."[387] This is the seventh implication of our Christian anthropology—closely allied to the sixth.

It is not, for example, any *government's* responsibility to see to our children's upbringing. As the Universal Declaration of Human Rights correctly (and biblically!) states, it's the *family* and not the state that is "the natural and fundamental group unit of society."[388] Families have then often sought "protection" by a state—to which protection they are indeed "entitled."[389] For "no one shall be subjected to arbitrary interference with his privacy, family, home."[390] This specifically includes interference with education: "parents have a prior right to choose the kind of education that shall be given to their children."[391]

Now Christian parents will of course need to draw on other people's help in educating their children. Each of us has our limits in terms of knowledge. So when it comes to exploring with our children all of creation's integrity and its beauty, for example (chapter 26), few of us will be able to do that well across the breadth of the sciences and the length of a pre-adult life. Likewise, few parents are well-equipped individually to take a child deeply into all of art, literature, and music. Yet a well-rounded grasp of God's world requires attention to all these subjects and more. So Christian parents will need other people's help. The question is: *which* people? And the answer, in ideal terms, is twofold. First, these will be friends who are on the same page as ourselves regarding the "what" and the "how" of bringing children up "in the discipline and instruction of the Lord." Secondly, they will be friends who can contribute their own expertise seamlessly to that great, integrative project.

A Christian school ideally conceived, for example, is a gathered group of people devoted to precisely such an enterprise. And that is a great environment for your child's continuing education outside your home—if you can find a school that is truly of this nature. Unfortunately, actual Christian education on the ground varies in its degree of proximity to the ideal. Its curriculum may for example not be holistic in a thoroughly Christian way, and it may not be taught in an integrative manner. At the extremes it may, on the one hand, be Christian and incredibly narrow in its outlook. On the other hand, it may be indistinguishable from secular education in almost every way, at least in the classroom—that is, not very Christian at all. For we do not make education "Christian" simply by putting that adjective before that noun, and then performing a few recurring religious activities throughout the school term. Nor do we achieve this goal of a Christian education merely by having Christian instructors teaching what is still essentially a "disintegrated" modern curriculum.

There are perhaps at least two reliable ways of discerning whether a particular school is doing better than that. The first is to take note of how well or badly it's doing as an institution in recognizing and dealing decisively with the cultural and political pressures of the day—whatever they may be. Is there evidence of a robust, Christian, institutional mind informing distinctively Christian institutional postures and behaviors—for example, regarding human rights or transgenderism? The second reliable way of discerning is to take note of which kinds of graduates the school produces. Do these graduates themselves possess a robust, critical Christian mind, melded with a warm Christian heart, and are they capable of bringing a lively Christian faith to bear on all areas of thought and life? Or do they graduate looking much the same as secular high school graduates? Are they, for example—like King Solomon—erudite in speaking "of beasts, and of birds, and of reptiles, and of fish," but lacking in the kind of biblical wisdom that sustains a long obedience in the same direction under God's rule?[392]

As parents, we need to know to whom we are entrusting our children when they are out of our line of sight, and what we can expect as a result. Even if we intend to choose a Christian school to help us in raising our children, we need to know this. But we *especially* need to know it if we intend to choose a state or fee-paying school that is secular in nature—and the fact is that many parents have no realistic options apart from these. Since the more commonly chosen of these two options is the non-fee-paying, state school, I shall focus my comments here on that reality.

What Christian parents will discover about state schools depends very much on exactly where and when they are raising their children. Until very recently in much of the Christianized world, for example, the ethos and curriculum of such schools was still very much informed by Christian faith. Therefore, the notion that the family is indeed "the natural and fundamental group unit of society" was widely accepted. So was the idea that schoolteachers stand *in loco parentis* (in the place of parents) with respect to children *only for particular purposes*. They "stand in" while teaching mathematics, for example—but not when it comes to educating children in sexual ethics. The religious and moral instruction offered in state schools, consequently, was minimalistic in nature, out of respect for the appropriate boundaries between school and home. Therefore, Christian parents could send their children to state schools with considerable confidence that they would receive a decent "common denominator" education in many subjects that could then be integrated without too much difficulty into the broader Christian curriculum being lived out and taught in the home. My own children went through this kind of state education in our own city as recently as the early 2000s, and my wife and I do not recall having to do too much "deprogramming" with them at the end of each day, so as to integrate their faith with their learning.

It's possible that you find yourself still living substantially in this kind of environment. In the Western world generally, however, the situation as a whole has changed radically and astonishingly quickly in our public education systems in the course of the past decade. State schools are populated by an increasing array (it seems) of confident, even dogmatic, adults possessing very clear ideas about exactly how they want to shape the young lives that have been handed into their care. They do not apparently regard themselves as standing *in loco parentis* in any meaningful sense at all. Many of them have instead inherited (perhaps unwittingly) the ideas of philosophers like Plato and Karl Marx (1818–83). They regard the children in their care, therefore, as first and foremost wards of *the state*, and only secondarily (and problematically) as the sons and daughters of parents. Parents are in fact viewed as obstacles in achieving the educational system's righteous goals for its students. Teacher knows best—on just about everything.

This mindset was well illustrated (in the US context) in the course of a rather infamous 2021 gubernatorial race in Virginia. During a debate, one of the candidates said: "I don't think parents should be telling schools what they should teach." If we're thinking about the specific content of a math module, then as a non-mathematician I certainly agree. The problem is, however, that what is being "taught" in state schools nowadays is frequently heavily ideological. Overt indoctrination has become as much a part of the state curriculum as education. Consider, for example, the "Sexual Orientation and Gender Identity" program (SOGI 123) recently introduced into schools where I live.[393] This program explicitly proposes that schoolchildren should decide for themselves their sexual orientation and gender identity, and that a parent's only role is to "open up the conversation and keep it open, by allowing [children] to question, express, and explore their individuality as they wish."[394] In line with this same belief, the policy of many school boards in Canada is to conceal it from parents *unless they have a child's consent* when that child identifies at school as transgender.[395] This applies to children as young as eight or nine years of age.

Summing up: it is a good thing to draw on other people's help in raising our children. But we need to be careful not to lose the plot of our Christian narrative in doing so. And we need to ensure that our children, under extensive and sometimes baleful influence during their long school week, do not lose the plot either. As soon as we involve the *secularized* world, in particular, in raising our children, we risk the UN Declaration's "interference with . . . family." This is not least because people in that secularized world may well be *contemptuous* of the institution of family, and they may be actively involved in trying to undermine it. Education, we must understand, is never "just education." It always takes place in the midst of a battle among "interested parties" for the hearts and minds of our children. It's not something to take at all lightly.

28

Church

"Let us consider how to stir up one another to love and good works, not neglecting to meet together, as is the habit of some."
(Hebrews 10:24–25)

AT VARIOUS POINTS IN this book I've touched on the deeply Christian idea that human beings are created by God as *social* beings.[396] Precisely because this is true, what people around us think, and how they behave, has a considerable impact on us—as we interact with school systems, for example (chapter 27). Psychological experiments have shown this to be true even when something quite "objective" is at issue, such as the length of a line in a vision test. Even in a case involving straightforward perception, "having social support is an important tool in combating conformity."[397]

The philosopher Hannah Arendt has developed this idea in writing about society more broadly.[398] Identity, she writes, is always social in nature, and not something that any individual can create in isolation. But faced with the modern world's complexity, people have tended increasingly to favor "the private world of introspection and the private pursuit of economic interests" over "the public sphere of action and speech."[399] Isolated in private spaces with only close intimates for company, focused on purely personal concerns in the mistaken belief that we shall thereby experience individual identity in a heightened manner, we ironically but inevitably suffer an identity crisis—the loss of a sense of self.

And this renders us susceptible, says Arendt, to the extremes of totalitarian ideology and practice on both the political left and the right. "The modern, isolated subject is vulnerable to the siren calls" of precisely these kinds of extreme ideology and the new forms of community that they offer.[400] Why? Because abandoning the public in favor of the private sphere—retreating inside my head, inside my home—does not in fact obliterate the human *need* for wider community, and for the personal identity that it shapes. That need must still be met. The attraction of totalitarian "community" in such a context is that it offers simplicity and clarity in this quest. It offers a large community (a state) that includes only people "like me" in terms of class, race, or whatever. Beyond these boundaries, tyrannical terror may then rightly be unleashed in various ways on those who do not "fit in."

My point here is that we are not designed by God to "go it alone." We are wired for community. And our deep human yearning for such community even in overtly highly individualistic cultures is so great that, when we find it, we tend to be keen to maintain our hold of it. This inevitably involves "fitting in"—and being seen to fit in—to a group. This can tend in very positive, but also in very negative, directions. It all depends on the nature of the group. At the darker end of the spectrum from good to bad, "the group" can implicate us not only in error, but even in madness. Discussing this reality, Doris Lessing writes perceptively about

> the effect on us of mass emotions and of social conditions from which it is almost impossible to detach ourselves. Often the mass emotions are those which seem the noblest, best and most beautiful. And yet, inside a year, five years, a decade, five decades, people will be asking, "How *could* they have believed that?"[401]

The reality is that we cannot do without "groups." The only questions are, "Which groups will they be?" and, "What is likely to be the effect of their inevitable social influence?"

This leads us beyond the question of the Christian family—the primary social group that can keep us on the right track, even when error, madness, and darkness press in from all sides—and on to the question of church. A church is a local Christian community on a larger scale than the Christian family. For individuals not embedded in Christian families, a church is in fact the primary such community or "family." All Christians, anyway, are called as Christ-followers to be active members of such a community, for their own good and for the common good. It is the primary, public means by which Christians gain social support with a view to combating conformity to what Paul describes to the Roman Christians as "this world." God gives us church as a gift that will help us not to conform, but instead to "be transformed by the renewal of your mind."[402] Using Arendt's vocabulary rather than Paul's, church is the necessary social context for Christian identity-formation, which can take place only in the company of others and "can be meaningful only when lived out amid others."[403] This being so, we must not neglect meeting together as church, "as is the habit of some." We must instead gather together in meaningful Christian community to remind each other what "love and good works" look like, and to "stir up one another" to do them.[404]

What will be the characteristics of a church that is able to provide Christ-followers with this kind of support? I want to propose three of these in the current chapter, delaying further comment on our lives "in Christ" until chapter 29.

First of all, the good church will be a Christian community that teaches in complete sincerity that Christian worship is a way of life, and whose worship gatherings reinforce this core biblical idea (along the lines described in chapter 21). Our involvement in a church that thinks and acts otherwise will not help to us in our own determination "to present our bodies as a living sacrifice."[405] So the gatherings of the good church will seek to engage the whole person in worship, neither neglecting beauty and imagination in favor of intellect, nor intellect in favor of emotion, nor promoting any other kind of unbiblical dichotomy. For if they do not engage the entire person in these ways, these gatherings will continually narrow our vision of the Christian faith rather than enlarge it. They will reduce, rather than expand, our ability to live a life of worship in our families and elsewhere.

Already implicit in these comments on worship is a second idea: that the good church will be committed to the *education* of the persons who comprise its membership. And this education, in order actually to be helpful, will necessarily not be smaller in scope, nor less holistic in approach, than the one that Christian parents are striving to offer to their own children (as described in chapters 26 and 27). The curriculum must therefore go well beyond mere "religious instruction." It must be expansive—designed to equip its members to think and live Christianly across the whole breadth of their daily lives. It must also be deep—at least as deep as the education that community members have received in the world outside the church community. Otherwise this allegedly "Christian" education will again continually narrow its members' vision rather than enlarge it. These churchgoers will have nothing to say, "Christianly," about large and important areas of human existence, and they will instead default to "the world" for their ideas about how to live in these zones.

My final proposal about the good church is that it will be a community that meets personally. Those who hold to a truly Christian anthropology believe that human beings, as image-bearers of God, are irreducibly *embodied* beings. We are not minds, or souls, or hearts, that just happen to be found in bodies, and that can just as easily do without those bodies. It is as *embodied* creatures that human beings are *social* creatures. From a Christian point of view, then, it is a contradiction in terms to refer to "virtual community." "Virtual community" is not real community, and only someone who has not experienced the latter can possibly confuse it with the former. I met quite a number of such people, unfortunately, during the COVID-19 crisis. They told me that their church had transitioned seamlessly from "live" to "virtual" mode, and that no one had noticed much of a difference. In fact, they claimed, "virtual church" had provided "better community" than before. I'm afraid that my response to them, in each case, was that the quality of their fellowship prior to 2019 must have been exceedingly poor.

At best "virtual community" is a temporary fix while real community happens to be impossible. I used to indulge in such fixes myself, from time to time, when I communicated via Zoom with my grandchildren who lived at that time in a different part of the country—but it's not *at all* the same as *being with them*. "Church," likewise, cannot be "virtual," any more than real education can occur "at a distance" (see chapter 45). The good church is one that meets personally—and *in the very act of doing so* reinforces in people's minds and hearts a Christian rather than an alien anthropology.

This is especially so *if* the church meets regularly—and not just once a week, for example (as if this represented any kind of rational response to the cultural tsunami now threatening to wash over the Western church, in particular). Even worse is the church that does not meet much or at all during secular holiday seasons. For that church thereby reveals that its operative understanding of itself (its "ecclesiology," or "doctrine of the church") is as the religious equivalent of a secular organization, offering religious "activities" at selected times of the year. I was once at a church service in August in my home city, in the course of which it was announced that the church would be "restarting" after the summer, along with the local schools, at the beginning of September. This does not reinforce, through practice, a biblical view of what "church" really is. Unfortunately, it actually reinforces, through practice, a false consciousness.

To sum up so far on "church," then: the eighth implication of a Christian anthropology is that we need to commit ourselves to the kind of local Christian community that will help us (and our children) maintain and develop our Christian identities, even under heavy cultural pressure.

29

In Christ

"There is neither Jew nor Greek, there is neither slave nor free,
there is no male and female, for you are all one in Christ Jesus."
(Galatians 3:27–28)

THE GOOD CHURCH MEETS in-person. Who are the "persons" involved? They are Christ-followers—people who are "in Christ Jesus."[406] We need to dwell on this point for longer than you may think necessary. Isn't it obvious? Perhaps it once was. But especially in a cultural moment in many parts of the world when "diversity" and "inclusion" are front and center in public discourse, it's all too easy for Christians, in thinking about Christian community, to lose the plot of their own narrative, and to begin to operate out of someone else's story.

The Christian community that is the church (globally) is certainly diverse, biblically speaking, in many important ways. So too, oftentimes, are local churches, although not every local church community is rooted in a strikingly diverse local environment to begin with. Local circumstances aside, however, what is entirely clear in the NT is that characteristics such as race, sex, and social class represent no barrier to a person's full membership of the universal church or a particular local expression of it. It does not matter whether one is Jew or Greek, slave or free, male or female—whether one is Roman or barbarian, wealthy or poor.[407] Every image-bearer of God, redeemed by and baptized into Christ, is equal in his or her "being" ("ontologically" equal, as theologians say) to every other.[408] And these image-bearers are expected, in the NT writings, not merely to believe this but also to act upon it in their community life together. No matter who they once were—in their lives in society before encountering Christ—they are now all "brothers" and "sisters" in a new "family" (the church). This is why Paul, for example, urges his friend Philemon to receive back his runaway slave Onesimus "no longer as a bondservant [slave] but . . . as a beloved brother."[409]

The originating point of this diversity lies in Jesus's "Great Commission" in Matthew 28: "Go therefore and make disciples of all nations, baptizing them . . . , teaching them to observe all that I have commanded you."[410] In obeying these instructions, Christ-followers have embraced, in addition to the "creation mandate" given to all image-bearers in Genesis 1–2 ("Be fruitful and multiply," and so on), this further "evangelism mandate." How are the two related? The first (Genesis) mandate describes the life that all image-bearers are supposed to live as they worship the one true God. The second (evangelism) mandate requires all worshipping image-bearers to call on every other human being to repent of his or her sins, to worship God instead of idols, and to follow God's plan for their lives rather than their own plan.

The necessary connection between these two mandates has unfortunately sometimes been obscured in Christian theology. For example, sometimes our gospel proclamation has communicated quite well what people are being saved *from* in Christ (principally the judgment of God), but it has not been quite so clear about the full dimensions of what they are being saved *for*. "Repent of your sins and be saved," we have urged. But what does it *mean* that people should repent of their sins? It *means* that, in turning from idols to worship the living God, they should turn *away* from a life *not* grounded in God's creation plan for us. It *means* that they should embrace instead a different way of life that *is* rooted in God's plan. The two biblical mandates are *intrinsically* connected. The very point of the evangelism is to call people back to the godliness *in all areas* of life for which they were created. Had they never sinned, evangelism would be unnecessary; if everyone were to get saved, it would once again become unnecessary. In some versions of Christian theology, Christ-followers would at this point find themselves at a loss for something to do. For "growing the church" has become their *purpose*. They don't have a meaningful *creation* theology to provide a larger context for their *redemption* theology.

One way or another, anyway, the consequence of Christian obedience to the Great Commission is that the church has always been an incredibly diverse body—"a great multitude that no one [can] number, from every nation, from all tribes and peoples and languages."[411] No one is excluded from this family who agrees to be included, on Christ's terms. Every individual who is included, on Christ's terms, must be treated equitably, justly, and with love, as brother or sister, without regard for race, sex, social class, and so on. There is diversity, and there is inclusion.

But what does it mean to be "included *on Christ's terms*"? It means, precisely, that one must have turned away from a way of life that was *not* being lived under his lordship, and must instead have embraced his rule. The inclusion in question is premised on having been "baptized into Christ" and having "put on Christ," which involves observing "all that I have commanded you."[412] It's an inclusion premised, therefore, not just on a confession, but on a commitment to be a "disciple." It entails, then, a personal commitment to "sound doctrine" in all aspects of thought and life.[413] To be "in Christ" is to have committed to putting "to death . . . sexual immorality, impurity, passion, evil desire, and covetousness, which is idolatry," along with "anger, wrath, malice, slander, and obscene talk" and lying.[414] It is, in fact, in the very context of exhorting the Colossian Christians that they should "put off the old self" and "put on the new self, which is being renewed in knowledge after the image of its creator," that the apostle Paul speaks to them about diversity in the church.[415] He clearly does not have in mind diversity of belief or behavior. *That* kind of diversity in the church is not, in biblical thinking, good.

The good church that meets personally is necessarily, then, a community with hard boundaries. Without them it could not be helpful to Christ-followers (and their children) who wish to maintain and develop their Christian identities under heavy cultural pressure. Those people need a community in which—wherever one turns, and whomever one's children meet—the same core beliefs and behavioral commitments are encountered, in worship, in education, and in personal interactions. It is precisely as this happens that the "plausibility" of Christian faith is increased on all sides. Community members reinforce again and again, to each other and to themselves, that "this way of thinking and living is true, and it's good." Our children, in particular, need this kind of consistent experience of Christian community. It is a wonderful thing—and I can testify to this as a parent—when one's wider "family" is populated by winsome adults of excellent Christian character who will reinforce rather than undermine your teenager's Christian faith. It's a particular blessing when they manage to do this even while listening to the teenager complaining to them about his or her completely unreasonable parents. Our children *need* this kind of consistent experience of Christian community. And this is true whether it's the plausibility of something hugely important that is in question—like a truly Christian view of sex and gender—or something of slightly less importance (like family rules concerning "screen time"). The functional Christian community helps youngsters, among other things, to see that their families are a lot less unusual (and even weird) than they might first have thought.

Perhaps the greatest contemporary threat to this kind of functional Christian community derives from the seemingly innocuous emphasis in some Christian circles on "hospitality." The danger here lies precisely in the fact that Scripture itself advocates hospitality, toward both fellow-believers and "strangers."[416] Who, then, can be against it? The problem is that the idea has recently been developed in strikingly unbiblical directions, particularly when it comes to hospitality toward "the marginalized." In this way of look- ing at things, "hospitality" gets interpreted as forbidding the drawing of any boundaries around our church communities that exclude people defined (or self-defining) in any way as marginalized or disadvantaged. And this includes people who embrace beliefs and practices (e.g., concerning sex and gender) that are impossible to reconcile with "sound doctrine." That is, they are not orthodox Christian believers.

This is a disastrous intellectual and moral development, which has compromised church community after community in recent times in terms of each one's ability to be a truly *Christian* church. Our first responsibil- ity as Christian parents and leaders is not to find a place inside Christian communities for the unbelieving "marginalized." Our first responsibility is to create and maintain communities within which Christian believers young and old (and diverse in so many other different ways) can grow and flourish in a biblically grounded faith. It's to build communities that support these persons in their pursuit of holiness.[417] And this is why Paul, faced with sexual immorality in the church in Corinth, instructs them to "purge the evil" from their midst.[418] He recognizes the danger to the en- tire community in any toleration of difference of core belief and practice within their boundaries. Consequently, he certainly does not recommend "hospitality." Nothing in biblical faith justifies *that* kind of "hospitality," since healthy Christian community cannot possibly coexist with it. This is also why in his letter to the church in Rome, in the midst of voluminous greetings to his fellow-Christians who are on the right path, Paul instructs them to "avoid" others who are not.[419]

So the ninth implication of a Christian anthropology—closely related to the eighth—is this: that we need to commit ourselves to a local Christian community that is deadly serious about maintaining strong and appropriate boundaries that are grounded in "sound doctrine." We'll return to the ques- tion of how a Christian community should then also relate to non-believing neighbors in chapter 33.

30

Work

*"In Christ Jesus . . . I have reason to be proud
of my work for God." (Romans 15:17)*

IF THE GREAT COMMISSION is aimed at calling image-bearers back to the
living God and to the fulfillment of his creation mandate, what exactly
does that mandate require of Christians as they participate, not only in
family and in church, but also in "society at large"? The next five chapters
of Part III will explore various aspects of this question. What are the implications of a Christian anthropology for how we think about work, generally (chapter 30), and about the creation of wealth, in particular (chapter
31), in the context of our care for "the environment" (chapter 32)? If our
first responsibility as Christian parents and leaders is not to find a place
inside our Christian communities for non-believing neighbors (see chapter 29), what *is* our responsibility toward them personally (chapter 33)
and politically (chapter 34)?

As we know from chapters 12 and 13, human beings are created to
work. Work is intrinsic to God's creation plan. It is one aspect of our worship of the Creator. We are designed to have dominion over and to subdue
the earth. As we saw in those chapters, how we read this language is important. It does not justify an exploitative human approach to creation, for
we are the image-bearing *representatives of* God. We are not created, then,
to exercise power unfettered by moral constraint—by God's character and
law. We must instead rule and subdue worshipfully, remembering that
God's other creatures are our co-worshippers. We must bear in mind that
we are as much priests as we are kings, called to serve and protect as much
as to rule. With all of that said, however, we *are* called to *act* in the world—
to work. In various ways creation does *require* "subduing" on our part,
as we go about our God-ordained business of creating and maintaining
"shalom." And all of this is true before we even get to the complications

introduced by the entrance of evil into our lives. The fall does complicate our work, just as much as anything else in our lives (including our "play"). But it is certainly not the case, biblically, that work is part of human existence only because of the fall.

Work is, instead, intrinsic to male and female existence in God's world. As such, it is from the beginning of the biblical narrative very broadly defined. Work is not in the first instance understood as particular "jobs" in particular zones of life called "workplaces." Rather, work is part of the human vocation in general. And then, as we embrace that general vocation, work takes shape in myriad particular tasks. Genesis 3 envisages some of these tasks—in the home (raising children) and outside it (working in the fields).[420] Both of these are *forms* of work, each involving—in a fallen world—new forms of *pain*. But in *every* area of life, and not just in these zones, human beings are called to exercise their royal and priestly responsibilities.

Eventually in the biblical story we read about some individuals who hold actual "positions" referred to as "king" and "priest." They do these political and religious "jobs"—but only as particular instances of the work assigned to humanity as a whole. We already saw in chapter 13 how the language in Numbers 3 concerning the work of the priests in the tabernacle directly reflects what Genesis 2 says about the priestly vocation of all human beings. Both humans in general, and priests in particular, are called to "work" in and to "keep" God's temple. The priests themselves are (naturally) only some of the Israelites who as an entire people-group are called to priesthood—to be "a kingdom of priests."[421] Less obviously, perhaps, notice how in Deuteronomy 17 the "job description" of the Israelite king seeks to ensure that he remains one "brother" among the many image-bearers who are called to rule, all the while remembering God's character and following his law. Measured against the norms of the surrounding ancient Near East cultures, the king in Deuteronomy 17 is scarcely a king at all. What this passage is really portraying is the leadership under God of one image-bearer among equals.[422]

Biblically-speaking, then, work is not in the first instance a set of particular activities carried out in "workplaces." Work is part of our general human vocation, subsequently taking shape in multitudes of particular tasks—in the home, in the field, in political and religious contexts, and so on. And no aspect of this work—all of it necessarily offered in worship "as a living sacrifice" to God—can be regarded as more or less spiritual, more or less important than any other. Our human tendency in this area of life, as in others, is toward dichotomy and hierarchy. "This is work and that is not," we say, and "this work is much more important than that work." With respect to *dichotomy*, running a business is work (for example), while being at home and raising children is not work, but "family." Spending one's day building cars is work, but spending the same day creating art is "play." With respect to *hierarchy*, manual work is far more important than intellectual work (it is said), a career in the caring professions is morally superior to one in business, and best of all is to find oneself in full-time pastoral ministry.

Underlying this kind of worldview is the same kind of unbiblical, dis-integrative approach to God's world in general, and to the human person in particular, that we have now touched upon many times in this book. At least some of it rests on a pronounced sacred/secular distinction of the type to which I objected in chapter 21, although in the world outside the church it survives in forms so mutated as to be unrecognizable. It is, anyway, precisely the kind of distinction—whether it appears in our thinking about worship, or about work, or about anything else—that Christians need to resist. We inhabit a biblical story, after all, in which it is not just full-time religious func-tionaries (priests) whose work is "spiritual," but also the work of someone like Bezalel. This was a man "filled . . . with the Spirit of God, with skill, with intelligence, with knowledge, and with all craftsmanship, to devise artistic designs, to work in gold and silver and bronze, in cutting stones for setting, and in carving wood, for work in every skilled craft."[423] And along with this Spirit-filled artisan worked many others into whom God had likewise "put skill and intelligence to know how to do any work in the construction of the sanctuary."[424] It was God who equipped them all to do precisely this impor-tant work—the work of the craftsman and the artist.

These are not by any means the only kinds of God-ordained tasks, at the level of individual "employment," that emerge in Holy Scripture as specific instances of the "work in general" that humanity is called to do in pursuit of what is good for creation. The tenth implication of a Christian anthropology is that we should commit ourselves to doing this good "work in general," embracing enthusiastically along the way all the many tasks that it will require of us. As we walk this path, shall we discover tasks that are "unspiritual," and should not be done? Yes! But they will not be "unspiri-tual" because they focus on ordinary, material life in creation rather than on "spiritual things." These tasks will not be "unspiritual" because they focus on what some people think of as the small and the mundane, rather than on the large and the glorious. They will not be unspiritual because they comprise manual labor (or because they do not), or because they represent "worldly" rather than "church" endeavors. The work of an evangelist is no more spiri-tual, in itself, than the work of a plumber. Work is "unspiritual" in God's good world only when it involves activities that stand in conflict with God's character and laws, and which therefore cannot rightly be offered to God as worship. It is work that it is done *in* creation in defiance of God's plan *for* creation, rather than in furtherance of that plan. In respect of *that* kind of work, we should heed the exhortation in Ephesians 5: "Take no part in the unfruitful works of darkness."[425]

There are many examples that we could explore of *that* kind of "dark" work. Consider some of the technological initiatives driven by the ideology of transhumanism, for example. There is nothing intrinsically wrong with technology, biblically speaking. Human beings have been using "tools" to help them in their ruling and subduing of creation from the start, and often to the evident benefit of both humanity and the rest of creation. But what about technological research and development now funded by people who are determined to deconstruct creation itself in its present form? What about technological research and development specifically aimed at producing a "post-humanity" populated either by radically enhanced humans, or by greater-than-human machine intelligence? That is a fundamentally anti-humanistic endeavor, and it's impossible to see how it could ever be described as "work for God."[426] The important point is this, however: it's unspiritual work precisely because it represents an assault on personal matter. It's not unspiritual work because it *involves* materiality. We'll think some more about this in chapters 44 and 45.

31

Wealth

"He will also bless the fruit of your womb and the fruit of your ground, your grain and your wine and your oil, the increase of your herds and the young of your flock." (Deuteronomy 7:13)

THE BIBLICAL VIEW OF work (chapter 30) is much more expansive than the one that many modern people hold. In the modern world, "work" tends to mean specifically "activity that makes me better off economically than I was before." In doing this work I have thereby created for myself—temporarily or more permanently, and in differing degrees—what we refer to as "wealth." This wealth can then be used to access commodities that other people, in turn, have worked to produce, and then to trade or sell. This is "work," nowadays. In biblical thinking, on the other hand—as we have seen—work is part of our general human vocation. It involves a wide range of tasks and activities across the breadth of God's creation—in the home, in the field, in political and religious contexts, and so on. Economic exchange leading to wealth is not intrinsic to the biblical concept of work.

It is worth developing this idea in terms of "church work" in the NT context, having already commented in the previous chapter on the community life of the OT people of God. What kind of work is the Christian envisaged as doing in Ephesians 4, for example? It is "the work of ministry" or "service" (Greek *diakonía*), aimed at "building up the body of Christ."[427] This term "service" is used in other NT passages for the apostle Paul's own work in the churches, and also for the labor of his coworkers.[428] It is extraordinarily demanding work, accomplished only "by great endurance, in afflictions, hardships, calamities, beatings, imprisonments," and so on.[429] However, it is crucially important, enabling other Christians in turn to bear fruit "in every good work."[430] None of this Christian "work of faith and labor of love and steadfastness of hope in our Lord Jesus Christ" is carried out with the purpose of gaining material benefit.[431] Paul is actually determined that the Thessalonians, in particular, should clearly understand that this is true of his own apostolic service. He pointedly reminds them that "we were not idle when we were with you, nor did we eat anyone's bread without paying for it, but with toil and labor we worked night and day, that we might not be a burden to any of you."[432]

Economic exchange leading to wealth is not intrinsic to the biblical concept of work. However, that Pauline reminder to the Thessalonians makes it clear that working for material benefit is indeed *part* of doing "the work of God" in his world. Paul and his companions engaged in *business* while they were working in other ways, accruing wealth that they subsequently spent on goods that other people sold them.[433] In Thessalonica, Corinth, Ephesus, and likely in many other places too, these early Christian leaders engaged in economic exchange. In Paul's case this was based on his own trade of tent-making (or perhaps, more generally, working with leather).[434]

Our own Christian duty to engage in the same kind of economic activity is described in numerous places elsewhere in the NT. The ex-thief is now to do "honest work with his own hands," Paul instructs the Ephesians.[435] He commands those Thessalonian Christians who are "not busy at work" that "in the Lord Jesus Christ" they are "to earn their own living."[436] Idleness was a longstanding problem in the Thessalonian community, leading to a previous Pauline instruction: "If anyone is not willing to work, let him not eat."[437] Striving to maintain oneself and one's family economically so as not to be a burden to others is simply one aspect of our Christian discipleship.[438] Succeeding in this task puts us, consequently, in a position to "share with anyone in need" and generally to do "the work of God" in the world more broadly.[439] So no one must be allowed to shirk responsibility in this area. This same apostolic perspective is evident in the early post-apostolic *Didache* (already mentioned in chapter 23), which is alert to the human attraction to freeloading. If a traveller wants to join a Christian community and is skilled in a craft, "let him work for his bread. But if he has no craft, make such provision for him as your intelligence approves, so that no one shall live with you in idleness as a Christian. If he refuses so to do, he is making merchandise of Christ; beware of such people."[440]

Work that generates wealth in this way is part of our Christian vocation—one aspect of the entirety of our work, which must be regarded as worship. This is actually true in the NT even when it is work for another person that is neither chosen nor paid. For this reason, Paul can exhort Christian slaves: "Whatever you do, work heartily, as for the Lord and not for men, knowing that from the Lord you will receive the inheritance as your reward."[441]

In various ways the important role of wealth-creation within the overall biblical conception of work has not been well understood, historically. In fact, many Christians have not been able to accept wealth-creation as a valid aspect of their Christian vocation at all. For some, the problem has lain simply in the fact that material wealth is indeed *material*, and thereby (allegedly) not *spiritual*—a variant of the problem discussed in chapter 30. Even when believers have not gone this far, biblical teaching about the possession of too much wealth having negative *spiritual effects* on humans has weighed on many minds. This has often led Christians of previous generations both to renounce their current material possessions, retreating into the desert or joining communities of monks and nuns, and to avoid wealth-creation in the future.[442]

In modern times this same negative approach to wealth has tended to reveal itself in its weaker forms in the preference mentioned in chapter 30 for the caring professions over careers in business. It has manifested itself more strongly and explicitly in assaults on the wealthy, the systems that help to create wealth, and the corporations that so successfully utilize those systems. In this way of approaching life, then, wealth-creation is either wrong—something that all true Christians must renounce—or it is not *necessarily* wrong, but nevertheless likely to produce problems for believers. Therefore, Christians should at least be cautious about it. But probably they should avoid it as much as possible, indulging in "business" only as a kind of accidental by-product of following a profession that focuses on higher things. And perhaps, more radically, they should even participate in pulling down the entire "capitalist system."

The problem with the stronger versions of this negative approach is that everything else we have been thinking about in this book, including the earlier content of the present chapter, forbids us from adopting an antagonistic attitude towards wealth-creation as such. Well before we get to the NT texts, we already know from the OT that the rightful work of image-bearers in God's good creation includes "economic" work, and that the worshipper of God can expect a material reward from God in doing this work well. For example, we read in Proverbs 28 that "whoever works his land will have plenty of bread."[443] Deuteronomy 7 likewise promises such worshippers that God will "bless the fruit of your womb and the fruit of your ground, your grain and your wine and your oil, the increase of your herds and the young of your flock."[444] In the light of such Scriptures, Christians cannot possibly understand wealth-creation as lying outside the bounds of a truly Christian vocation, or even view it as an inferior form of Christian vocation when compared to others. We would do well to ponder this matter, among others, very carefully when we are tempted to involve ourselves in the kinds of social and political activism described in chapter 48, which tends to draw its inspiration from Karl Marx much more than from Holy Scripture.

If we should not be antagonistic towards wealth-creation as such, should we be hostile nevertheless towards certain forms of it? Yes! Not all wealth-creation is consistent with our human calling under God to look after our fellow-creatures. Not all wealth-creation takes place within the bounds that God has ordained for creation more generally. There *is* wealth-creation that is founded on dishonesty and greed. There *is* wealth-creation that is rapacious in nature, "creating wealth for stockholders, even though they already have more wealth than they know what to do with, by stealing the resources of the poor and the powerless."[445]

Should the *possession* of wealth, once it has been created, be regarded as an obstacle to the progress of the Christian believer through life? Absolutely! There are many warnings in the Bible about this reality. Wealth is for sharing, not for keeping, since it comes to us from God, and it remains God's more than it becomes ours. We are the representatives of God in distributing it to others. One is reminded here of a saying attributed to John Wesley, who urged Christians to earn all they can, save all they can, and give away all they can. The believer's relationship with wealth *can* become an obstacle to faith—but this is by no means inevitable. It is the *love* of money that is the root of all evil, not money itself.[446]

Arising out of all of this: the eleventh implication of a Christian anthropology is that the good work of God in the world in which we should participate must necessarily include a righteous wealth-creation that always attends to the full dimensions of the larger biblical story in which we find ourselves.

32

Creation Care

"The land mourns, and all who dwell in it languish, and also the beasts of the field and the birds of the heavens, and even the fish of the sea are taken away." (Hosea 4:3)

THE LARGER BIBLICAL STORY in which we find ourselves, in its full dimensions, is a narrative not just about human beings, but about the entirety of creation.[447] In thinking about work and wealth-creation, then, we must at the same time think about what secular people call "the environment" and "environmental issues." We work and we create wealth in this "environment," impacting it in various ways that (other) animals cannot, and being impacted by it in return. As creatures wielding "dominion," living in a world that is subject to change, the situation could not be otherwise. But what difference does it make to our thinking about these realities that Christians regard "the environment" as, in fact, "creation"? What does a Christian anthropology demand from us in thinking about, and then living out, "creation care"?

A considerable number of people have been seriously concerned for some time now about our current human relationship with our planetary environment. In the modern period, it is obvious that humanity has steadily been changing this environment far more significantly than ever before. The concern now is that we have gone too far, and that—for the sake of all creatures—we must constrain our activities and alter our habits. One aspect of this concern relates to the impact of human wealth-creation on the earth's climate. But that is only one issue among many.

Responses from Christians on this raft of environmental issues have often been deeply inconsistent with biblical teaching, and unfortunately these responses possess longstanding historical roots in Christian theology. The influential medieval thinker Thomas Aquinas, for example, believed that "the entire changeable universe is finally for the sake of the human good and species."[448] The Protestant Reformer John Calvin—although I commended him above Francis Bacon in chapter 13—did undeniably write that the "end for which all things were created . . . [was] that none of the conveniences and necessaries of life might be wanting to men."[449] This is a creation theology that has already placed humanity at the center of creation in a manner that is to varying degrees unbiblical—most centrally in proposing that other creatures exist merely for the sake of humans. This kind of *creation* theology has then often been wedded to a view of redemption that focuses entirely or mainly on *human salvation* and says little or nothing about the cosmos as a whole. In its most *radically* unbiblical form, salvation becomes all about human *souls* escaping their imprisonment in evil matter—from their incarceration in *bodies.*

One way or another, in all of this, the material creation as such becomes of little or no importance—not even our *human* material form. In the words of the fairly contemporary song mentioned in chapter 8, we are souls trapped for the moment in a body, waiting for rescue.[450] That rescue will take place when, as Peter writes, "the heavenly bodies will be burned up and dissolved, and the earth and the works that are done on it will be exposed."[451] Our souls (the story goes) will then enter a much better, spiritual eternity. Even in its less unbiblical forms, the point about this kind of anthropology is that it provides very little reason to look after creation. "It's all going to burn anyway," as some have said, "so why worry too much about it?" Why get interested in global warming for any other reason than its (alleged) signposting of the end-times? Why bother passing legislation designed to protect the environment? These are cogent questions if the earth is "merely a temporary way station on the road to eternal life, . . . unimportant except as a place of testing to get into heaven." It's hard to argue a different view if the earth is created only for the faithful to "use for profitable purposes on their way to the hereafter."[452]

The Christian anthropology presented in this book, however, carries very different implications. In this *biblical* anthropology, human beings are called to care for the whole of creation as it waits for its final redemption. God cares about it all, and so should we. Human beings wait for a coming redemption that involves the resurrection of the body. Non-human creation, currently "groaning . . . in the pains of childbirth," also looks for that same "revealing of the sons of God" on the way to the birth of a new heaven and a new earth.[453] Humans do not "escape" the remainder of creation in the course of these events. "Just as the resurrection hope is hope of a resurrection body, so resurrection life is to be part of a complete creation"—and this new creation stands in significant continuity with the present one.[454] A text like 2 Peter 3 might at first appear to tell us, instead, about a complete disjunction between them. But that would put it in serious tension with other biblical texts that clearly deny this reality. Our resurrection bodies, for example (if they are at all like Jesus's body) will be similar to, as well as different from, our present ones. There is continuity. The present world may well be destined for "fire"—but only so that it becomes a more purified version of its previous self.[455] Notice in this regard that the new heaven and the new earth are indeed just *that*—and not something utterly different.[456] Notice, too, that in that new creation human beings will still be "kings and priests," just as we are now.[457]

A genuinely Christian anthropology, then, requires that we love, not only our image-bearing neighbors, but also the remainder of what we rightly think of as God's creation—and not merely as "the environment." So it is that "whoever is righteous," biblically, "has regard for the life of his beast" (or, "the righteous care for the needs of their animals").[458] In this biblical anthropology, the well-being of the remainder of creation is in fact intrinsically bound up with our own and our neighbors' well-being. Both Holy Scripture and our own experience teach us about this. For it is evidently and especially the poorest people in creation who suffer most quickly and most devastatingly from negative "ecological" developments.[459]

All of this means, necessarily, that we must consider carefully whether we have ever made mistakes (and/or are now making them) in our exercise of "dominion" over the earth. Have we made mistakes that have harmed and are still harming creation at large—and thereby our human neighbors as well? We cannot just dismiss such questions as if they did not matter—for example, the question of whether certain approaches to modern wealth-creation have contributed to unusual and dangerous warming in the global climate. We only need to review the opening lines of Hosea 4 to discover the innately biblical character of this kind of idea—that human failures *can* result in damage to the rest of God's creation. The only questions, then, are *whether* any failures of ours have produced such results in our case, and what we can *do* about it.

Here I simply want to comment on a couple of important matters. The first pertains to the question of "trusting science" that I raised in chapter 4. The scientific evidence pertaining to the "whether we have contributed to climate change" question appears to be overwhelmingly supportive of a positive answer.[460] Yes, we have contributed. Yet recent polling figures from the USA, for example, suggest that a great many Christians do not even believe that global warming is a serious problem, much less that it is in some measure "our fault."[461] We may of course choose to adopt a skeptical posture toward the scientific community on such a matter. However, we must recognize the risk in doing so without very good reason (see once again our chapter 4). How shall we ever know whether we have made mistakes as image-bearers if we are not open to evidence that touches on that question? Would we not *want* to know, so that we can repent?

Of course, even if there *were* any doubt about the extent of global warming and its main causes (secondly), we should still be obliged by Holy Scripture to respond as creatively and constructively as we can to its negative effects, so far as we could ascertain them. As people holding to a Christian anthropology, that's part of our job. Global warming, *to the extent that it is happening* and *regardless of the precise nature of its causes*, ought to matter to biblical Christians. We *ought* to be fully engaged with others in responding to its challenges, as best we can. And this means that in the realm of public discourse, for example, we should be urging our politicians to consider, in all of their decision-making, the common good not only of all *people*, but of all *creatures*. At the same time, we should be insisting—as those called to be people-keepers as well as earth-keepers—that our leaders must continue to consider the good of all human beings *along with* the good of non-human creation. That imperative is *also* one to ponder carefully when we are tempted to involve ourselves in the kinds of social and political activism described in chapter 48, which tends toward one-sided recklessness in its demands.

The twelfth implication of a Christian anthropology is precisely that we must think about wealth-creation in the context of the whole of creation, as well as the importance of wealth-creation *to* the whole of creation—and then do good work to the glory of the Creator.

33

Love

"If you really fulfill the royal law according to the Scripture,
'You shall love your neighbor as yourself,' you are doing well."
(James 2:8)

I HOPE THAT IT is now clearer what it means to be a "working person," biblically-speaking. It may not always be easy to identify the particular work that you should be doing in God's world. But the framework provided in the previous three chapters should certainly help you in wrestling with the question of where all your work fits into the divine scheme of things, and how to do it all to the glory of God. My experience is that the wrestling will get us there in the end, even if the process is challenging. I recall a story a pastor friend told me about a woman in his community who had deeply grasped the idea that her Christian faith should affect every aspect of her life, including how she regarded her work. She was struggling, however, with the specific question of how to interpret "Christianly" her "work for profit" as an accountant. One day she excitedly told her pastor that she had worked it out: "My job as an accountant is to imitate the Creator God in bringing order out of chaos."

In the present chapter I'm going to develop the idea of our Christian work in God's world specifically along the lines of our social responsibility toward people outside the believing Christian community. In chapter 29 I made a proposal about what that certainly does *not* involve. But what *does* it involve? Here we must delve more deeply into the business of "loving our neighbor." I first discussed this duty in chapter 15, relating it to the business of "keeping" people, introduced in Genesis 4. We are to treat all our neighbors properly—the people in our proximity, including our enemies—as image-bearers of God, just like us. But what does this mean in practice?

It may seem "obvious" to you what it means. No doubt each of us already has in mind a whole range of attitudes and actions that fall within or outside

137

the scope of "love." The question is: how far are we *correct* in this assessment of what love of neighbor requires of us? Does our understanding of love really arise out of biblical teaching, or does at least some of it actually derive from elsewhere? After all, numerous contemporary Christians appear to believe that love of neighbor always requires "inclusion in," and forbids "exclusion from," Christian communities. But we have already seen that, biblically, this is not true. As 1 Corinthians 5 shows us, the truth is that our love of some neighbors may actually require the exclusion of others, at least temporarily. That exclusion itself may indeed be the most loving thing that can be done, in the long run, for the excluded: "so that his spirit may be saved in the day of the Lord."[462] So this business of loving one's neighbor is not so straightforward as we sometimes think. Like every other implication flowing out of a Christian anthropology, it requires some careful reflection.

As we begin, the most important thing to notice about the biblical love of neighbor is its close association with love for God: "you shall love the Lord your God . . . and your neighbor as yourself."[463] We must always assess what counts as "love of neighbor" in terms of our relationship with and commitment to God. We must "read" the command to love our neighbor in the context of the entire story of God in which all of humanity is caught up. What matters is not what we first *assume* that love looks like, or whether we *feel* loving in pursuing a certain course of action, or whether those around us in society necessarily *agree* that what we're doing is loving. What matters is whether our treatment of others does *in fact* count as love, given everything that we believe about God, ourselves, and creation at large. It is only in considering Paul's apparently harsh advice to the Corinthians in this context that we can possibly understand it—correctly—as neighbor-love, and not as something else. He loves both the church community and the individual Corinthian who must be excluded. He loves everyone enough to advocate (no doubt emotionally difficult) steps *on the part* of the community *in pursuit of* everyone's short-term and long-term good.

Biblical love is not indulgent; it is hard-edged. It has nothing to do with misty-eyed sentimentality that blinds us to reality and disables us from dealing with it well. At the very heart of biblical love lies, instead, the ability to see things as they actually are, and then to act morally on that basis. Biblical love is as "wise as serpents and innocent as doves" as it navigates a world inhabited by a considerable number of neighborly "wolves."[464] It is shrewd. It is marked not by weakness, but by strength—the strength of character that pursues what is good for others, no matter what. Biblical love is certainly bound up with compassion—with what *Merriam Webster* defines as "sympathetic consciousness of others' distress together with a desire to alleviate it." The Good Samaritan is said have possessed this deep inner sympathy with the victim that he encountered on the road to Jericho. It led him to attend to the man's needs as his neighbor (literally) got back on his feet. But biblical compassion does indeed lead people to do such *biblical* actions—not just any kinds of action that "feel compassionate" (such as putting that man out of his misery by killing him).

Our social responsibility toward people outside the believing Christian community is to love them with this kind of love—with righteous, compassionate love. By way of clarifying what this looks like, let me now briefly contrast it with a couple of perspectives found in contemporary society about what "compassion" (specifically) demands.

The first relates to the Samaritan case just mentioned. Contemporary "compassion," uninformed by biblical faith, demands that we take a very liberal approach to end-of-life issues, since people should not have to endure (it is said) what they consider to be intolerable suffering. Everyone should have the right to take action (and get help) in ending such suffering. Defendants in euthanasia court cases, prior to changes in the law in different countries that made at least some "mercy-killing" legal, often cited "compassion" as their defence. Conversely, Christian love demands that we try to help our neighbors to see their lives as precious gifts of God who alone gives life and rightly takes it away. It also demands that we support them in tangible ways in following the right path in this respect. It requires that we offer them the care they need to complete their journey to the end.

Contemporary "compassion," uninformed by biblical faith, also demands, secondly, that we look after, in an ongoing way, "the marginalized" in society. We need to care for those who find themselves significantly disadvantaged in various ways, and even in dire straits—lacking food and shelter, perhaps, or addicted to alcohol and drugs, and so on. Well, Christian love agrees that we have a duty to help the needy, while they are in great need. But Christian love also, necessarily, resists any idea that their intrinsic nature consists in being "helpless victims" rather than "image-bearers of God." Christian love empathizes with their plight, and (for example) feeds them when they have no food of their own. But it also calls them to—and supports them in—Christian discipleship. In this life of discipleship they once again become able (for example) to feed *others*, out of their own resources, rather than being fed. Christian love is necessarily hostile, then, to codependent organizations (including some churches, unfortunately) that help to keep "the marginalized" in their marginalized state in the long term, even while claiming to look after their best interests. Sometimes there are clearly financial incentives to do this. These are the "clients" without whose ongoing existence an organization's funding would dry up.

In these two cases, and in many others concerning "neighbors," what people think "compassion" involves is intrinsically bound up with the larger story that they think they inhabit. This is inevitable, although it is a truth self-consciously suppressed in some modern approaches to religion. I have written elsewhere, for example, about the way in which people enamored with the so-called "Axial Age hypothesis," such as the writer Karen Armstrong, have tried to argue that all religions essentially teach the same thing—that is, the virtue of compassion.[465] This is, I'm afraid, nonsense. Different religions and philosophies provide *very* different answers to a great number of important questions. These include, "What *is* compassion?" We Christians need to be sure, then, that our own beliefs about such matters really do arise from our own biblical story, and not from somewhere else.

So the thirteenth implication of a Christian anthropology is that we should "love" our neighbors outside the church. But what does that mean? Are we really loving them in our own social programs, for example, if these are essentially designed to leave them on the streets rather than moving them onwards? Are we really loving them if we ease our social consciences by giving street beggars money that they then spend on drugs, or by feeding them so that they are able to spend on the same drugs the money they get from other sources? Are soup kitchens a good idea, and why? And how are our social programs to be balanced anyway with our evangelism? For at the end of the day what fallen image-bearers really "need" is to turn to Christ. Are we really loving our neighbors if we don't prioritize putting *that* challenge before them? If we give them bread *instead* of the gospel? Contemporary culture will of course applaud us if we make that choice; it already does, when it sees us choosing that path. But in what sense does *that* choice flow out of a genuinely Christian view of the human person?

34

Politics

*"I saw the holy city, new Jerusalem, coming down out
of heaven from God, prepared as a bride adorned for
her husband." (Revelation 21:2)*

As we move toward the end of Part III, I want to say a few words about politics.[466] Jesus's Great Commission is aimed at calling image-bearers back to God and to his creation mandate (chapter 29). What exactly does that mandate require of Christians as they participate in "society at large," not only one-on-one with neighbors, but also at the level of larger community structures?

Many Christians appear to hold the opinion that they should stay entirely out of politics. If they mean by this that the Christian church should not aspire to be the federal government of a state (for example), then I agree. If they mean that a Christian's primary loyalty should be to Christ, and not to any political movement or party, I also agree. The Christian's first duty is to be a Christian, and not something else. The church's first responsibility is to be the church, and not something else.

But what if politics will not stay out of the church? For example: what if the federal government of my state (or any level of government, for that matter) announces its intention of passing legislation that amounts to the imposition on Christians of a particular set of beliefs and values that they must necessarily reject? What if politics itself has essentially become a particular kind of intolerant religion, intent on repressing its competitors? It was the Bolshevik revolutionary Leon Trotsky who allegedly once said, "You may not be interested in war, but war is interested in you." Likewise, you may not be interested in politics—but what if politics is interested in *you*, and your family, and your church? What if politics is knocking on your door and demanding entry into your home, and indeed your church. What if it intends to interfere with the way you raise your children, or counsel your flock? You cannot stay "out of" something when you are already immersed *in* it—and when it is intent on drowning you and those around you. Love of Christian neighbor, if nothing else—including the neighbors who are your children—forbids passivity in such a case. Concern for our legitimate interests as Christians, alluded to by the apostle Paul in writing to the Christians in Philippi, forbids it.[467] We need to be actively engaged in politics—in debating with other people what a "good city" (Greek *polis*) looks like, and in helping to construct it.

But this engagement ought to be premised on more than simply our legitimate self-interest. The entirety of Paul's text runs like this: "Let each of you look not *only* to his own interests, but *also to the interests of others*" (my emphasis). The fact is that our duty of love for neighbors outside the church *also* demands that we take an active interest in politics. It is a great Christian work genuinely to help the homeless neighbors whom we find on our city's streets. But doesn't our duty to our unchurched neighbors also involve discovering all the societal dysfunctions that may have contributed either to their being on the streets in the first place, or to keeping them there now? Doesn't Christian love involve, not only dealing compassionately with the consequences of bad social planning (for example), but also trying to replace it with good planning? Jeremiah was called, while in exile, to "seek the welfare of the city where I have sent you."[468] The book of Daniel provides us with an extended narrative example of someone who responded to this calling. Are Christians not likewise called, as people in "exile," to live not only for ourselves, but also for others, in the public realm?[469]

Holy Scripture does indeed provide us with more than enough reason to engage in such a "politics of exile." The foundation for this politics rests on what we learn from the Bible about God's own interactions with the world that is not yet fully his kingdom—the world as it exists now, before the new Jerusalem arrives. This is of course a present world deeply corrupted by evil. But God, who is incomparably good, commits himself to working in it *for* its good. He does this in largely non-coercive ways that respect the moral freedom of his frequently wicked image-bearers. From the beginning of Genesis onwards, in fact, God continually finds ways of turning the evil that he discovers the world—and in his own people—to good.

For example, Abraham and Sarah are far from ideal carriers of his covenant promise, morally speaking. But the promise survives, because it is *God's* promise and not theirs. Later in the Genesis story, God works with Jacob, Leah, and Rachel, even though their "society" is *also* significantly dysfunctional. The society of *Jacob's children* is similarly problematic, as the family baggage gets passed down from one generation to the next. But Joseph eventually recognizes explicitly what God has been doing with them all. Addressing his murderous brothers, he tells them, "You meant evil against me, but God meant it for good, to bring it about that many people should be kept alive."[470] The Joseph story begins in chaos, but because of what "God meant" in it all, the narrative ends in "shalom." It is a divine comedy (chapter 19).

And this is also how the biblical story continues into Exodus and beyond—not least in the societal framework that God builds around his chosen people Israel. The law that lies at the heart of these provisions is not designed for righteous people, but for sinners. God weaves an orderly legal framework around his sinful people that is designed largely to contain their moral chaos while the redemptive story continues. There is a striking pragmatism in his actions. God does not attempt to bring his kingdom into being, suddenly and all at one time, by creating law. Instead, mindful of the raw human material at his disposal, he nudges the Israelites gently in the direction of the new Jerusalem. He does this while creating a societal framework for them that prevents them in the meantime from completely self-destructing. These are pragmatic, rather than a utopian politics.

All of this is instructive for us. Human beings are God's image-bearers, called to work in God's entire creation for its good. This includes what we sometimes sloppily call "secular society" (as if God were somewhere *else*). As image-bearers we are constantly exhorted in the biblical tradition to "be like God" precisely by being involved in the world.[471] This implies involvement in the political as much as any other sphere of life. In fact, it implies a certain *kind* of political engagement. From the beginning of the biblical story God does not relate to the world in an all-or-nothing way, but in a "realistic" way. He assesses what can realistically be achieved in a society largely populated by people who will not follow his ways. This is a suggestive paradigm for us as image-bearers. It suggests a politics inspired and informed by our vision of the kingdom of God, but likewise realistic about what can be achieved in a currently "plural" environment in our various societies. It also models an unwillingness to abandon the political realm merely because it is inevitably marked by compromise.

The fourteenth implication of a Christian anthropology, then, is that Christians need to exercise such "dominion" as they can in the public, political sphere—as much as any other sphere of life—while seeking "the welfare of the city." In doing so we shall, "like God," look to nudge society as much as possible toward righteousness, to restrain and minimize evil as much as we can, and (where possible) to turn evil toward the good. We shall do this doggedly, and for the sake of *all* our neighbors, not just our Christian ones.

We need not think—and we *should not think*—of this "politics" as involving only large-scale political involvement of the kind that makes the news. For most of us, our engagement in the realm of public discourse will be at a much less spectacular level—but not for that reason any less important. In many parts of the world getting elected to school boards, for example, is one of the most important goals that a parent can strive to attain. Indeed, in many contexts it would frankly be reckless to continue to send one's children to public school if one were *not* willing to getting involved in "the politics" of that system. We need to ensure that our children and others will be morally safer in those environments than would otherwise be the case. We must at all costs never underestimate any of the "small things" that we do for God, in this area or in any other. I am reminded in this regard of the closing sections of the novel *Middlemarch* by George Eliot. Dorothea, the main character, has suffered much disappointment in her life, but her impact as she gets on regardless with "small things" is significant:

> Her full nature . . . spent itself in channels which had no great name on the earth. But the effect of her being on those around her was incalculably diffusive: for the growing good of the world is partly dependent on unhistoric acts; and that things are not so ill with you and me as they might have been, is half owing to the number who lived faithfully a hidden life, and rest in unvisited tombs.[472]

This is not the ill-considered, romantic, and utopian politics that aims to pull down entire economic "systems" in the interests of "freedom," with no sober thought for what comes next (chapters 31 and 48). This is also not the reckless utopian politics that gives no thought to the consequences of radical "save the planet" ideology for our vulnerable human neighbors (chapters 32 and 49). It is not the kind of politics, for example, that insists that "we need to change everything because right now our current system is on a collision course with the future of humanity and the future of our civilization," but possesses not a single coherent idea about what will replace the allegedly "oppressive and racist" capitalist system that needs to be overthrown.[473] Biblically grounded politics is different. It is the sober politics of those who understand that the kingdom of God is "not yet"—but who *in that context*, and in ways that are consistent with the current fallen, complicated state of affairs in the world, certainly pursue kingdom ideals as far as is possible.

35

Committing

"The one who doubts is like a wave of the sea that is driven and tossed by the wind, . . . he is a double-minded man, unstable in all his ways." (James 1:6–8)

WE ARE NOW AT the end of Part III, which has drawn out some important implications of embracing a truly biblical account of "the fundamentals of humanness" (as outlined in Part II). I emphasized at the end of Part II the importance of actively *embracing* a Christian understanding of these fundamentals. I suggested that they will not find their way to the core of our being without some effort on our part. The same is true of the *implications* of these fundamentals.

This is (again) because we all live in fallen societies that in one way or another are built, not on the rock of God's truth about our humanity, but on the shifting sands of mere human opinion. They are built in all kinds of ways on understandings of humanness that are different from our own. All of this is true, whether or not our neighbors could ever articulate exactly what their own anthropologies are, and why they believe in them. Nevertheless, there is always a "philosophy" that informs their beliefs and their behavior—and it may well be significantly out of step with a Christian worldview. So in such fallen societies, people may well have no compelling reason to stand up for the rights of babies in the womb, or to oppose the liberalization of opinion and law concerning end-of-life issues. They may consider it the most natural thing in the world for their neighbors to engage in all kinds of sexual activities outside the bounds of a male-female marriage, and indeed for individuals to choose which of "male" and "female" they would like to be. And so on. At the root of it all, they may live their lives indifferent or hostile to the idea that there is one, living Triune God, and they may regard as ridiculous the idea that human life should be conceived as "worship" of this God.

Christians live in such fallen cultures, and these cultures "scream" the following message at us every day: "Your view of the human person is absurd; why don't you adopt ours instead?" How they do this, exactly, depends to some extent on the *particular* culture we're considering, but of course there are also *global* realities beyond the local ones: cable and satellite television, internet, and social media. Research suggests that many people quite enjoy listening to cultural screaming in these virtual forms, and that they do it a *lot*. By way of example, in Canada over 93 percent of adults have at least one television in their home, on which they watch just under four hours of "product" (on average) each day.[474] Furthermore, 75 percent of Canadians also browse the internet while watching television. And 73 percent spend at least three to four hours each day online, while 66 percent spend at least one hour each day online watching television or movies. The formative power of all this interaction with the digital world is *massive*. The general cultural environment seeps into even our "private" spaces by these means, imperceptibly shaping over time our understanding of reality, our imaginations, and our desires. In the process it leads us, inexorably, toward (perhaps subliminal) conclusions about what is "normal" in the world.

All of this need not to be a matter of conscious intent in order for it to have profound effects on people, leading them to firm opinions concerning "what everyone believes" and *should* believe. But there *is* certainly conscious intent in the mix as well. Politicians would like us to see the world in ways that are advantageous to them. Businesspeople hope to get us to buy their products. Social activists desire to transform our hearts and minds in ways that will make it easier for them to change the world in their chosen direction. None of these people any longer needs us to go outside our homes, physically, in order to sell us their goods. We are their captive audiences and customers in our own homes. From the start it was the intent of companies like Facebook to captivate us in this way. As Sean Parker (the company's founding president) has admitted, their goal was to consume "as much of your time and conscious attention as possible," exploiting in the process an obvious "vulnerability in human psychology."[475]

It is possible for us to underestimate the extent of our vulnerability, as innately social creatures, to these evangelistic strategies—the extent of the control that they exercise over us. For as author and media activist Duane Elgin pointed out in 2008, "To control a society, you don't need to control its courts, you don't need to control its armies, all you need to do is control its stories. And it's television and Madison Avenue that is telling us most of the stories, most of the time, to most of the people."[476] It's possible to underestimate the extent of our vulnerability to all this cultural "screaming."

It's possible to underestimate, in particular, the extent to which constant exposure to it can render the gospel implausible even to those who claim to have received it, causing us in the words of James to become "like a wave of the sea that is driven and tossed by the wind"—a "double-minded" person.[477] Judging by what happens in many of our homes, it's *certainly* possible for parents to fail to understand the extent to which exposure to "cultural screaming" can render the gospel implausible to our *children*, wiring their very brains in ways that threaten gradually to inoculate them against biblical truth. In chapter 27, I proposed that it is *our* responsibility as parents, and no one else's responsibility, to see to it that our children are brought up "in the discipline and instruction of the Lord." We cannot simply delegate away that responsibility to others. I had in mind, in that chapter, schoolteachers. But it's equally true that we cannot—*should* not—delegate our parenting responsibility away to talking *screens* of any kind. In fact, we need to limit our children's access to such screens as rigorously and for as long as we can.

When my own children were young, we had one television in one room of the house, and we watched (together) one program each week (*Star Trek*). *Star Trek* had its own propagandistic edge, of course—but it was *relatively* harmless. And its message was in any case overwhelmed by those of all the good books we read, together and separately, back then. Parents nowadays find themselves in a more challenging general environment when it comes to screens, but the principle remains the same. If we don't take this issue seriously, we shall find ourselves *thinking* that *we* are the ones raising our children, when *in fact* they are being brought up by the people they encounter on their mobile phones.

This is the family version of a larger problem in many of our church communities—that pastors imagine that it's the church that is catechizing the flock, whereas in fact it's Netflix. It could hardly be otherwise in churches whose leadership apparently believes that, in response to the many, many hours that even Christians are spending absorbed in the digital world, it still makes sense to "do church" in a traditional manner that involves one worship meeting each week for everyone (maybe), and an extra midweek gathering for keeners.

To repeat: Christians live in fallen cultures that scream at us every hour of every day, "Your view of the human person is absurd." We need, then, both to limit our exposure to the screaming as much as possible—understanding it for what it is—and at the same time *very deliberately and counter-culturally* to work out, actively, the implications of our Christian anthropology in our lives. Instead of allowing our minds to be filled with other people's perspectives on humanness, becoming "conformed to this world," we must commit instead to filling them with Christian truth. We must reflect on this and converse about it "when you sit in your house, and when you walk by the way, and when you lie down, and when you rise"— throughout the day in all its aspects.[478] And we must teach it "diligently to your children," in pursuit of their transformation "by the renewal of your mind," and of their discernment, too, of "the will of God, what is good and acceptable and perfect."[479]

It will be helpful to us in this quest to stand firm, counter-culturally, in our Christian faith, if we're able not just to recognize elements of foreign anthropology in our thinking, but also to assign them to where they rightly belong in the intellectual world. It will help us if we can "put them in their place." This leads us on to Part IV of the book, which adds to the proclamation of *truth* about being human, in Parts II and III, an analysis of many prevailing, contemporary *lies* about it, and where they come from. *This* is where the cuckoos get their moment in the limelight! Christian persons, as creatures determined to protect the integrity of our Christian "nest" and to see its rightful inhabitants flourish, need to know as much as possible about the cuckoos that threaten it, including their "natural habitats." It's all part of the process through which we come to see clearly which of the anthropological birds in our nest are not our own, even though they may *look* very much like our own. And this will help us to do a better job of removing such cuckoos from our thinking. In Part IV of this book, therefore, we'll spend some time conducting an identification parade. We'll go deeper into the analysis of some of the "foreign bodies" that show up in various ways in our Christian nest when it come to anthropology, and we'll be doing some focused work on where they come from.

PART IV

Foreign Bodies

36

Follow the Science

*". . . to make you know what is right and true, that you may
give a true answer to those who sent you." (Proverbs 22:21)*

AS WE GET GOING on Part IV, let me say something similar to what I stated
just prior to Part II, which for many readers (in the language of *Star Wars*)
may feel like a long time ago in a galaxy far, far away. Some readers are
going to find Part IV quite challenging. This is because, in the course of
their Christian journey so far, they have had little to no exposure to the
history of ideas. If this describes *you*, then I urge you to "stick with" these
final chapters—difficult or not—all the way to the end. For if we are to
combat the cuckoos in our nest effectively, we need to understand their
points of origin and their evolution. So if you find the material difficult,
"Don't Panic!"[480] Slow and steady is once again the way to go. And "going"
with a group of friends may (again) be wiser than "going it alone," so that
you can help each other with problems and questions that you may have.
Above all, *keep* going. Don't stop because you can't work something out,
but park the problem on a mental shelf in a mental cupboard with a label
on it saying, "To be picked up later"—and come back to it down the road
somewhere. Stick with these chapters, and you'll be glad that you did. And
hopefully you'll find it easier to trust me when I say this about Part IV
than you did when I said it about Part II—because you've discovered that
I was telling you the truth about Part II!

I want to begin by circling back to Part I and to the human being
as a "knowing" person.[481] So if you skipped chapters 3 to 6 the first time
through, this is the moment to go back and read them. These chapters
represent a good place to start in Part IV, because one of the reasons why
contemporary Christians find it difficult to commit to the biblical view of
the human person is that (without necessarily realizing it) they have been
deeply shaped by certain modern ideas concerning how we gain reliable

knowledge. In reality these modern ideas *come from somewhere*. They possess "natural habitats." But this is not necessarily clear to people accustomed simply to "seeing them around the place." We are social creatures; we take our lead from others in forming our opinions. And "what everyone knows" in contemporary society about gaining reliable knowledge of the world is that our "legitimate authorities" do not include the Bible. Interacting daily with the impressive body of knowledge that modern science in particular has assembled, Christians can easily come to feel that appeals to Scripture on topics like human nature are "weak." And that is not a good starting point for the development of a robust Christian anthropology.

It was not always this way. The Bible used to be widely regarded (at least in "Christendom") in a radically different way—as virtually an encyclopedia of all true knowledge. But when modern science began to challenge this settled opinion, some Christians responded in an unfortunate way. Rather than welcoming the new scientific knowledge about the world and trying to integrate it into their larger Christian idea of truth, they set their face against it. This undoubtedly then accelerated a trend in post-Reformation Europe toward understanding Holy Scripture and emerging science as being necessarily at war with one another. This was the age of "Enlightenment," which in Immanuel Kant's view (1784) was about "humanity's release from self-imposed tutelage to external authority and readiness to use its independent reason."[482] Enlightened people had gradually come to realize (they said) that scientific method must now become the primary "legitimate authority" with respect to knowledge. Knowledge must be based on "empirical" enquiry (involving observation and experience) that gathered together "facts" and assigned them a place within a matrix of scientific "laws." What secular people call "Nature" must now provide the framework within which biblical truth claims could be assessed and pronounced to be helpful or unhelpful.

This is the natural habitat out of which has emerged some important "common knowledge" that many of our contemporaries now possess. They know, on the one hand, that the Bible is largely or completely untrue and, on the other hand, that only human reason, working with empirically established facts, can provide us with reliable knowledge. In its most extreme form this approach to life is known as "scientism," with its almost complete contempt for truth claims that cannot be verified by empirical testing and its almost religious faith in science alone as the path to true knowledge. When we encounter this philosophical bird, borne along on the powerful winds of "facts," over-wintering on our Christian shores or even turning up in our Christian nest, it is precisely its massive self-confidence that can lead us to doubt the validity of our own "flimsy," faith-based convictions. "Science has spoken," so very confidently; what can faith possibly add?

It is important when we find ourselves thinking in this way to remember our discussion in chapters 4 and 5 about physics and metaphysics. We need to recall the way in which physics is *in fact*—despite the imperialist claims of scientism—only able to provide us with certain kinds of important knowledge. Science can tell us a considerable amount about the physical world, and we should be grateful for it. But science cannot do what scientism has apparently deluded many modern people into *thinking* it can do. It cannot provide us with knowledge about what is "right," for example—how human beings *ought* to live. Many modern people apparently assume the opposite, and they believe therefore that they can do without the inconveniencies of realities like religion. They assume that "right" can be deduced from what is "normal" in the world—what is "natural" to certain smaller groups of people, in the first instance, and then to larger groups all the way up to "humanity as a whole." But this is not true.

Only a moment's critical thought will reveal this to us, although as a witty and wise man once said, a moment is a long time and thinking is painful.[483] Let us embrace this short-lived pain with joy, however. First, suppose that scientific enquiry has established that it is natural to certain groups of people to practice cannibalism. Does that make cannibalism *right*, even for those groups? How do we get from "is" to "ought"—from what they actually *do* to what they *ought* to do? But then suppose, secondly, that scientific enquiry were somehow able to discover that *all* human beings possess a "natural tendency" in the same cannibalistic direction? Or alternatively, that human beings, as an entire class, are selfish by nature? If both cannibalism and selfishness are intrinsic to *human* nature, would both be right, and would vegetarianism and generosity be wrong? This makes no moral or logical sense. And of course, thirdly, the task of discovering empirically what might be "natural" to *all* human beings is in reality impossibly difficult. How could we ever succeed in such an endeavor? What kind of research strategy would we need to develop?

Science as science, in its passion to discover what *is* the case, is not capable of delivering authoritative statements on how human beings *ought* to live. And this helps to explain why, when we carefully examine modern statements that claim to ground in "Nature" various exhortations about what is right, we always find that these claims are not *in fact* rooted in physics at all, but instead in metaphysics. In other words, these modern claims about the nature of "Nature" are not what they first appear to be. It may not be Christian faith—at least, not overtly—that provides them with their foundation, but it is certainly a non-empirically-derived "philosophy" of some kind.

Consider, for example, the American Declaration of Independence (1776). Near its beginning we read about "laws of Nature and of Nature's God" that "entitle" a certain people-group to assume among other nations a "separate and equal station." But how exactly do the laws of Nature "entitle" anyone to anything? The appeal to "Nature" makes it seem at first that this and others of the Declaration's assertions are grounded in scientific endeavor. But in reality they are not grounded in such scientific endeavor at all, and they *could not* be. The "truths" articulated in this document are instead asserted to be "self-evident"—among them, "that all men are created equal" and that they are "endowed . . . with certain unalienable rights." And now it becomes particularly clear that science is not running the show. For *actual* scientific research reveals that the great majority of people throughout history have not believed that "all men are created equal," nor that they are "endowed . . . with certain unalienable rights."

Now I agree, regardless, that human beings do possess rights, and I argued that point of view in chapter 22. But notice that, in that chapter, I appealed to Holy Scripture to ground these rights, and indeed to discover what human rights truly *are*. The right to die is not, for example, one of them (chapter 24), no matter which assertions people make about this topic. The authors of the Declaration, influenced by the European developments described above, do not want to go the way of Scripture. They are looking for what they think of as a stronger authority to undergird their claims: the laws of Nature (with "Nature's God" slipping in as a footnote). But what they are actually doing in this Declaration, in invoking these "laws of Nature," is *pretending* to make scientific claims about "rights" while in reality grounding them in obviously metaphysical claims—and hoping that no one will notice. Unfortunately, this has set a precedent, whereby nowadays all sorts of people simply *assert* that something new is a "right," and dare people to call them on it—a kind of poker player's bluff.

This is how scientism necessarily proceeds. And we must not be intimidated by it into thinking that our appeals to Scripture, in all the domains that Scripture rightfully addresses, are weak. Everyone necessarily—and whether or not they realize or admit it—interprets physics within the context of metaphysics. They may do it well or badly—but they certainly *do* it. Bringing our specifically *Christian* faith to bear on science is no more or less problematic than bringing in any other philosophy or "faith." And, of course, we believe that we have particularly good *reasons* to hold that our Christian metaphysics are *true*. Many notable modern scientists have believed the same.

My point in writing in this way is not just to alert you to a philosophical cuckoo—the Follow the Science Cuckoo—that often turns up in the Christian nest concerning how we arrive at reliable knowledge. That's important, of course. Next time you hear someone in your church community advocating belief or action on the basis of what science has "proved" to be true about "human nature," you should certainly challenge that assertion. A cuckoo has revealed itself that needs to be ejected from the Christian nest. For Christians, what is natural to humanity—even if it could genuinely be discovered (e.g., selfishness)—would provide no secure guidance about how we should live.

But more than this: I'm also concerned to show you just how logically incoherent "scientism" is, on its *own* terms, and why there is nothing to fear in it. So next time someone *outside* your Christian community urges you simply to "follow the science" on some subject or other, may I suggest that you respond, first, by saying that as a matter of principle you always take very seriously what scientists say within their various areas of expertise. *But then* (may I suggest), consider following up with this: "But I don't intend simply to accept without discussion the metaphysics (e.g., the ethics and the politics) that you appear to be smuggling into this conversation along with the science." This will either end the conversation quickly, or it will make it much better.

37

Gut Feelings

"They should seek God, and perhaps feel their way
toward him and find him. Yet he is actually not far
from each one of us." (Acts 17:27)

AS MODERN PEOPLE ENTERED the nineteenth century, many of them found themselves satisfied that the new scientific method and its consequent technologies were "delivering the goods." But when everything in the world is governed by reason, facts, law, and calculation, what gets lost? Charles Dickens explores this question in his novel *Hard Times*. The misguided schoolteacher Mr. Gradgrind, who lives in the industrial north of England, possesses utter confidence in facts and calculation; this is all that *exists*. Here we encounter scientism with a vengeance. Discovering that his children have attended a rehearsal at the nearby circus, he is dismayed. "I should as soon have expected to find my children reading poetry," he complains to his wife.[484] Unsurprisingly, his family's story does not end well.

This is the background against which, in continuing our reflections on the "knowing" person, we must try to understand what is called "Romanticism." This was an influential, largely nineteenth-century movement that touched various aspects of culture, including literature, art, and music. The Romantics focused on what *they* believed had been lost in modernity, emphasizing over against the scientific mindset the individual spirit, the subjective, the irrational, the imaginative, the spontaneous, and the emotional.

For example, the German artist Caspar David Friedrich (1774–1840) produced one of *the* iconic Romantic paintings: "Wanderer above the Sea of Fog" (1818). He captures the thrust of the movement in these famous words: "The artist should not only paint what he sees before him, but also what he sees in himself. If, however, he sees nothing within him, then he should also refrain from painting what he sees before him."[485] The subject in the "Wanderer" stands alone atop one of the strange rock formations found in beautiful Swiss Saxony. He is out of doors, away from urban, mechanized life. He is not *analyzing* Nature, but instead he stands *in* Nature as *part* of it, mesmerized by the haze of the fog in front of him. His back is to us, not to shut us out of the spiritual experience he is having, but so that we may share in it by seeing the world through his eyes.

Romantics such as Friedrich were skeptical about the ability of reason to deliver many important human goods, and they did not appeal to it as an authority. The kind of understanding of the world that they promoted was not rational, but empathetic. It had to do with feeling more than with thinking. As the "proto-Romantic" German author Johann Gottfried von Herder (1744–1803) once said: "Feeling is the way of understanding."[486] The Englishman William Wordsworth's poem "The Tables Turned" pursues the same line. His reader is urged to "quit your books" and get outside, permitting "Nature [to] be your teacher" as she endows him with "spontaneous wisdom." "One impulse from a vernal wood," the poet claims, "may teach you more of man, of moral evil and of good, than all the sages can." We need only restrain "our meddling intellect" and promote instead "a heart that watches and receives."[487]

This is the natural habitat for the second main idea that has shaped our contemporary mindset concerning how we gain reliable knowledge—the Look Inside Yourself Cuckoo. The "legitimate authority" in this case is no longer Nature dissected by reason in the form of science—what Wordsworth refers to as "murder" by dissection. Now it is Nature apprehended by intuition, imagination, and emotion. And it is (in Friedrich's words) not only Nature as it lies *before* the person contemplating it, but also as (s)he discovers it *within*. It has made a long flight, this Romantic bird, to get to our own particular shores, and it has changed its colors somewhat along the way, as we shall see—but it is still recognizable for what it is.

The problem with Romanticism from a Christian point of view is not that it encourages us to remember that we are more than simply "minds in bodies." That is an appropriate intervention. We do need to remember that beauty is important, and that it is good to get outdoors and learn things from creation. We would all be vastly impoverished, moreover, if we lacked all the manifold gifts that Romantic musicians, authors, artists, and so on, have bequeathed us. In these respects, Romanticism is unproblematic. The problem with Romanticism lies, as in scientism, in overreach. Romantic "method," like scientific method, possesses its proper domain in the world. But the problem with both "methods," in their (customary) post-Christian forms, is that they do not respect the borders of these domains.

Insofar as Romanticism remains at all serious about retaining a *connection* between the worlds "outside" and "within," Wordsworth's poem provides us with a great example of the difficulty. He proposes that hanging out in a forest in springtime will teach us more about our human nature, and about good and evil, than all our interactions with wise human authors through the ages. But how can Nature possibly communicate such truths? We already discussed this general problem in the previous chapter. What is new in Wordsworth is that he now portrays Nature as a kind of personal divinity. But this does not help us toward a solution to our problem, especially since he does not bother to tell us why we should accept his novel religion. Nor is it helpful for him to suggest that in listening to this alleged goddess, Nature, we should empty our minds—that we should suppress our "meddling intellects." Will these empty minds mysteriously fill up again, and how—and who will be doing the filling?

So even when Romanticism remains serious about retaining a connection between the outer and inner "worlds," it is problematic. But in practice this approach to reality has often *not* remained serious along such lines. The result is that *everything* becomes about what I find "within." In contemporary culture, it is certainly a person's subjective testimony to this *interior* reality that carries the greatest amount of weight. It is the personal declaration of the human "nature" that I discover when I look inside myself. Notice the evolution of ideas here. It is no longer a matter of truths being self-evident to the many ("we") who connect either intellectually (chapter 36) or intuitively with the *cosmos*. These truths are now self-evident only to the single person ("I") who ponders the *self*.

In this evolved, differently colored Romantic cuckoo, we are still dealing nevertheless with *markedly religious sentiments*. Its brightest, most garish colors are found in its most extreme (but common) contemporary form, known as narcissism: "a mental condition in which people have an inflated sense of their own importance [and] a deep need for excessive attention and admiration."[488] It is a *holy* moment in contemporary culture when individuals, having looked within, disclose the truth about their individual human nature to others. This is why to question nowadays a person's subjective account of "who they really are" is in many quarters virtually tantamount to blasphemy (i.e., a religious crime). In several countries citizens are in fact essentially *forbidden* to question this personal testimony by new laws passed in pursuit of freedom of (this contemporary kind of) religion. So there is strong social and indeed legal pressure to regard as self-evidently right the assertion that people's claims about their "natural selves" are self-evidently true. And with so many of our contemporaries apparently so deeply convinced in this way that personal introspection is the best—and perhaps the only—route to discovering "who I really am," it's not surprising (again) that Christians can easily come to feel that appeals to Scripture on such a topic are "weak."

Once again, however, we must not be intimidated. The weakness lies entirely on the other side. For "interior human nature" is simply part of Nature at large, and like Nature at large it cannot help us answer a whole range of important questions about our humanness. For what *is* the case does not by itself prescribe what *ought* to be the case. So when faced with the question of "natural" desires, for example, our Christian question ought to the same as before: why should we believe that these desires offer us a reliable guide for life? It may well be natural for me to want to do all sorts of things. But which of these natural things *ought* I to do, and which ought I *not* to do, and why?

This is an important distinction drawn by most human beings—Christians or not—in at least some parts of their lives. Most people possess strong convictions about which desires they and others should not act upon—indeed, which kinds of actions are not only unethical, but should also be illegal. Are there really people prepared to argue consistently that what is *good* is simply what an individual feels to be *natural*? If they do exist, and if they are determined to live consistently with that philosophy, all I can say is that the rest of us would be well advised to avoid them. They can only do us harm.

No matter what *other people* believe, anyway, it is clear that truly Christian people cannot base *their* self-understanding on the results of introspective enquiry into what is "natural." From a Christian point of view, what we feel to be natural is entirely irrelevant when it comes to deciding the question of how we should construe our human identity and live it out before God. So when church communities make space for this alien, Romantic idea—when they imitate the surrounding culture in ascribing the status of revelation to the self-reporting of neighbors concerning "their truth"—they have seriously lost the plot of the gospel. They have allowed a gigantic Look Inside Yourself Cuckoo not only to take up residence in their Christian nest, but to flourish there. And if it is left there undisturbed, profoundly negative consequences will inevitably follow for the faith and life of the rightful inhabitants of the nest who are committed to following *the* Truth. Cuckoos do serious damage.

38

The Power of Choice

*"I have set before you life and death, blessing and curse.
Therefore choose life." (Deuteronomy 30:19)*

THE TWO MODERN, PHILOSOPHICAL cuckoos discussed in chapters 36 and 37 fail in their quest somehow to ground in "Nature" the knowledge of what human beings are, and how they should live. Precisely at their moment of failure, a significant, third bird shows up. This one has nothing to say about how we gain secure knowledge. It's important for us to recognize, however, its connection with the other two, and the effect that it has tended to have on society.

This cuckoo begins with the same musical idea as its relatives—that we certainly cannot depend on Holy Scripture for reliable instruction in matters like ethics or politics. But its melody and the accompanying lyrics then take off in a different direction, for in this song we cannot depend on Nature either. What is left to us is *choice*. We must abandon our quest to grasp hold of objective knowledge, and we must accept the necessity simply of exercising choice and getting on with our lives. The Good is whatever human beings *will* it to be. We are on our own, and we must *construct* our own reality. It is not "given."

The first natural habitat of this idea was ancient Greece around the fifth century BC. Here itinerant teachers known as Sophists—men like Protagoras and Thrasymachus—would travel around teaching young men, for payment, how to debate effectively. They believed that there exists no ultimate distinction between things as they really are ("nature," Greek *phýsis*) and mere convention ("law," Greek *nómos*). The implication for teachers and students of rhetoric, specifically, is that we need not concern ourselves about a correspondence between our words and any external reality to which they might refer. The Sophists taught rhetoric merely as a craft, then—a set of skills that might help a speaker achieve whichever goals he desired. The point was simply to win debates—irrespective of the speaker's knowledge about a particular subject, irrespective of truthfulness, and irrespective certainly of virtue. As Protagorus put it (as quoted in Plato's *Theaetetus*), "man is the measure of all things"—the willing, speaking, choosing man.

There is no Nature to which a human being is accountable in these activities, although as a debater he obviously functions as a member of a society of humans who are also willing, speaking, and choosing. Out of this process there does emerge, as an expression of the will of a particular group, social convention—there does emerge "law." But there is nothing *beyond* this "will of the people"—whoever the "people" might be. So there can be no appeal to any higher authority, such as a transcendental "justice"—because none exists. The will of the people is everything. As Thrasymachus understood, in this scenario justice can be nothing other than obedience to the laws of society, which the powerful have willed into existence because they *can*. Might is right. The same basic idea later appears in Marxist thinking. Here "law" is understood merely as an instrument in the service of those who exercise dictatorship in a society by way of control of the means of production. The *Communist Manifesto* (1848) is explicit on this point, attacking "bourgeois notions of freedom, culture, law," and so on, as merely "the outgrowth of the conditions of your bourgeois production and bourgeois property, just as your jurisprudence is but the will of your class made into a law for all."[489]

It was precisely this focus on the craft of rhetoric, detached from knowledge, truth, and virtue, that Plato (following Socrates) so deeply disliked about the Sophists. It led him to a consequential attempt to ground these realities once again in transcendence—as we shall see in chapter 41. These Platonic efforts were later synthesized with a Christian faith that also grounded itself in transcendence. The consequence was a situation in Christendom where, for a long time, Sophistic ideas about "nature" and "law" could not get much traction.

However, they show up again rather famously in the sixteenth century, in the thinking of the Italian politician Niccolò Machiavelli (1469–1527). In his book *The Prince* (1513), Machiavelli advocates for realism or pragmatism in politics. The prince should do what is necessary in order to take control of his destiny, leaving aside philosophical and theological ideas that get in the way. Machiavelli regarded Christian faith, in particular, as dissipating the vigor that this prince requires in order to succeed. Concentrating on the way things *are* in the world, and not on how they *should or might be*, the prince must simply do what needs to be done in order to establish his position in the world.

Sophistic/Machiavellian ideas later fluttered around an increasingly post-Christian Europe, touching down here and there, until they found an established home with the German philosopher Friedrich Nietzsche (1844–1900). Nietzsche famously proclaimed in 1882 that God was dead. In a world shaped by Enlightenment and scientific thought, there was no longer a place for him. And with the death of God came the collapse of all the metaphysical and theological foundations of Western culture. "Truth" consisted in what we could now clearly perceive as merely "conventions" invented for practical purposes. And there was no morality applicable to all human beings, either. There existed only a series of moralities plural, each appropriate for a particular social role.

This collapse of the foundations of Western culture was a good thing, Nietzsche claimed. For at the heart of all life there is a "will to power," which Christianity—with its promotion of charity, humility, and obedience—had for too long repressed. From a Christian point of view, these are virtues. But in Nietzsche's opinion they were the very symptoms of a declining life. So Nietzsche's hero is not Jesus, but Zarathustra—a strong-willed, self-mastering sage who models the "new man" in post-Christian times. This new man Nietzsche labels "superhuman" (German *übermenschlich*). The superman exercises his own will to power in order to rise above the masses. They are constrained by traditional religion and convention. The superman freely *chooses*, instead, to live a noble life.

Nietzsche's philosophy, with its very particular view of what it means to be human, has proved extraordinarily influential, especially in the Western world. All kinds of people who have lost confidence in "the knowledge project," and who therefore risk succumbing to the nihilism that Nietzsche predicted would follow that loss, have found "the will project" to be an attractive alternative. It provides in its own way a certain kind of meaning and fulfillment. Its adherents have made their peace with there being no Truth, but only truths; no facts, but only interpretations; and no right and wrong beyond what the group or the individual *assert* to be right and wrong. The deficit is made up by way of self-expression, self-fulfillment, and self-actualization—in many ways the "values" that lie at the heart of our contemporary cultural agenda.

Our enormous cultural emphasis on the sanctity of "personal choice," for example (as described in chapters 23–24, for instance), is testimony to the influence of Nietzsche's ideas. This is often not "choice in line with God's commandments" (Deuteronomy 30:19), or "choice in conformity with Nature," or even "choice in conformity with my own *personal* nature." It is instead what we might call *naked* personal choice. This is where people routinely go, nowadays, when all arguments about right and wrong on the basis of objective reality fail—or when they can't be bothered to look for them: "well, it's my choice." This is also where we go when we don't want to hold *someone else* accountable for *their* behavior: "well, it's his choice." The fact that such statements have a ring of self-evident truth about them—that there is, in the language of Genesis 2, nakedness and no shame—has a lot to do with our cultural buy-in to Nietzsche's philosophy.

Thankfully, I don't believe that most people are capable consistently of looking at the world in this Sophistic/Nietzschean manner for any great length of time. They may well espouse a "constructionist" approach to reality while dining with their sophisticated friends. Beyond that, they may well quite like the freedom that this philosophy gives them in various areas of their own lives, when things are going well. But just let them suffer at the hands of someone *else* operating on the same ethical basis, and typically you will hear a very different story. Then the language of objective reality, including objective right and wrong, will suddenly reappear with a vengeance. "That's a lie!" "What you did was wrong!"

It's just as well that we keep getting called back to reality in these ways. For to the extent that people *have* ever truly followed the Sophistic/Nietzschean line, or have allowed other people to take power who *are actually committed* to following it—to that extent, the world has only ever become a very dark place. This is true whether we consider Marxist regimes on the left or fascist regimes on the right. The will to power inevitably favors, in the end, the people with the most power. And those people tend to be nowhere near as naïve about the implications of this philosophy as the majority who are focused, at a vastly more superficial level, on their personal self-construction—and who are thereby distracted from what is really going on in the world. This is precisely one of the reasons *why* Nietzsche's superman is able to rise above "the last men" in the first place—the great mass of the population, in Nietzsche's portrayal of reality, who are tired of life, risk-averse, and addicted to comfort and security.

We Christians are not above being compromised by elements of this Sophistic/Nietzschean thinking. For example, the next time someone in your Christian community recommends a ballot of "stakeholders" so that "the people" may determine the view to be taken on this or that pressing moral issue, be aware that a cuckoo is singing, and take robust steps to eject it from the nest. You will recognize a Freedom to Choose Cuckoo, at least in its specifically Nietzschean form, by its prominent moustache and its dark, brooding visage.

39

A Mare's Nest

*"For although they knew God, they did not honor him as God
or give thanks to him, but they became futile in their thinking,
and their foolish hearts were darkened." (Romans 1:21)*

LEAVING ASIDE FOR A moment the infiltration of our own Christian nest,
one of the things that makes challenging the important task of identifying
the three philosophical cuckoos described in chapters 36–38 is that they
are difficult to differentiate even "at a distance" in the contemporary "cultural nest." *Is* that the Follow the Science Cuckoo? I thought it was—but
its song now makes it sound more like the Look Inside Yourself Cuckoo.
And now that I listen again, the melody appears very much like that of the
Freedom to Choose variety.

The modern world often seems in this way to be a veritable "mare's
nest"—that is, "a place, condition, or situation of great disorder or confusion" (*Merriam Webster*). Characterized by what Paul refers to in Romans
1 as futility of thought, the last thing that contemporary culture offers is
any kind of consistency of intellectual approach to any question. To the
contrary, it seems that we are often dealing simply with varying modes of
desire, which then select from among the available "legitimate authorities"
the one that looks like working best for its present purposes. But in the very
next moment it will select a different authority altogether, without pausing
to give any defensible reason for doing so.

Allow me to illustrate this confusing, "pastiche" reality by describing
some aspects of recent federal politics in my own country of Canada. My
question is this: so far as we can tell from observing the government of
Canada in action over the last few years, is something "right" in my home
country because it is in harmony with Nature, because it corresponds to gut
feelings, or because it expresses individual or group will?

The answer is, "it all depends." During the COVID crisis in 2019–2022, for example, the government's oft-repeated mantra when justifying its recommendations and requirements was that they were only "following the science." It *could* never have been quite as simple as that, of course, for the reasons explored in chapter 36. Science can tell us a lot about "Nature," including how a coronavirus works. But even when there is no serious conflict among scientists about the science—which in the case of COVID-19 was not the case—the ethical and political decisions that are made subsequent to the acquisition of scientific knowledge never flow "self-evidently" out of that knowledge. And it is disingenuous to suggest that they do.

Nevertheless, let's acknowledge that the Canadian government did state clearly in this case to which "authority" it was appealing. But if it believes that "following the science" is such an important principle, we might reasonably expect to find the same principle also fundamentally informing the government's approach to legislation in other areas of Canadian life. Such reasonable expectations are quickly confounded. Consider the legislation passed early in 2022 concerning "conversion therapy." This legislation ("Bill C4") criminalized, among other activities, any that are designed to "change a person's gender identity to cisgender." The word "cisgender" refers to a gender identity that corresponds to sex at birth. The underlying belief here is that there *exists*, objectively-speaking, such a thing as a gender identity that does *not* correspond to sex at birth. But was this conclusion reached by "following the science"? It was not. There is not a scrap of scientific evidence in favor of this assertion. Notable scientists were indeed among the many professional people who, in the committee stage of the discussion of Bill C4, urged the government not to go ahead with the legislation in its current form. The actual science pertaining to gender dysphoria was clearly presented in this context—and the government ignored it.[490] The "gut feelings" of some Canadians were more important. This was the "legitimate authority" that "desire" selected concerning the new offence of conversion therapy—wrongdoing so broadly defined in the legislation as to potentially criminalize all kinds of Canadian citizens simply going about their ordinary business.

So "follow the science," when it suits you—but stop following when it gets in your way, and go instead with the "gut feeling" of those with whom you empathize, even though science suggests that for most people such feelings are temporary.[491] And then, thirdly, appeal when necessary to "freedom of choice"—but only selectively. For example, in 2021 the Canadian government passed new legislation pertaining to medical assistance in dying (MAID). In introducing this "service" to the public, it reassured Canadian citizens that it was "committed to ensuring our laws . . .

support [Canadians'] *autonomy and freedom of choice*" (my own italics).[492] But *whose* autonomy and freedom of choice? In 2022 one member of Parliament who was concerned about the wide-ranging implications of the new legislation introduced a bill that was very much about autonomy and freedom of choice. It was designed to protect medical professionals legally from having to participate directly or indirectly in MAID. She was intent on ensuring that their "conscience rights" were respected. This bill failed in Parliament—because the current federal government is interested only in protecting the autonomy and freedom of choice of some Canadians, and not of others. And this despite the fact that the Canadian Charter of Rights and Freedoms explicitly mentions freedom of conscience as one of a citizen's "fundamental freedoms."

The present Canadian government has shown itself to be remarkably casual about other Charter freedoms as well. For example, the Charter guarantees Canadian citizens the freedom "to enter, remain in and leave Canada." In recent history, however, this has only applied in real life to those who have accepted the government's interpretation of what "following the science" on COVID-19 entails. Likewise, it is only when the government has approved of the causes espoused by Canadians exercising freedom of "peaceful assembly" that it has expressed enthusiasm for, and ultimately upheld, such freedom. For example, before the many ordinary Canadians involved in the 2022 Truckers' Convoy protest even arrived in Canada's capital, Prime Minister Justin Trudeau dismissed them contemptuously as

> the small fringe minority of people who are on their way to Ottawa, who are holding unacceptable views that they are expressing, [and who] do not represent the views of Canadians who have been there for each other, who know that following the science and stepping up to protect each other is the best way to ensure our rights, our freedoms, our values as a country.[493]

In other words, real Canadians don't hold opinions like that, and they don't express their freedom of choice in that manner. The prime minister knows who "his people" really are, it seems; he incarnates their beliefs and values; and he ultimately both speaks for them and expresses their "will" in his own—with all the acts of power that follow. This kind of appeal to a "will of the people" in the abstract, which inevitably overrides the wills of actual individuals or groups of citizens in the flesh, is common in contemporary politics, and not only in Canada. It is often even more overt than in the specific case I have described. The reason is this: that if the will of the people can be established somehow as favorable to a proposed policy—and the opinion poll industry has emerged in the West as a major contributor to the cause in this regard—then it is obvious (isn't it?) that the policy is "right." For "right" *is* a matter of will (right?).

I happen to have drawn my illustration from the realm of Canadian politics, but my intention is to conjure up a broader societal reality. There is very little consistency or coherence in how contemporary society approaches questions of truth and falsehood, right and wrong—the question of "the Good." There is only disorder and confusion in the societal nest. It is extremely important, then, that Christians become increasingly skilled in differentiating from each other the three cuckoos we've been discussing, and in discerning what they are up to at any given moment. It is all part of being proactive in preventing their migration and intrusion, in whatever guise, into our own Christian nest.

And we need to teach our children to become adept in the same ways. We need to teach them, as a basic life-skill, critical thinking. Do they understand how far to "follow the science" when it claims to speak authoritatively about their human identity, and can they spot overreach? Do they understand how unhelpful it is, and indeed how dangerous to one's health, to consult one's "gut feelings" on identity questions? Do they understand why they absolutely must not choose the constructionist, Nietzschean alternative, comprehending all the darkness that lies on that pathway through life? Overall, are our children able to see with clarity how none of these three cuckoos can deliver what each one claims to offer in its song? Do they grasp that none of them offers a viable alternative to biblical revelation as a basis for human self-understanding?

If our children can grasp all of this, then they will be much better able to resist these siren, cuckoo calls. For they will resist, then, *not* just because their elders have advised them that Christian faith *requires* resistance, but also because they can see for themselves that it is *the rational, good thing to do*. They will understand that it is in their own best interests to resist, and that it would be stupid not to do so. For no sensible person would join in the singing of these cuckoo songs.

When youngsters equipped with critical tools in this way begin to "get it"—truly to understand why they do not have to "give in to the cuckoos" that chirp at them every day about their human identity—it can be transformative. I remember a young teenager at one of my presentations who was asked to report on the most important thing that he had learned from it. "I've learned that no matter what anyone says, I don't need to look inside myself to discover who I am," he replied. "It's such a relief."

40

The God Delusion

"We are in him who is true, in his Son Jesus Christ.
He is the true God and eternal life. Little children,
keep yourselves from idols." (1 John 5:20–21)

IN THE REMAINING CHAPTERS we're moving on from "foreign bodies" that influence our Christian thinking about reliable knowledge to those that look to infiltrate our Christian nest in pursuit of other goals. We begin in the present chapter by discussing further the subject of God, following on especially from chapters 14 and 21. For as surprising as it may at first sound, "God" can be a cuckoo in our nest. Or to be more precise: *a god* can be a cuckoo in our nest. What I mean is that the "god" whom we worship may turn out, after critical enquiry, not to be the living God revealed in Scripture who became incarnate in Jesus Christ. Our operative idea of God may come from "somewhere else."

After all, people mean all sorts of things when they say that they believe in "God." This is a problem with opinion polls that simply ask: "Do you believe in God?" A large number of people in the thoroughly Christianized country of the USA (for example), when asked, will unsurprisingly agree that they believe in God. But what does this mean? A survey published in 2006 by Baylor University tried to find out, enquiring further about the *kind of God* in whom people believed. It turned out that around 41 percent of the US population believed at that time in a god who is significantly *unlike* the God revealed in Christ and in Holy Scripture. There was already a cuckoo in the avowedly Christian nest. And it is still with us.

Its natural habitat lies, first of all, in ancient Greece among the followers of a philosopher named Epicurus (341–270 BC). Epicurus inherited earlier, "revolutionary" philosophical thought in Greece that rejected the kind of view of the Greek gods presented by writers such as Homer and Hesiod. Epicureans held that there *are* gods, but that they are not interested in us. They do not "act" in our world. For the Epicureans this was good news, because it meant that human beings, like the gods, could simply get on with the pursuit of happiness, unencumbered by the concerns and needs of the world and having nothing to fear from the gods, either in the present or in the future. The gods themselves show us, they said, that we should live lives detached from the world, in pursuit of "tranquility" (Greek *ataraxia*).

In our modern world, we have typically received this general way of thinking about "far-off divinity" through the medium of deism. Deism was a religious system developed in the Enlightenment in order to conform Christian faith to the emerging, thoroughly rationalistic outlook of those times. Deism retained aspects of traditional Christian teaching that were perceived as compatible with the new perspective, while rejecting others. For example, in deism there is a supreme deity who ought to be worshipped, and people ought to repent of their sins in the belief that there is reward and punishment both in this life and afterwards. So obviously this Enlightenment philosophy is in various respects *unlike* pre-Christian Epicureanism. However, Epicurus's core idea of divinity as "distant" is certainly also a core idea in deism. The god of deism is a supreme intelligence who does possess an overall plan for creation—but he does not "interfere" with the watch-like, intricate machine that he has created, with all its natural laws. As the transcendent cause of the universe, God "winds it up" at the beginning, but then he puts it down again and leaves it alone to run.

This is the god in whom all those Christianized Americans mentioned earlier actually believed—a god who is aloof, otherworldly, and unconcerned with the affairs of humanity. A popular label nowadays attached to this kind of thinking is "Moralistic Therapeutic Deism" (MTD). The author of a more recent study of MTD (2021) suggests that its popularity resides in the fact that it "asks little of its followers while providing the comfort, convenience, and community they long for."[494] For the distant god asks only that we should be happy, feel good about ourselves, and in a general sense "be good" to each other—in which case we shall be allowed into heaven. One of the key statistics of this research, for our purposes, is this: that 74 percent of those who embrace MTD consider themselves to be Christians. They do so even though the overlap between MTD and truly Christian faith is very limited. In particular, a staggering 91 percent of MTD people do not believe that they are sinful and in need of salvation through Christ. So MTD people say that they believe in "God"—but they are actually worshipping an idol.

This is not the only species of God Cuckoo that exists. Let me mention just one more by way of illustration. In this second way of thinking, divinity is not distant, but near. But it is "impersonally" near. "God" is a kind of "force" in the cosmos that is all *around* us, and also *within* us, so

that in the end there is no distinction between ourselves and "god." This
is also an idea that was already being explored back in ancient Greece. It
is associated with a man named Zeno (335–265 BC) and the movement
he founded: Stoicism. The Stoics believed that the universe is a single and
ordered whole, ruled by a supreme cosmic power called *Logos*—"Divine
Reason" (DR). This DR is the organizing, integrating, and energizing principle of the entire universe. Each human soul, the Stoics believed, is a
fragment of DR, inhabiting its own body. The essential nature of human
beings is therefore to reason, and so to live in harmony with one's own
nature and with the nature of the cosmos. Predictably, salvation for the
Stoics is to depart from the irrational—from all passions and emotions—
and to arrive at a state of indifference toward such things as pleasure and
pain, wealth and poverty, fortune and misfortune.

Stoicism is a Western philosophy with very clear connections to all
kinds of Eastern philosophy, whose various forms also provide "natural
habitats" for this kind of cuckoo. Its song can be heard in the Christian nest
wherever God is conceived of and worshipped not as a Trinity of persons,
but (for example) as a great Ocean of Being destined to absorb all the scat-
tered drops of water that are human "beings." This cuckoo song is also present, perhaps unnoticed, wherever "meditation" is practiced, in its Eastern
religious forms, in Christian circles, in preference to, or alongside, Christian
prayer. People who say and do such things may claim to be worshipping
God, but they are actually worshipping an idol.

Perhaps you think it's strange that I'm focusing on theology—on the
nature of God—at this point in a book about humanness. I have good reason for doing so, however. Theology and anthropology, in all systems of
thought, are intimately related to each other. What we think divinity *is*,
and how we believe it *behaves*, determines who we think *we* are, and how
we ought to behave. This is already clear from the preceding discussion,
but let me now unpack it further.

First of all, if your God is not the Triune God, but a "distant" Ep-
icurean-style god, there is a "street-value" (as it were) to your belief. It
inevitably affects how you view yourself, your neighbor, and the entirety
of your existence. You will inevitably see yourself as an autonomous being,
accountable to no higher authority, and you will understand your goal
in life as the personal pursuit of happiness. In order to ensure the presence of personal "tranquility," you will deliberately detach yourself from
every person and from everything in the world that disturbs your serenity.
You will live a fundamentally self-interested life that is designed to ensure "freedom from fear and anxiety."[495] Epicurus himself embraced only
the virtues that were "needed in order to live an untroubled life."[496] Even

friendship was important to him primarily for the security that it provided *him*. We are a long way here from the biblical love of neighbor that flows out of the character of the living, Triune God. And the Christianized form of this kind of thinking (MTD) is not much of an improvement on its ancient ancestor. In this Christianized system of thought there is admittedly at least some accountability to a higher authority, in the sense that one needs to be "good" in order to get into "heaven." But the ethic is still fundamentally self-centered, nevertheless.

Secondly, if your God is not the Triune God, but a Stoic divinity, there is also a "street-value" to your belief. The Stoics held that dispassionate reason should be the guiding principle that we should all embrace in our relationships—whether with DR, with our fellow human beings, or indeed with other creatures. Therefore, they regarded things like pity, grief, and sorrow as deformations of the soul. This is an entirely different perspective from that of biblical faith. Furthermore, whereas believers in the living, Triune God—because of their belief in human image-bearing—have typically looked with horror on both abortion and infanticide, the Stoics were happy to endorse both practices as "reasonable." A different view of divinity leads to very a different view of human life.

So it really matters whether we have God Cuckoos in our Christian nest. They're difficult to spot, though, when they've been living there for some time. They look like members of the family. Perhaps the best way of exposing them is to give attention to how we're living. What does our life imply about the nature of the god whom we are really worshipping?

41

Matter Doesn't Matter

"And God saw everything that he had made, and behold,
it was very good." (Genesis 1:31)

IN THIS CHAPTER WE turn our attention away from cuckoos that sing about God, and we begin to consider cuckoos whose melody concerns creation.[497] In doing so we're first going to circle back to the Greek Sophists discussed in chapter 38. You'll recall that they were already *disputing* in the fifth century BC the existence of a transcendental basis for the conventions or laws of society. Now we need to familiarize ourselves in some depth with their major critic, and the precursor of both Epicurus and Zeno. This is the Greek philosopher Plato, who followed other, pre-Socratic philosophers in seeking to *establish* the existence of a transcendental basis for the conventions or laws of society.

Plato believed in an eternal, unchanging world populated by "Forms." These are the perfect originals of the various imperfect realities in the visible world. For example, in our world we see many different kinds of dog. These are all representations of the perfect, divine Form of the Dog. This and other Forms can be conceptualized in our minds, but we cannot perceive them through our senses (such as sight and smell); for example, any attempt to "see" the Form of the Dog would fail, because our senses are incapable of accessing the Forms. Rational contemplation (*thinking*) is our only means of gaining access to the Forms, the most important of which is the "Form of the Good." This is the final cause of all the other Forms and of their knowability by us. The Form of the Good is ultimate reality—the highest idea of what is good, beautiful, and true.

How did we get into this situation? Plato's story is that our "sensible" world (the world accessible to our senses) came into being when a "craftsman" got to work. Using the building plans represented by the Forms, he created the material world. This is a world that is as good as he could make it. But it is certainly not perfect, because matter resisted his attempts to bring perfect order to it. Being recalcitrant or stubborn, it did not "play along."

What is a human being, specifically, in Plato's thinking? It is a creature made by lesser gods to whom the craftsman delegated this task. Once upon a time all human souls lived as eternal, divine entities in the world of the Forms. Then the gods took these individual, pre-existing souls and placed them in physical bodies. What are the implications of this move? Well, the fusion of soul with body has created a problem for the soul. The soul is now like a man sitting in a cave beside a fire, facing the cave wall. He is able to contemplate reality outside the cave only by gazing at the shadows thrown up on the wall by the fire. That is to say: burdened by physicality in the shadow world that we see, touch, and smell (the cave), the human soul only dimly remembers its true home (the world of the Forms). We vaguely recall this "real world" whenever we see something in the shadow-world that reminds us of it—for example, a cat reminds us of the Form of the Cat—but that is all. Philosophy, for Plato, is all about our attempt to rise, through pure thought, from *opinions* about the appearance of things (in this present world of shadows) to the *knowledge* of reality itself (which lies outside the cave). Philosophy is the pathway by which the soul finds enlightenment, recovering its understanding of the true nature of things. If we pursue this pathway to its end, ultimately our soul will escape its bodily confinement. In Plato's thinking, this will take place at the end of a long series of reincarnations.

This is the "natural habitat" of the core idea that I mentioned and rejected in chapters 8 and 9—the idea that human beings are essentially eternal, immortal souls only currently residing inside bodies. This is where the idea ultimately comes from that human beings possess a transcendental "bit"—currently stranded on an island of skin and bones—that survives our physical death and flies off to heaven (hopefully) to be with God. Plato was in many ways a natural conversation partner for the early Christians, fundamentally because he did believe—as other Greeks did not—in an objectively existing, divine reality separate in being ("ontologically" distinct) from our own. He was useful, therefore, to the early Christian apologists, as they tried to explain Christian faith to their pagan neighbors. Of course, when faith builds a bridge to culture in this manner, the traffic flows in both directions—and there is always a danger of ideas coming back across that bridge that will bend our Christian thinking out of shape. This has certainly happened in the case of the Platonic understanding of the soul. All too often sitting unnoticed in the Christian nest, disguised as a Christian bird, the Platonic Cuckoo has frequently bent our Christian anthropology badly out of shape.

The third-century Christian writer Origen, for example, was certainly capable of disagreeing with Plato. But consider this: he believed that God's first creation comprised disembodied minds that became souls, designed for endless contemplation of the divine. Weariness with this task then led to their "fall," and their subsequent embodiment. The saved soul must now ascend by degrees once again to a state of pure mind—an ascent to God. In other words, Origen held a deeply Platonic understanding of the human journey. Inevitably, then, although Origen affirms here and there in his writings the doctrine of the resurrection of the body, he does not appear to mean by this what the apostles mean. For apostolic doctrine on this point is ultimately incompatible with Platonic Christianity, in which there *can* be no true and lasting place for a resurrected body, as apostolic teaching describes it. Why would you need one?

An earlier and even more problematic version of this kind of Christianity/Platonism synthesis was the range of views known by modern scholars as Gnosticism. Here, too, the spiritual realm was separated from the material realm, and the soul, which was good, was separated as far as possible from the body. But in the gnostic systems matter was understood as resolutely evil (and not just recalcitrant, as in Plato). In fact, the gnostics regarded the entire material world as having arisen from an error on the part of the craftsman. In this range of philosophies the craftsman has evolved into a divinity lower down the chain of being than the absolute, transcendent God—the "Unknown" God—who did not approve at all of the creation project. The gnostics tended to believe that this disapproving God was the God of love and mercy revealed in the NT, while the craftsman was the inferior, angry, and violent god of the OT. Naturally, there is no fall after creation in this ideology. Creation itself is the fall—a fall away from spiritual purity and into material reality. Gnostic views of salvation are correspondingly very different from the one taught by the apostles. Gnostic salvation usually consists in the immortal soul escaping the material world and returning to the spiritual realm of the supreme God. The escape-mechanism is "knowledge" (Greek *gnōsis*), or enlightenment. Salvation is about freeing the spirit from the prison of matter. It is worth underlining that this gnostic environment generated not only a particular evolution of the Platonic Cuckoo, but also other cuckoos that have unsettled the Christian nest since that time. For example, consider the quite common quasi-Christian insistence, at different points in history, that the God of the OT is quite different from the God of the NT—with its accompanying idea that the NT is properly Christian Scripture, whereas the OT is not.

Although they expressed the idea in differing ways, the Epicureans and the Stoics agreed with Plato (and the gnostics) that matter did not ultimately matter. In particular, they too had no place for individual bodies in any kind of afterlife. And this is why, when the apostle Paul was attempting in Athens to communicate his message about Jesus and the resurrection, the assembled listeners (including Epicurean and Stoic philosophers) could not comprehend what he was talking about.[498] Unsurprisingly, even when Paul clarified what he was saying, "some mocked."[499] It's actually surprising that more of them did *not* make fun of him, given their understandings of the world.

Throughout the book I've already touched on all kinds of problems that arise in Christian thinking and living when the Platonic Cuckoo—especially in its gnostic evolution—is not identified in the Christian nest and expelled. When matter fundamentally matters, this leads to a very different approach to *the entirety of human existence* compared to when matter fundamentally does not matter. I want to end this chapter by drawing your attention to a particular danger in failing to act decisively in this area. In doing so I'm temporarily swapping out my "nest" metaphor in favor of my earlier "bridge" metaphor. Here's my observation: that when the Platonic/gnostic idea of the soul manages to cross the doctrinal bridge and to get firmly "dug in" on our side of it, it creates a bridgehead that makes it easier for other similar ideas to cross over behind it. For once the first wrong idea has settled into our community, these further ideas don't seem quite as strange to us—absurd even—as they otherwise might.

So on the one hand, it becomes easier for gnostically inclined people in Christian communities to embrace Eastern religious ideas. Consider Hinduism, for example, in which the body is also only the shell inside which the soul resides in the course of its onward journey toward salvation. Here, too, salvation is conceived of as escaping the material world. In all honesty, such a religion views the world in terms that are *radically* different from truly Christian faith. But to someone who has already drunk deeply from the wells of the Platonic-gnostic-Christian synthesis, Eastern ideas can look strangely familiar. So it is that people arrive at the deadly, utterly mistaken conclusion that "all religions are essentially the same," and they begin to adopt Eastern spiritual practices alongside or instead of Christian ones (chapter 33).

But on the Western side of the equation, consider finally how the already deeply embedded belief, inherited from Plato, that "my real self exists inside my body," makes it so much easier than it would be otherwise to embrace the kind of Romanticism (indeed the narcissistic individualism) that we discussed in chapter 37. The first cuckoo has been left undisturbed, and now it welcomes in its friends.

42

Art

"I will stretch out my hand against the Philistines."
(Ezekiel 25:16)

WE ESTABLISHED IN EARLIER chapters that human beings, since they are "like God," are beautiful creatures capable of appreciating beauty, and that one aspect of the worship that arises in response to beauty is the creation of art.[500] We encounter *literary* art in the poetry of the Psalms and the Song of Songs, for example, and we read about *architectural* and other art in the building and furnishing of the tabernacle. And wherever and whenever Christians have not been completely seduced by the cuckoo in the nest that has denigrated matter in relation to soul—proclaiming a gnostic rather than an orthodox gospel—they too have produced art of all kinds. It is part of our human vocation not only to *respond* to the beauty of God's creation, but also to *create* beautiful artifacts in *imitation* of our Creator—books, music, buildings, and all the rest of it.

Saint Augustine was one of the most influential of the early theologians in shaping Christian understandings of art in the long centuries prior to the rise of modernity. He believed that true art is in fact science, precisely because it is grounded in the reality of God's creation. For example, the principles of good musical modulation and its appreciation are the same mathematical principles employed by God in bringing order out of chaos in the first place. The notes on a musical scale are separated by mathematical proportions (2:1 is an octave, 3:2 is a fifth, and so on), and sounds conforming to these ratios create beautiful harmonies that echo ultimate, cosmic harmony. But this applies to the visual arts as well. The mathematical ratios marked off by divisions on a musical string also appear as proportions between different parts of a line on a page or in a building. So music and architecture, for example, are siblings. The first echoes eternal harmony aurally, and the second mirrors it visually. Beauty cannot emerge in either domain unless the mathematical rules have been followed, whether consciously or not.[501]

Augustine's perspective deeply shaped the medieval world, not least in the construction of the great cathedrals like Chartres from the twelfth century onwards. Here the musical proportions employed by the great Composer (God) in writing his cosmic symphony are the very same as the ones used by the medieval architects in building their churches.[502] The ideal church—medieval Christians naturally thought—should be constructed according to the laws of the universe. This same conviction— that beauty is objectively anchored in given metaphysical and physical reality—has necessarily continued to mark all authentically Christian approaches to art since that time as well. This has been true even when artists have declined to adopt Augustine's particularly Platonic, and in some respects restrictive, way of thinking about art.

For example, modern harmony is largely indebted to Johann Sebastian Bach (1685–1750). Bach was an innovator in this respect and in many others, but he was nevertheless someone who firmly believed that "the aim and final end of all music should be none other than the glory of God and the refreshment of the soul."[503] Many listeners to and players of his music over the centuries, whether "religious" people or not, have commented on the way in which his music lifts them up "into heaven," as it were. This has included many accomplished composers who understand more than most people what it takes to write outstanding music. Ludwig van Beethoven (1770–1827), for example, once said of Bach's music in general that his own heart beat "only for the High Great Art of this forefather of harmony." Robert Schumann (1810–56) said of Bach's famous Well-Tempered Klavier (BWV 846–893), in particular, that "its benefits are great, and it seems to have a morally strengthening effect . . . as if it were written for eternity."[504] These are the very kinds of comment that one also tends to hear from visitors, whether religious or not, to Chartres Cathedral. The art itself, rooted in transcendence, functions as a bridge into that transcendence, whether people "believe in all that religious stuff" or not. In the case of Bach we see this startlingly illustrated by the rather strong atheist Richard Dawkins, who once chose as one of eight records he would take with him to a desert island the aria "Mache dich, mein Herze, rein," from the *St. Matthew Passion* (BWV 244). The text in translation runs as follows: "Make yourself pure, my heart, I want to bury Jesus myself. For from now on he shall have in me, forever and ever, his sweet rest. World, get out, let Jesus in!"[505]

However, while many people in Christendom in the eighteenth century, like Bach, still sought to interpret the entirety of life, personally and culturally, in the light of Christian faith, and their heirs were still making

this attempt in the nineteenth century, the new, "modern" way of thinking about the world was already gaining traction. And this has produced
significant changes in how many people in post-Christendom think of art.
It has birthed three particular ideas about art that can show up as cuckoos
in the Christian nest.

The first is the child of scientism (chapter 36), and I'm going to name
it the Philistine Cuckoo. Philistinism is a resolutely negative posture toward
the arts by "materialistic person[s] . . . disdainful of intellectual or artistic values" (*Merriam Webster*). Charles Dickens' Mr. Gradgrind, obsessed
with facts and calculations and with no time for poetry, is one of these.
Then there are also all those modern politicians and businessmen who so
frequently attack as "useless" an education in the humanities that does not
train a person for a particular role in a workforce. But Philistine *Christians*
also exist—believers who cannot understand why their fellows should write
and read poetry and other literature, or "waste time" on landscape painting—or who, when planning a new church building, are only interested in
pragmatics, and not in beauty. These are the Christians whose *own* commitment to business-like, programmatic efficiency in their own (church)
community, in pursuit of narrowly "spiritual" goals, makes art at best a little
splash of color to help "get the message across."

The second cuckoo I want to mention here is the child of constructionist, "will-to-power" ideology (chapter 38), and we'll call this one simply the Nietzsche Cuckoo. Its distinctive plumage is not disdain for art,
but the detachment of art from the transcendental. It can be detected in
the Christian nest (or elsewhere) whenever we encounter an opinion like
"texts (including the Bible) mean whatever people want them to mean."
This is its *literary* incarnation. Once upon a time we lived in "the age of the
author"—which encompasses most of Western history right down into the
twentieth century—in which the task of a reader was to discover the truth
that the author wanted to communicate in a text. But then "structuralism"
arose, in which the emphasis lay on texts rather than their authors—"the
age of the text." And now we live in "the age of the reader," populated
by poststructuralists who explore how readers *construct* meaning in the
course of reading texts. This is the process by which Nietzsche eventually
gets to tell us how to read books.

But this same constructionist approach to meaning is found right
across the spectrum of contemporary art. We see it in the Theatre of the
Absurd (in the plays of Samuel Beckett, for instance), which invite audiences
to reflect on being alone in a meaningless world. We encounter it in postmodern music that locates meaning and structure in listeners rather than
in musical scores. It is also evident in the postmodern visual art that rejects

notions of objective truth and prioritizes instead individual experience and our interpretation of it. In all of this, art is no longer grounded in objective meaning, and it is no longer a window into objective beauty, or an expression of that beauty. Beauty lies only in the eye of the beholder. Art in this mode certainly has nothing at all to do with glorifying God, or even with providing us with glimpses of "the Good." In fact, constructionist art is vastly better at portraying darkness than it is at communicating light. What it "constructs" is typically an exceedingly bleak world in which it is difficult to live—the kind of world in which Nietzsche himself went (literally) quite mad.

Unable to look into the constructionist void for too long without freaking out, postmodern people like to spend at least some of their time listening to a third cuckoo singing a somewhat different song about art. This is the Romantic Look Inside Yourself Cuckoo discussed in chapter 37, which is intent on trying to apprehend Nature by way of gut-feeling. I'll call this the Caspar Cuckoo in honor of the artist mentioned in chapter 37. This cuckoo also detaches art from the transcendental, but it tries to find some firm ground to stand upon, at least for a moment, on the slippery slope that leads straight to constructionism. This firm ground is, of course, my inner self. This is a self that is able to *feel* things about art; to be momentarily entertained by it, at least; to get meaning from it that is not merely "constructed," but has a more quasi-religious aspect to it. It is still "what the art means *to me*" that's important—objective meaning and beauty do not exist. But the "me" in this sentence is the *feeling* "me," not just the *constructing*, "me." It is the self that will not give up on some kind of mystical, religious truth in it all. The presence in the Christian nest of this third cuckoo can be detected wherever we no longer find in the Christian community any robust notion of art as the vehicle for transcendent truth and beauty. Art is celebrated instead (as it is in the culture at large) only "because it makes me feel good"—whether it is that "nice" painting over there, or that "fun" romantic comedy that I saw on Netflix last week.

A truly Christian understanding of the human being requires that we take art much more seriously than in all these cases. We should neither be Philistines, nor Constructionists, nor Romantics, when it comes to art.

43

Innocence

"If we say we have no sin, we deceive ourselves, and the truth is not in us. If we confess our sins, he is faithful and just to forgive us our sins and to cleanse us from all unrighteousness." (1 John 1:8–9)

In the course of our discussion of the fundamentals of a Christian anthropology in chapter 17, we considered the important idea that humanity is *fallen*.[506] In all kinds of ways, and with terrible consequences, humanity has been compromised by evil—the heart of which is self-worship. One early biblical example relates to our previous chapter, because it illustrates the way in which this inward, idolatrous turn affects art. In Genesis 4 Lamech kills a man for wounding (Hebrew *peṣaʿ*) and injuring him (Hebrew *ḥabbûrâ*,).[507] In killing in this way he is certainly not responding to or reflecting divine justice, which sets clear and equitable limits in such matters: "if there is harm, then you shall pay life for life, . . . wound for wound (Hebrew *peṣaʿ*), stripe for stripe (Hebrew *ḥabbûrâ*)."[508] Lamech has become his own god, possessing his own law—and notice that he celebrates this idolatry in the Bible's first poem! Already, near the beginning of the human story, art has ceased to reflect objective beauty, and it has come to express the human will to power. Constructionism has begun.

The origins of the human problem lie earlier, however. From almost the beginning of our story (Genesis 3 tells us), humanity as a whole has been compromised by evil. And then each one of us individually, before we are even conscious of this reality, is also compromised by it. This happens simply by virtue of being born into, and then raised in, fallen human culture. We inherit "baggage" created by the poor decisions of our ancestors, and we are given still more of it to carry by those whose company we keep in our families and other groups. But then we ourselves, individually, begin to participate actively in the chaos and the darkness as well, and in various ways we add to it. Humanity has been characterized by fallenness almost from the beginning, Holy Scripture teaches us, and every individual human participates in that fallenness. This is why everyone needs to be saved from sin (chapter 18).

This important aspect of a truly Christian understanding of the human condition is, of course, not widely accepted as truth in contemporary culture. In that culture, lack of self-esteem is considered just about the worst evil that exists in the world, and those who cause it are some of the worst people. Much more compelling in this contemporary context, then, is the idea that human beings are fundamentally and naturally good. Other people are generally good, and I myself am pretty good. I certainly don't need to be saved—as a woman I recently met at a wedding told me, within seconds of our conversation beginning, and upon learning that I am a biblical scholar. She was emphatic on the point, and this was not very surprising for someone who did not claim to be a Christian. However, this idea of natural human goodness is not only widely found among the non-churchgoing population. As we saw in chapter 40, the great majority of MTD adherents also espouse this idea. So the Innocence Cuckoo is another bird that we need to consider in this part of the book.

The most important "natural habitat" of this cuckoo is the Romantic movement that we've already encountered in earlier chapters, including chapter 42. Over against Enlightenment ideas about progress that entailed a negative assessment of "primitive peoples" whom progress had left behind, the Romantics developed a narrative in which those pre-Enlightenment peoples were actually the fortunate ones who lived in a golden age before regress set in. In "the state of nature" (i.e., before they became part of civilized society) human beings did not live as solitary, brutish beings (as Thomas Hobbes had argued in his important book *Leviathan*). They did not live as "fallen" beings. Instead, they lived in pre-civilizational, Eden-like bliss.

As examples to illustrate their point, Romantic writers often referred to the native peoples of the world that Europeans had recently encountered in their travels, especially in North America. They frequently compared such native societies favorably to European civilization, which they described as being in various ways corrupt and unjust. Already in John Dryden's 1672 play, *The Conquest of Granada*, the hero Almanzor asserts: "I am as free as Nature first made man 'ere the base Laws of Servitude began when wild in the woods the noble Savage ran."[509] Likewise, Baron de Lahontan writes in a 1703 travelogue that "the savage obeys the will of Nature . . . therefore he is happy. It is the civilized folk who are the real barbarians."[510] At a more serious, philosophical level, the exceedingly influential "Father of Romanticism" Jean-Jacques Rousseau (1712–78) presented the state of nature as a morally neutral and peaceful condition marked by a lack of pride, envy, or fear of others, as well as by compassion.

In this kind of Romantic narrative, "the fall" is long delayed in the human story. It does not occur until the blessed human creature living in the state of nature is "spoiled" by civilization. Civilization, not sin, then becomes the entity from which the individual needs to be saved—the corrupting institutions of especially urban society. Salvation is achieved by turning back to, and reconnecting with, Nature—both internally and externally. In particular, what is *inside* a person must be allowed *out*. If human beings were indeed inherently sinful, then our gut feelings would obviously need be handled carefully, and on many occasions ignored and even repressed. But since we are characterized by natural goodness (Romantics claim), our gut feelings can be trusted. Indeed, they should be constantly analyzed for revelatory value concerning what is good. In the interests of authenticity in the midst of a repressive, false society, this revelation should then be shared with everyone else. Self-dramatization was already a favorite activity of the Romantic Lord Byron, long before it was the preferred mode of expression in postmodern, narcissistic individualism.

So much for the lyrics of the Innocence Cuckoo's song. There is, of course, no reason at all to take this song seriously. This is not least the case because the Romantic account of the "pre-civilizational" peoples who are so important to its perspective is entirely ungrounded in any evidence. I know that many contemporary people, especially in a country like Canada, believe something very like this account of history in general. They have certainly heard it often enough—rehearsed again and again in contemporary discourse about the state of our planet. "Once there was a golden age, populated by people living in blissful harmony with Nature. Then came civilization, and everything went to the dogs." We shall return to this Romantic narrative in relation to the *planet* in chapter 49. For the moment let's stick more narrowly to the question of human innocence, choosing for critical analysis just one of Rousseau's claims about the state of nature. This is the claim that the state of nature is a *peaceful* condition. What evidence is there that such a general state of peace ever existed in human history? What is the science on this topic? And since science requires hard data to work with, let me be more precise. We have indigenous peoples still living among us at the present time, and we've certainly also had them living among us in the more recent, documentable, and recoverable past. Do the lives of these modern "primitive peoples" (as some call them), with their lines of continuity stretching back into the past, suggest that there has ever been anything like a non-violent, peaceable "state of nature"?

The answer is, categorically, "no." In his book *Constant Battles*, Steven LeBlanc traces the human liking for warfare from the Paleolithic period onwards, moving chronologically from groups of hunter-gatherers to complex human societies. His discussion of tribal warfare in recent times in the New Guinea highlands is particularly striking: "This last place on Earth to have remained unaffected by modern society," LeBlanc affirms, "was not the most peaceful but one of the most warlike ever encountered."[511] He cites this and all the evidence in his book precisely to dispel the misconception that human beings are "peaceful by nature and . . . have been so for millions of years."[512] People in the past were in fact "in conflict and competition most of the time."[513] This reality was underlined in the significantly titled 1993 symposium, "Crime in Prehistory." This conference "challenge[d], as simplified and distorted, views that portray prehistory as peopled exclusively by members of happy, peaceful communities, living in harmony with each other and with their environment."[514]

In short, both Christian theology and modern scientific enquiry call into question the Romantic narrative concerning "the state of nature." It turns out that this narrative is driven by precisely the cavalier approach to historical facts that the Romantic poet Friedrich Schiller—author of the lyrics to "Ode to Joy" (the modern European anthem)—already described in 1788: "I will always be a poor source for any prospective historian unfortunate enough to approach me. . . . History is only a magazine for my imagination, and the objects have to put up with what they become in my hands."[515] Over against such an imaginative approach to history, scientific enquiry suggests a real human past that is deeply marked by human fallenness as well as by goodness "all the way down." This is the kind of world that Holy Scripture also describes. That contemporary people outside the church cannot see that *the present moment* is likewise marked by deeply rooted sinfulness—sinfulness that is not simply a matter of poor education or faulty institutions—should not be especially surprising to Bible-readers. They above all should understand that one of the core aspects of human fallenness is a major disturbance precisely in our human capacity even to *think* clearly about our true moral state.[516] We'll return to this important matter in chapter 48. One way or another, for the moment, it's not particularly shocking that Romantically inclined contemporary people outside the church should have been seduced by the Innocence Cuckoo. What is unconscionable is that we Christians should ourselves have listened so intently to its song, to the extent of finding ourselves among those who "say we have no sin," thereby deceiving ourselves and revealing that "the truth is not in us."[517]

44

Information

"The beginning of wisdom is this: Get wisdom, and
whatever you get, get insight." (Proverbs 4:7)

ATLANTIC CITY (1980) IS a deservedly obscure movie, and I don't recommend it. But it does possess one excellent moment of insight. "Teach me things," says a younger woman to an older man. "What do you want," he replies, "information or wisdom?" This reply indicates an awareness of a qualitative difference between these two entities. There is something much better than information on offer here. It is the *wisdom* that this man has accumulated over many years as a result of reflecting on information *and* experience, coming to understand their significance, and learning to make good judgments about them in pursuit of virtue. Which one does she want—information or wisdom?

You might think that the correct answer is obvious. Wisdom is surely more important than information. Holy Scripture agrees, and so do I.[518] But my observation is that many of us seem to have difficulty in thinking and living as if this were really true. We don't find it easy to spot the Information Cuckoo in the Christian nest that is constantly seeking to usurp wisdom's place at the center of our affections. And one consequence of this bird-spotting failure is that we can accidentally end up with a sub-Christian rather than a properly Christian view of education (as I described it in chapters 26–27). It will help us to avoid this kind of outcome if we are aware both of Information Cuckoo's provenance and of the damage that it has already done to its own habitat.

First we need to understand that prior to the rise of the modern world the great majority of people capable of reflecting on information and wisdom would have agreed with Christian faith on their relative importance. The accumulated wisdom of the ages, stretching back through time (they would have affirmed), provides the foundation for our lives. But already in the writings of the English philosopher Francis Bacon in the early seventeenth century we find a different idea beginning to take a hold of the European imagination (chapter 13).[519] In this way of thinking, reason exploring Nature, untroubled by any previous form of tradition, is the path to true knowledge. And this true knowledge is desirable, not so that humanity may live in greater *harmony* with Nature, but so that we may more efficiently *control* it. In other words, a utopian project has now emerged, requiring in the pursuit of "progress" the bending of everything in Nature to human ends by way of reductionistic science. Mr. Gradgrind's "facts"—information—are the paving stones on the path that inevitably gets us there.

In due course this way of thinking has created a world dominated by information technology, which lies at the heart of all kinds of astonishingly rapid, recent change in the world. It is also the key that powerful people in modern society hope to employ in attaining their *future* goals. In this quest, further advances in areas like artificial intelligence will (they predict)) deliver to humanity (or more accurately, to them) still greater control over Nature. Specifically, as discussed briefly in chapter 1, it will allow us/them to assume greater control over *human* nature, overcoming the "problems" created by our physical embodiment. The society that is in the process of emerging as we begin to tread this path is well described by Henry Kissinger:

> The internet age in which we already live prefigures some of the questions and issues that AI [artificial intelligence] will only make more acute. . . . The internet's purpose is to ratify knowledge through the accumulation and manipulation of ever expanding data. Human cognition loses its personal character. Individuals turn into data, and data become regnant. Users of the internet emphasize retrieving and manipulating information over contextualizing or conceptualizing its meaning. They rarely interrogate history or philosophy; as a rule, they demand information relevant to their immediate practical needs. . . . Truth becomes relative. *Information threatens to overwhelm wisdom* [my own italics].[520]

Inevitably, one of the major casualties already resulting from these developments has been Christianly conceived education. In the Christian way of thinking, education has always been about wise persons *forming* other persons by way of induction into a broad and integrated body of knowledge. All the subjects in a curriculum were recruited in pursuit of this goal. As one noted German humanist of the sixteenth century put it, "nothing less should be learned from the Latin language than wisdom, righteousness, religion, prudence, good government, and good morals."[521] *Where* should such learning take place? In a series of *personal encounters.* For the Christians agreed with their pagan Greek predecessors such as Socrates that "wisdom . . . must be developed in conversation with wise teachers and fellow students."[522] The Sophists at this time, we recall, were traveling around the ancient world communicating to students merely technical knowledge that was divorced from any concern about their formation in truth and virtue. For Socrates and Plato, on the other hand, a real education required *time* spent in a *place*—an academy (college/university), such as the one founded by Plato in Athens in 387 BC. Real education required wrestling in a *social* context, in that time and place, with a range of difficult questions that could not be quickly or easily answered—much more important questions than "what are the best techniques for winning arguments?"

For a while, this same traditional view of education managed to survive the pressures of modernity in the West well enough, even when, in the aftermath of the Enlightenment, educators increasingly embraced a secular rather than a Christian humanism. For a while, universities and colleges still existed "for the training of character, for the nurturing of those intellectual and moral habits that together form the basis for living the best life that one can."[523] But beginning in the nineteenth century, humanities scholarship, under pressure from the hard sciences to justify its value in the modern world, began to redefine itself in increasingly "scientific" ways. It became specialist and fact-centered, rather than generalist and wisdom-centered. The research humanities scholar was born, whose purpose was no longer to help students grapple with the meaning of life across a broad range of disciplines, but to seek out fresh information in a narrow field of study and then to share it with everyone else.

So it was that information-seeking and information-sharing became the heart of education across a broad spectrum, but with this important caveat: in the humanities it was increasingly embedded in a Nietzschean worldview in which (remember) there are no facts, only interpretations, and no truth, but only many truths (see Kissinger above). This in turn encouraged the idea, across the board, that there is no such reality as objective virtue to which the members of an academic community might commonly aspire. So it is that, for many contemporary "educators" (if they deserve that name), education is no longer even about producing well-rounded, broadly educated, critical-thinking citizens. On the one hand, education is now about the inculcation of ideology. On the other hand, it is about training students in skills that enable them later to flourish in particular forms of paid employment, and thereby to contribute both to the modern "project of control" and to the net worth of their company. This is an extraordinarily debased understanding of education, in which information has *already* overwhelmed wisdom. The consequence is that, if one is wise, one does not attend most universities or colleges nowadays to gain wisdom. For their purpose is certainly not to explain to you the meaning of life.

The Christian vision of education is obviously very different from this degraded version—but the Information Cuckoo often distracts us from it, and we too fall under its spell. Consider for example the way in which Kissinger's "demand for information relevant to . . . immediate practical needs" marks to a considerable degree contemporary discourse in the church concerning the education of pastors. It is in fact often the *governing* idea—that what pastors need to acquire above all from their education is a range of skills designed to make them useful in the Christian employment market. This is a direct reflection of the "worldly" attitudes toward education that each of us naturally encounters as we go about our daily business in society. The most crucial people who encounter it in that context are precisely those who fund, and exercise governance in, Christian educational institutions.

This inevitably leads to demands for curricula focused on "training people to do the tasks of a pastor," from which long-esteemed subjects now considered "insufficiently practical" and "too difficult" are gradually excluded. Gutting the curriculum, along with making the requirements pertaining to what remains more "flexible," allows seminaries and colleges in turn both to shorten their degrees and to allow students to study only the subjects that *they consider* most relevant to *their goals*. Students are thereby able to complete their studies as quickly and "efficiently" as possible and to get back out into the job market, which even Christians often refer to (and this is deeply ironic) as "the real world." God forbid that these students should ever linger too long in their studies and learn something that they did not already know.

The entire enterprise is *evidently* no longer grounded fundamentally in a vision for theological education whose main emphasis lies on inducting students, over time, into a broad and integrated body of knowledge, in pursuit of spiritual and moral formation. And this is, frankly, a disaster for the church, which has always needed, and will always need, pastors who are broadly and deeply educated and able to do much more than carry out a range of professionally oriented "tasks." It used to be commonly assumed, therefore, that they would need an education that wrestled with more important questions than the Sophistic "what are the best techniques for winning arguments, or for that matter for preaching, or for running a board meeting?" But that was when we knew we wanted prophets rather than technicians—visionary leaders rather than managers.

My conclusion is this: that in order to protect and sustain our distinctive Christian vision of education, the Information Cuckoo that has already created a thoroughgoing caricature of education in its *own* nest needs to be clearly seen for what it is, and to be thrown out of *our* nest— before it can do any more damage than it already has.

45

Zion

"Escape to Zion, you who dwell with the daughter of Babylon."
(Zechariah 2:7)

IN CHAPTERS 28 AND 29, in the context of the deeply Christian idea that human beings are created by God as *social* beings, we considered the idea of church. All Christians, I proposed, are called as Christ-followers to be active members of a local, Christian community—both for their own good and for the common good. It is worth emphasizing this second aspect in the present chapter, since I did not do so earlier. Jesus did say that "where two or three are gathered in my name, there am I among them."[524] But there's nothing to suggest in the remainder of the NT that having coffee with two like-minded friends in Starbucks, or in your home, in any way counts as "church." There's no reason to see this as, in any way, a valid alternative to membership of a larger, diverse Christian community that includes members whom you almost certainly do not like, but who need your support in their Christian lives. It's not all about you (and your friends). This being the case, we must not neglect meeting together as church, "as is the habit of some."[525]

One of the characteristics of the good church that we considered back in those earlier chapters (28 and 29) is its commitment to a proper Christian *education*, as described in chapters 26 and 27, along with its antithesis now in chapter 44. This proper education is deep and expansive in nature, offered in pursuit of wisdom for every area of life. Another characteristic is that the good church meets *personally*. Those who hold to a truly Christian anthropology believe that human beings are irreducibly *embodied* beings. We are not minds, nor souls, nor hearts that happen to be found in bodies and can just as easily do without them. From a Christian point of view, then—I suggested earlier—it's a contradiction in terms to refer to "virtual community." I now want to develop this line of thought further in saying more about the Information Cuckoo identified in chapter 44.

I'm picking up here, in particular, a thread from chapter 26 about the necessary integration of the "what" and the "how" in our Christian thinking about education. We teach children—and now I want to add "adults as well"—what we really believe, theologically and anthropologically, as much by *how* as by *what* we teach. So if we desire to teach, over against all kinds of Gnosticism, the utter importance of our embodied nature as social beings, but we choose to do this by way of disembodied communication over the internet, we have tripped over the first hurdle in the race, and we shall not finish it well (if at all). In divorcing *form* from *content* in this way we have encouraged our students, by our example, to do the same. This inevitably leads them to conclude that the content (the information) we are "delivering" is the real deal, and that the remainder is only "delivery method." In-person, face-to-face teaching (we proclaim loudly by our practice) is only one such "delivery method." There are many other, equally valid ways of going about the business of education.

The very language itself should alert us to the massive change that has now occurred in our thinking. Once our language was that of a gathered community of friends sharing life together in pursuit of wisdom.[526] Now we are using the language of Amazon. We have become Sophists in our thinking—although they at least showed up bodily to work. We have come to believe that education can be "conveyed" like a product directly from a teacher to a student, with resulting "measurable outcomes." We have thereby abandoned Socrates, who believed that "education was a more mysterious affair [than this], requiring the degree of patience and encouragement of a midwife." The midwife could help to birth it, but not "by preaching to the mothers, drawing diagrams, and providing them with birthing manuals— the equivalent of lecturing, sending out PowerPoint slides, and providing so-called study guides" in contemporary online learning.[527] The midwife had to *be there*, in person, for the entire affair.

So it is, in this abandonment, that we arrive at the "distance education" (DE) that is currently so ubiquitous in the world—a contradiction in terms if ever there was one. This is one step further on (and down) from the situation described in the previous chapter. In that chapter I described a time when students still attended universities or colleges in order to receive the admittedly debased education in which information had already overwhelmed wisdom. But now, increasingly, they do not "attend" at all, because people in all parts of the educational world have come to believe that there is little to no point in "attending." All the "educational" goals espoused in the Information Cuckoo's song, in response to the demand for information relevant to students' immediate practical needs, can be achieved more efficiently and more cheaply by other means. And educational institutions have been falling over themselves to meet this demand. They have scrambled to offer their curricula in ever more reduced, distant, dumbed-down, and therefore cheaper and more "accessible" forms. They have not usually done this out of any genuine conviction that the education they now offer is better than before, or even just as good—although that is what they inevitably *claim* in "talking up" the product. Rather, they have been sucked into this digital world by what they imagine is economic necessity. Their unprincipled scrambling represents simply their best hope (they think) of surviving the prolonged race to the bottom of the educational market that they have now entered. The grim logic of that market has now tightened its grip.

What results is an even more attenuated modern form of "education" than the non-stellar version that was available shortly beforehand. Admittedly—as in the case of the "virtual church" described in the previous chapter—it's more than possible not to notice this development, if your previous educational experience was sufficiently negative. But the fact of the matter is that with the realization that "persons in embodied community" are no longer at all necessary to the educational project, the destruction of real education is now complete. The graveyard marking its burial place comprises half empty or deserted colleges populated by professors—if they are not yet "working from home" by themselves—whose business is increasingly not to share their lives with others in that time and place in pursuit of wisdom. It is instead to sit in front of computer screens in "virtual" contact with students elsewhere. These students are, in turn, only in "virtual" contact with each other. And once this new reality takes root, it is very difficult to reverse the situation—not least because many students profess to like it, and they will protest loudly about their "rights" if what they have come to like is threatened.[528]

What students can ever "learn" in all of this is exceedingly limited. Students who still hanker nostalgically after something better may "choose" to drag their bodies to a physical space in the graveyard—if that "option" is offered to them. If it *is* offered, it is assuredly portrayed as just one of various equally valid choices that can be made in "accessing" education. But even so, perhaps the "option" at least exists in some institutions. The problem is that those who choose it are often rewarded for doing so by being forced in any case to interact with other students online in a "hybrid" environment, overseen by teachers who cannot possibly give the persons right in front of them the full attention they so richly deserve for their effort. Promised an "in-person experience," they get cheated out of precisely that. It is one of the striking features of this entire drama that "freedom of choice" is one of DE's big marketing lines—but the one thing that you can no longer easily choose is a proper education.

Everything about this brave, new digital world screams out that we *are*, after all, just minds, or souls, or hearts that *happen* to be found in bodies, and that we *can* just as easily do without these bodies. And this is, of course, exactly what the gurus of this brave new world, with their glorious plans for our inhuman future, want us to believe. Plato's academy it is not, this "virtual education." Proper education it is not. And it opens us up to worse realities to come. True Christians should have nothing to do with it, except as a temporary, very short-term measure to be resorted to when nothing more satisfactory can be done in the meantime (e.g., because of an outbreak of plague). It's fundamentally contrary to our core Christian beliefs about the nature of our humanity, which at all times we need to nourish and protect from erosion by attending not only to *what we believe* but also to *how we live*. In everything we must insist that human beings are irreducibly *embodied, social* image-bearers of God. In every way, correspondingly, our Christian communities must seek to give embodiment to that message. This will often make these communities profoundly counter-cultural—and that is certainly true in respect of our present, in many ways anti-human, culture.

I am often reminded in thinking about this reality of the 1999 movie, *The Matrix*. The surface-world is dominated by machines possessing an artificial intelligence that was originally created by humans, but ultimately came to dominate them. The great majority of the surviving humans are now plugged into "the Matrix." In it they are used by the machines as a source of energy—although they are unaware of this, because they exist mentally in a virtual reality. But a smaller group of humans remain free in their bodies *and* minds, and they understand the way things really are in the world. They exist underground in an embodied community known as "Zion." One of their day-jobs is to unplug people from the Matrix, returning them to reality, while they wait for a savior figure whom they hope will bring down the machine world.

Likewise, we Christians are called as an "underground" movement to keep the true understanding of human personhood alive, while waiting for a Savior. We are called to do this in a world increasingly and disturbingly abandoning a true anthropology. It is a world dominated by the digital and the virtual, and it is populated by humans who typically have no idea what is really going on, because they are plugged into a false consciousness. We are called, in this situation, to be "Zion," providing refuge for all who want to escape Babylon.[529]

46

Jerusalem

"Take away from me the noise of your songs; to the melody of your harps I will not listen." (Amos 5:23)

IN DEVELOPING MY COMMENTARY on the Information Cuckoo in the previous chapter, I reminded you of two of the three characteristics of the good church. These are its commitment to a proper Christian *education* and its determination to meet *personally*. In the present chapter, the *third* characteristic first introduced in chapter 28 will be front and center. The good church teaches that worship is a way of life, and its worship-gatherings reinforce (rather than undermine), through their "worship activities," this core biblical idea.

This is above all where that helpful analogy to *The Matrix* offered in the previous chapter completely breaks down. Hollywood, just like the constructionist art mentioned in chapter 42, is much better at portraying darkness rather than light, evil rather than good. It is unsurprising, then, that the high point of Zion's community life in *The Matrix*, when its members are not fighting evil, is a rather banal and ghastly disco. It is as close as one can get to a worship gathering, apparently, in that worldview, and the positive vision of life that these "worship activities" reflect is narrow, superficial, and dispiriting.

Christian faith, conversely, casts a glorious, expansive vision of the underground, human counter-culture that opposes the anti-human one. Throughout this book I have unpacked what this looks like in our home life and our family relationships, in our broader social relationships, in our work and our play, our intellectual engagement, our music, our art, and so on. This is what I shall now refer to—in order to get decisively beyond the Zion of *The Matrix*—as "Jerusalem's vision" of life as worship. And it is this vision that should inform our Christian gatherings as they seek to engage the whole person in worship. I briefly described in chapter 21 some central aspects of how the early church attempted to do this, referring in particular to Justin Martyr's *First Apology*. I now want to say more about this historical reality, comparing it with our own contemporary approaches to "worship activities." My purpose is to introduce you to another problematic intruder in the Christian nest. It is the Worship Cuckoo, whose practices are precisely those that fail to promote "worship activities" that support "worship as life."

As to the history, we know from Justin, first, that the early Christians read Scripture together "as long as time permits," locating themselves within God's story. Our own approach nowadays is much more minimalistic, especially in churches outside the mainline denominations with their lectionary tradition (set Scripture readings each week). Old Testament "lessons" have all but disappeared from our worship gatherings, and even the NT is typically read out publicly only in small pieces that are directly related to the upcoming sermon. These practices are worthy of some reflection in the light of the apostolic injunction to "devote yourself to the public reading of Scripture."[530] Do we perhaps need less help than the early Christians in locating ourselves in the biblical story? Or is there some other reason why the public reading of Scripture is no longer important to us?

Secondly, the early Christians listened to sermons explaining the Scriptures to them and exhorting them to live out the Christian story. But as with the *reading* of Scripture, so too we have seen a decline in recent times, in churches of all kinds, in the importance of *preaching* Scripture. We have encountered a move to the visual image over against the spoken word, and to the topical sermon over against the text-based sermon. In some cases, we have seen a move almost completely to break the connection between the Scriptures and the sermon, as the latter becomes little more than a motivational talk, and the former is reduced to little more than a convenient resource from which to plunder one-liners, wrenched out of context, for the purposes of illustration. Is this not problematic?

Thirdly, the early Christians prayed, partly to remind themselves of the mighty works of God in the world and to thank God for these and for all his gifts, and partly also to confess their sins, to ask for things, and to intercede for others. But in recent times there has been a vast reduction in the amount of prayer offered in public worship. There are fewer prayers than there used to be, and they are much shorter than before, covering much less of the Christian story. Why is that? Does it matter?

Fourthly, the early Christians celebrated the Eucharist together weekly. For many contemporary Christians, on the other hand, the Eucharist is not one of our regular, habitual practices—nor is the saying of a creed. Are modern Christians in less need than our ancestors of reciting and acting out our faith? Why would that be?

In relation to all four points, I want to underline that, in terms of its impact on our understanding and practice, it's what we do together regularly and with emphasis that's most important. These are the activities that inevitably "preach" most powerfully to us their theology and their anthropology, telling us who we are and shaping our life of worship. The greatest impact does not arise from the realities upon which we place no great emphasis, nor from the activities that we only do from time to time. This brings me to consider, fifthly, the "worship activity" of music/singing. Holy Scripture may not be read out publicly very much nowadays, nor preached very seriously; public prayers may be few and brief; the Eucharist may not be celebrated, and no creed may be recited. But there will certainly be a substantial amount of music/singing in the worship gathering. Music/singing has thereby become—in a way that was not true of the early church—*the primary reinforcer* of the Christian community's theology. Existing as our main, regular, habitual practice, it has become a powerful influence upon us with respect to our identity-formation. And what is its character?

Music/singing existed in the early church, we recall from chapter 21, to facilitate confession of faith by the gathered people of God. But what is often evident in worship-gatherings nowadays is just how *passive* people are with respect to the music/singing. The model for what is happening is in fact more "concert" than "community singing." People are gathering to observe the performance of a "band" on a "stage," rather to participate in a group activity. The sheer volume of the music is often a significant part of the problem: when you can't hear yourself singing, why even try? So if music/singing is about facilitating confession of faith by the gathered people of God, our first question ought to concern *participation*.

Our second question ought to concern *form and content*. It is just a fact, historically, that the music and songs favored in Christian worship-gatherings have often been written and performed in only one musical style. But such a restricted *form* cannot represent the great and varied story of God in which we are all caught up. It cannot bring enough truth to the table. Likewise, many Christian communities sing from a remarkably narrow canon of songs, and it is impossible for such a canon to capture the fullness in *content* of the Christian story. Many of our gatherings are dominated by songs focused, for example, on adoration, which is certainly one important aspect of true Christian worship. But when this becomes the only theme in our singing, other important themes (such as lament) get lost. The whole person is no longer allowed to bring the entire self to God. This problem would not be quite so serious if modern songs addressed further aspects of the biblical story even while pursuing one theme (such as adoration). But in reality they are often incredibly brief and do not actually "say" much at all. This typically means that one feels obliged, almost out of politeness, to sing them more than once—several times, indeed. The result is that one finds oneself singing, more than once, a composition that did not have very much to say to begin with.

This is a strange thing to do, and it is only the disengagement of our minds from the process of singing that could possibly prevent us from *seeing* it as strange. And this brings us right to the edge of something that is not truly Christian worship at all—something that has much more of Eastern spirituality about it. In this mode, we engage in repetitive singing with a view to *escaping* our minds and our bodies. We sing mantras in order to enter a trance-like state in which we float off for a while into a spiritual realm that is "other" than the world in which we live. And in doing so we reinforce the false theology that we've encountered throughout the book, which takes it most toxic Western form in Gnosticism.

The Worship Cuckoo is real, and it is dangerous. We need to insist on asking ourselves the kinds of questions that will flush it out into the open from wherever it is hiding in our unexamined practices. Why do we not any longer engage very much in many of the "worship activities" of our forebears in the faith? And in terms of what we do instead (or more often), does that count as Christian worship, or is it something else? How can we tell? Could we do certain things differently and better? For example, wouldn't it be better to read Scripture and to pray more, and to sing less? When we sing, would it not be better to sing a greater variety of songs, touching on a wider range of doctrines, rather than the same song, touching one subject, over and over? For *Christian* worship is, among other things, about the whole person singing out the whole faith—and thinking about it, and remembering it, as he or she goes along. The good *church* is one that meets personally, and *in the very act of doing so*—including its "worship activities"—reinforces in people's minds and hearts *a specifically Christian* rather than an alien anthropology.

47

Justice

"What does the LORD require of you but to do justice, and to love kindness, and to walk humbly with your God?" (Micah 6:8)

SPOTTING CUCKOOS IN OUR Christian nest is an important task, but it can also be tricky. Indeed, the more that a particular cuckoo looks and sounds like a genuinely Christian bird, the trickier it is. And yet: it is especially important to be able to tell the difference in these tricky cases, particularly when we want to ally with people outside the church on matters of common societal and political concern (chapter 34). To return for a moment to my "bridge" metaphor from chapter 41: building a bridge to the culture in such cases requires the appointment of particularly keen-eyed gatekeepers on our own side of the bridge who can prevent the unobserved passage of dangerous goods from the other side into the heart of our own city. We all remember the story of the Trojan Horse, and how badly that ended for the city of Troy. It is with this in mind that I want to spend the next three chapters considering justice and environment.[531]

We live in a time when the issue of "justice" lies right at the top of many people's agenda. Everyone is talking about, and indeed demanding, justice. But how do we know what justice looks like? True Christians ought of course to take their lead from Holy Scripture in answering this question, so let's begin there. Justice is grounded in God's own character—it is transcendentally rooted. God is just—and that is why those who are in a right relationship with him are called to "do justice" to their image-bearing neighbors "and to love kindness, and to walk humbly with your God."[532] We understand what justice *is* and we are motivated to *do* it by being in relationship with God. We also comprehend the *lack* of justice in the world in this same context. The world is unjust because God's human creatures have rejected the one true God, and in so doing have inevitably become to varying degrees unjust. They have often then gone on to build relatively or entirely unjust systems and structures across the planet (in such areas as criminal justice, commerce, and employment). The evil that has thus worked its way into the world is now deep, complex, and intractable. Only God can and eventually will save us from it.

But this does not justify passivity on our part. In the Bible we encounter God's repeated identification in the present with those who suffer injustice, and his calling of his people to do the same. As we live out our lives as God's image-bearers this necessitates standing up for the human rights of every one of our precious, fellow image-bearers. This includes, for example, their right to be treated equally under the law (justly), regardless of wealth, class, race, or sex (chapter 22). Our calling as God's people involves especially speaking up "for the mute" (those who cannot speak for themselves) and defending "the rights of the poor and needy." For if we don't advocate for those who presently lack power, there will not be (for example) equality under the law.[533] These kinds of neighbors, in particular, require our attention.

This is what justice is, briefly and biblically speaking. It is not what our secular contemporaries mean by justice, and it *could* not be—not least because they do not believe that there are transcendent, moral absolutes in which justice can be grounded. This creates difficulties right away in terms of what the human rights *are* that we—and the justice systems we design—should set out to protect. There are of course many people in the world who share with those of properly Christian faith a strong commitment to individual, human rights. But how many such rights are there, and how do we know?

"Libertarians" contend for a small number of "freedom" rights (e.g., rights to free speech, property, and religion), but "liberals" tend to add to these numerous social and economic rights (e.g., the right to an education, or to medical care). The two groups also disagree on the role of the state in fostering and protecting these rights. Libertarians are highly individualistic, and they usually understand "freedom" in entirely negative terms (e.g., freedom *from* realities like taxation). Liberals tend to think more corporately. Agreeing with libertarians, for example, that a free market is the best way to create wealth that can then be fairly shared, they nevertheless see an important role for the state in supervising that sharing, precisely in the interest of fairness of outcome. Justice, on both views, comes down one way or another to the strong defence of individual rights—but which rights?

And in either case, why should we regard any of them as rights in the first place, and seek to protect them? Neither philosophy provides a satisfactory answer to this question. This is predictable, for having left behind the Christian nest where both were born, each philosophy finds itself unable to make a satisfactory home anywhere else. Whether their current proponents understand it or not, both these "liberty" approaches to justice (as I shall now call them for simplicity's sake) depend on the biblical idea of human rights and freedoms *as contextualized within the biblical story*. And when these rights and freedoms are removed from that context, it becomes impossible truly and objectively to *ground* them anywhere. They certainly cannot be grounded in "Nature," since what is "natural" is not thereby self-evidently good (cf., e.g., chapter 36).

Lacking such grounding, these rights and freedoms then tend to evolve into entities that no longer bear much resemblance to their biblical ancestors. This may be why their point of origin gets forgotten. In particular, the biblical idea of the importance of the individual devolves into mere *individualism*, with its *idolatrous* commitment to freedoms economic, social, and other. Freedom in Holy Scripture is *for* something—for loving God, and our neighbor, and other creatures. But divorced from the balancing biblical idea of obligation to family and community, freedom soon becomes about autonomy. This is why post-Christian "liberty societies" eventually experience the fragmentation of families, neighborhoods, and institutions. The truth is that these liberty philosophies have only ever actually "worked" in societies where Christian faith has remained strong enough to compensate for the selfishness that individualism produces. Uprooting this faith clears the field for the plants that then grow from the seeds of liberty's own destruction. For idealistic people eventually come along who are well aware of the inability of liberty philosophers to ground their fundamental ideas objectively. They are also sickened by the selfishness and greed that these ideas have produced, along with the accompanying hard-heartedness toward those who have suffered most from them. And a revolutionary spirit emerges, of the kind that we shall explore in chapter 48.

Before that, and for the sake of completeness: a third contemporary way of looking at justice tries to avoid the problems associated with grounding it in "Nature" by conceding that rights are not "natural," but arguing that we ought to defend them, anyway, out of rational self-interest. These are the rights (the argument goes) that we ourselves would like to be accorded if we were disadvantaged in some way (e.g., if we could not afford medical care). But if rational self-interest is really our driver, why not set up a society that deliberately exploits the poor in order to benefit the rest of society, and simply ensure that we have sufficient wealth and power to avoid ever becoming one of those poor? And if the answer to this question is that oppressing the poor is wrong, then we are back to where we started: *Why* is it wrong? Why is justice not, in fact, simply power? Chapter 48 once again beckons us.

A fourth (and for the moment final) contemporary way of looking at justice also tries to avoid the problems associated with grounding it in

"Nature," but in a different way. Advocates of this view argue that justice is *the greatest happiness of the greatest number of people* ("utilitarianism"). If something makes the majority happy, then it is just, within the limits set by the so-called "harm principle"—that our behavior should not harm others. This is of course problematic. Just because something makes a person happy, that does not make it right. And any agreement among large groups of people—majorities—about what makes *them* happy does not equate to justice either. For example, slavery made the citizens of ancient Athens very happy—but Athenian society was in this respect massively unjust. And as this example also demonstrates, the "harm principle" is actually useless in itself as a restraint on majority views, because one's view of what "harm" looks like depends on one's view of human nature, and on some understanding of right and wrong, which one needs to "borrow" from elsewhere. For the Athenians, slaves were *by nature* slaves—so slavery was not harmful to the slaves. All in all, utilitarianism is an utterly unacceptable way of thinking about justice, from a Christian point of view, since it erodes the rights of individual image-bearers in favor of the group or "the people." Do the elderly still have a right to life on this view, for example, if the majority have become unhappy with having so many of them around? Why, or why not?

So "let justice roll down like waters, and righteousness like an ever-flowing stream," as the book of Amos exhorts. Who can possibly be against justice? But let's be very clear about what we mean by the word. All sorts of people would like to recruit Christians in support of *their* notions of justice—and perhaps on this or that issue we should indeed support them. But let's not switch off our brains as we do this, and start writing other people "blank cheques" in support of whichever "justice" they happen to approve of at any particular moment in time. There is such a thing as the Justice Cuckoo, and it has the capacity to cause considerable trouble. In the worst-case scenario we may well discover, after critical reflection, that the "justice" for which others are asking us to fight is not justice, biblically speaking, at all.

48

Revolution

"But you have turned justice into poison and the fruit
of righteousness into wormwood." (Amos 6:12)

THE CLOSING CAVEAT OF my previous chapter applies as much to *postmodern* ideas of justice as to any other. This is a way of thinking that arises out of postmodern critical theory. It is quite different from "liberty" thinking, and indeed it typically sets itself up aggressively in opposition to liberty philosophies, point by point, and to the societal realities constructed on their foundation. Our question as we remain on the lookout for the Justice Cuckoo must nevertheless be the same: how far are these postmodern ideas about justice consistent with biblical teaching? However, as we pursue this question in the present chapter, we shall discover that we are not actually dealing with the Justice Cuckoo any longer, but instead with a Revolution Cuckoo.

The key elements of postmodern thinking about justice are as follows. First, it is even more focused than liberal (as opposed to libertarian) thinking on the question of societal "outcomes," refusing to accept inequalities in power, wealth, and well-being in society. But in distinction from liberalism, it explains these negative outcomes as arising largely from unjust social structures and systems rather than from other sources (e.g., individual industry or laziness; differences in individual ability). Since the root problems are structural and systemic in nature, it stands to reason that the only way to resolve them on behalf of the disadvantaged is through social policy. The solution is never (for example) to ask individuals to change their behavior. We achieve "social" justice—and the addition of this adjective to our noun is characteristic of this way of approaching reality—by changing structures and systems.

Pressing deeper (secondly): what is the nature of the society that must be changed? It is characterized most fundamentally by inequality of power. Achieving justice is therefore most fundamentally about solving this problem. The power-relations in our currently unjust society must first be described by way of analyzing "intersectionality." "The concept of intersectionality describes the ways in which systems of inequality based on gender, race, ethnicity, sexual orientation, gender identity, disability, class . . . 'intersect' to create unique dynamics and effects."[534] Persons in such individual categories are already lacking in power, and joint membership in other categories increases their powerlessness. The intersectional map lays bare the truth of all these power dynamics, thereby revealing to us the people in contemporary society who possess the least power—those most in need of social justice.

This intersectional map, thirdly, reveals the truth in ways that "dominant discourses" cannot. "Dominant discourses" are the truth-claims of currently powerful groups, typically grounded in reason and science or in religion. The point about language is that it does not merely *describe* reality. Rather, it *constructs* or creates it in the interests of masking power structures (cf. chapters 38 and 42). For example, academics and scientists conceal unjust structures behind talk of "academic freedom" and "empirical objectivity," respectively. Therefore, the reconstruction of society in a just manner requires the subversion of dominant discourses. This in turn necessitates taking control of, rather than permitting freedom of, speech. Even reasoned debate that touches on "wrong" ideas cannot be permitted, because this only provides unjust discourses with space in which to grow ever more dominant. The powerful (the "privileged"), blinded by their own social location, must simply be silent, creating space in which the powerless can speak—especially the people at the furthest end of the intersectional spectrum. These extremely marginalized people are, above all, able to see the way things truly are in the world, and to speak with moral authority about it.

The problem goes deeper than language, however. Fourthly, "all art, religion, philosophy, morality, law, media, politics, education, and forms of the family" are likewise "determined, not by reason or truth but by social forces. . . . Everything is determined by your class consciousness and social location."[535] Everything must be "unmasked" and deconstructed in pursuit of justice.

In the post-Christian West, especially, this way of thinking about justice has become increasingly influential in the last several decades. The "woke" revolution that it demands—the destruction of Western society and its re-creation from ground zero upwards—appears in many respects to be well under way.[536] Each day, it sometimes seems, it advances one step further, claiming another institution or organization. Its success in winning hearts and minds has a lot to do with the weaknesses of the "liberty" societies described in chapter 47. It has also not helped that for a long time now we have permitted advocates of Nietzschean constructionism (as well as of Marxism), as described in chapters 38 and 42, unrestricted, unopposed access to huge numbers of impressionable young people in the course of their education. The politics that we are presently discussing represent merely the predictable result of that kind of uncritically assimilated indoctrination. So it is that many Millennials and their heirs, both outside and inside the church, regard "social justice thinking" as the self-evidently *right* way of thinking about justice issues.

It is important, then, to be clear concerning the deep intellectual and moral incoherence of this way of thinking about reality, to which I shall return in the final chapter. Leaving that issue aside for the moment, it is especially important that we comprehend the striking incompatibility, in any case, between the ideas we've been discussing in this chapter and biblical ideas of justice. Let me make just two sets of observations along these lines.

First of all, it is impossible for a truly Christian point of view to accept the hopelessly Romantic postmodern account of good and evil at the heart of this perspective. Many of its advocates assume exactly what Rousseau (and indeed Marx) first assumed, that evil is instilled in naturally good human beings by "civilization." Change the present structures, therefore, and you will solve the problem of injustice. But biblical faith insists that evil resides *inside* as well as *outside* each of us. It has always done so—and science agrees (see chapter 43). Nothing in Holy Scripture or history suggests that we can eradicate injustice merely by changing societal structures. To the contrary, there is considerable historical evidence in favor of the contention that, in reality, when we change even quite unsatisfactory societal structures we can create more injustice than first existed. The truth is that our salvation necessarily involves dealing comprehensively with the problematic reality that is *actually* "systemic" in creation—the problem of sin. This is a problem that affects *all* people and *everything*, including our ability even to analyze our own situation accurately. Believing this, Christians are also obliged to reject the postmodern idea that people with less power than others are innately capable of seeing things more clearly because of their oppressed state. There is no good reason, biblically or indeed empirically, to endorse such a generalization.

Following on from this, secondly, Holy Scripture emphasizes that each fallen person is primarily an individual made in God's image, ontologically equal to every other human individual. It is not of *primary* importance that each of us is also a member of a sex, a race, or a nationality (and so on). This is what obliges me to love every other human being as my neighbor, irrespective of what differentiates another person from me. It is what obliges me to treat every other individual indiscriminately justly. The postmodern view, conversely, makes primary one's racial or group-identity rather than one's merely human identity. In this way of thinking, therefore, when matters of justice and injustice are raised, individuals are always treated as members of a class. The question is not, for example, *whether* you as an individual are guilty, demonstrably and objectively, of behaving unjustly toward others. As a matter of fact you *are* guilty of injustice merely by virtue of being a member of the powerful rather than of the powerless classes, as revealed by the intersectional map. One of the implications of this is that you have no right, as the member of a privileged group, to complain about being discriminated against. Social justice people have no problem with (e.g., racial) discrimination, just so long as it is directed against class enemies. Justice does not mean in this philosophy "treating individual persons justly" irrespective of their gender and race, and so on. It typically means precisely the opposite. And so we return to what I wrote earlier in this chapter: we are not in fact dealing with a Justice Cuckoo here at all, but with something else. Truly justice has been turned "into poison" (Amos 6:12).

There is much more that could be said on this topic, including the important point that in the postmodern way of thinking there can obviously be no individual atonement for the guilty, followed by restitution to a larger community of forgiven sinners. There is "no way out" of your tribal box. Actually, forgiveness, peace, and reconciliation among "groups" within their boxes is *also* impossible. As Miroslav Volf has discerningly written about this kind of tribal mentality: "Forgiveness flounders because I exclude the enemy from the community of humans even as I exclude myself from the community of sinners."[537] And of course, this exclusion of the self from the community of sinners is very much in evidence among advocates of postmodern justice theory. Many of them exude the distasteful, uncritical self-righteousness of crusaders at war with (external) evil who are determined to press on with the battle until the enemy is destroyed—by shaming, othering, denouncing, or whatever other weapon lies to hand. Their "gospel" is very different from the Christian gospel, point by point— even though they may be found "attending" churches.

In sum, biblical people *should* be passionately interested in justice. But the church must always be, first of all, the church, and not merely the religious wing of some other ideological movement, whether liberal or antiliberal. Avoiding this fate necessarily involves, among other things, being able to spot and resist the Revolution Cuckoo. A sure sign that a Christian community is failing in this task is when the language of "social justice" has become endemic within it. Another is when it shares with the surrounding culture shameful practices like discriminating against currently unfavored groups in the employment market, or when admitting students to a university or college.[538] Injustice is injustice, no matter how hard you may try to disguise it with the cunning use of adjectives. Injustice is injustice, no matter the sex, skin-color, or whatever, of the individual victim.

49

Environment

"The creation itself will be set free from its bondage to corruption and obtain the freedom of the glory of the children of God." (Romans 8:21)

ALONGSIDE JUSTICE, "THE ENVIRONMENT" is one of the issues currently grabbing hold of people's attention worldwide.[539] We saw in chapters 12 and 13 that a Christian anthropology requires that we too care deeply about what *we* call human and non-human *creation*. No doubt this further requires us to make common cause from time to time with all kinds of "environmentalists" possessing their own various, legitimate concerns. But once again, we must we wise about these alliances, remaining aware at all times of the ways in which "environmentalism" is not, in fact, biblical creation care, but a cuckoo whose song can take us off in very wrong directions.

Romanticism is once again one of the great dangers in this area of our Christian lives—and you have probably picked up by this point in the book my strong conviction that this is one of the core contemporary ideologies about which Christians *must* become well educated. Romanticism is important when it comes to environmental issues precisely because we *should* agree with our secular contemporaries in being appalled by the scientistic pragmatism of someone like Francis Bacon (chapter 13). The problem is that the mainstream reaction against scientism, in this area as in others, has been heavily influenced by Romantic ideas. The uncritical Christian mind can therefore find itself too much persuaded by *this kind* of response to scientism, failing as a result to offer a distinctively *Christian* response. In particular, we can find ourselves agreeing with the Environment Cuckoo's oft-stated allegation that it is not Bacon's "hijacking" of Genesis, but Genesis itself, that has led to our current "ecological crisis."[540] And, as a consequence, we may find ourselves living out of a Romantic "counter-narrative" about the planet, instead of our own biblical story, in approaching environmental issues.

The allegation in question has taken shape most famously in a still-influential essay written by Lynn White in 1967.[541] White's view of what Genesis 1–2 has to say involves God's planning creation "explicitly for man's benefit and rule: no item in the physical creation had any purpose save to serve man's purposes." Christianity, he claims—especially in its Western form—"is the most anthropocentric religion the world has seen."[542] To put it mildly, this is a problematic account of Genesis 1–2. But having described in earlier chapters what Genesis *really* has to say, I won't repeat myself here. The most important thing about White's essay is this: that although he is not correct in his claim about Christianity's thoroughly anthropocentric nature, many people have *believed* that he is. This perspective has in fact regularly reappeared in "green" publications ever since. James Lovelock once proposed, for example, that "our religions have not yet given us the rules and guidance" we need for forming a viable relationship with other creatures. He specifically believed that "the Christian concept of steward-ship" is problematic because it is "flawed by unconscious hubris."[543] In such biblical thinking (in his view), human beings are conceptually simply too high up in the hierarchy of being—and people agreeing with Scripture in this perspective are going to be the last people to care for non-human creation. We need (he proposes) a different story.

This is where Romanticism comes in, providing us with the counter-narrative to which I partially alluded in chapter 43—what I call "the myth of the dark green golden age." Long ago before the advent of agriculture (so this story goes), human beings lived according to the rhythms of the cycles of Nature. This was a time before hierarchy and patriarchy, in which we lived in harmony with Nature and in equality with each other. We possessed deep wisdom about how to live well in the world, and also a natural predisposition to sympathy and compassion for all creatures. Then there arose "civilization," accompanied by "world religions" that reduced the importance of "place" (unless it was in a spiritual afterlife). Much of what is wrong with contemporary human life results from this embrace of civilization. We must now retrace our steps, reconnecting with our hunter-gatherer ancestors in the state of nature. This is where we shall find the Nature-spirituality that we need in order to navigate the world. This reconnection will necessarily be achieved through the mediation of surviving indigenous peoples not yet entirely absorbed into civilizational reality. Even down to the present time they have lived more world-affirming, contented, equitable, wealthy, and peaceable lives than the rest of us, informed by a much more authentic, organic spirituality than ours. In particular, they have displayed impressive ecological knowledge. It is by listening to their wisdom, thereby reconnecting to our deepest past, that we can save ourselves and the planet.

This narrative has proved to be extraordinarily influential in recent times, and not just in creating the conditions for the modern revival (or, more accurately, reinvention) of ancient, pagan religion and in shaping our societal discourse about the environment. For example, when "social justice" people identify "civilization" as the reality that distorts a "natural" order marked by egalitarianism, shared wealth, peace, and general contentment, and they urge us to overthrow civilization "right now" so that this natural order can once again emerge—well, this is the "green" back-story upon which they are drawing, whether they realize it or not.

The problem is, of course, that there is no reason at all to regard this back-story as true. If the lives of modern indigenous peoples have anything to teach us about our Paleolithic, hunter-gatherer past, it is certainly *not* that we once inhabited such a dark green golden age. It is untrue, for example—as we saw in chapter 43—that hunter-gatherer societies have been less violent than their successors. It is moreover not the case that they have been more egalitarian and less hierarchical. And specifically in relation to the present chapter, it is also not true that they have been more ecologically sensitive than those who have followed them. All of these claims result from Schiller-like acts of the imagination. You will find in my book *Convenient Myths* a substantial number of specific examples that make this clear, often directly contradicting the "common knowledge" of our own times.[544]

It is often said, for example, that the indigenous peoples of North America followed "conservation practices" in their hunting. They killed only to meet their immediate needs in terms of food and clothing, and they made sure that nothing was wasted. Yet the truth is that when "the buffalo window" opened on the plains each year, the Plains Indians would kill buffalo in large numbers in a short period of time, often eating only the best parts and leaving the rest to decay on the ground. It all depended on factors like the distance to their camp and the available means of transportation. Where the geography allowed it, they were also known simply to stampede entire herds of buffalo over cliff-edges in order to get access to some of the dead for food.

This is completely understandable. Their main concern was to eat buffalo-parts while they had the chance, without themselves being killed by these very large and aggressive animals. Living in a harsh environment with meagre edible plant life, they were concerned not about the waste that was created by their hunting success, but about the lack of food that would result from its failure. "Nature" is something that only modern Romantics in their comfortable homes, casting upon their mental walls romantic projections of ancient people-groups, can afford to be romantic about. These *real* hunter-gatherers could not afford such romance. They were *struggling* with Nature, as human beings have almost always had to do. Survival, rather than sympathy and compassion for all creatures, was their main concern. Not for the first time in this book we discover that Romanticism does not necessarily represent things as they really are (or were). This was, incidentally, Johann Wolfgang von Goethe's objection to the paintings of Caspar David Friedrich (chapter 37), of which he once famously said (somewhat unfairly) that one might as well view them upside down.[545]

What we call "ecological wisdom" did not come into it—for these or other "traditional" societies. A comprehensive modern study has in fact demonstrated that people in such societies "do not . . . express a widely held conservation ethic."[546] Their often-low ecological impact results, "not from conscious conservation efforts, but from various combinations of low population density, inefficient extraction technology, and lack of profitable markets for extracted resources."[547] Consequently (as Thomas Neumann writes), it is "important to surrender the image of the aboriginal peoples living in idyllic harmony with host ecological systems."[548]

It is particularly important that our thinking is "the right way up" on this question of the ecologically noble ancestor because of the consequences that always follow from our core beliefs about reality. As one scholar working in this area has put it, "Romantic misconceptions might not matter, except that the conventional wisdoms arising from them generate normative prescriptions."[549] In particular, "current strategies of environmental and conservation education reflect our faith in such ideals."[550] When we misunderstand the past, it all too easily leads to our doing damage in the present, even as we imagine that we are doing good. In the final chapter of *Convenient Myths* I illustrate this reality in two ways with respect to the idea of the ecologically noble ancestor: how it has proved detrimental both to the human rights of native populations in Latin America and to sensible wilderness care in the United States.[551] It really does matter whether our readings of the past are true, and not simply romantic retrojections. We contribute neither to human flourishing nor to "saving the planet" by romanticizing the past.

In sum, in thinking about the care of creation we need to learn to ignore the Environment Cuckoo, and to get on with the task on the basis of our own true, biblical story about the world and its Creator. In spite of what Lynn White and others say about this biblical story, the fact is that it teaches us that "the environment" is in reality sacred, created space for whose wellbeing our Creator holds us accountable. And in spite of what they claim about the *effects* of the biblical narrative, the fact is that people who believe it to be true are not going to be the *last* people to take the steps necessary to care for *all* of "the environment's" creatures, but very likely among the *first*.

50

Conclusion

"The end of the matter; all has been heard. Fear God
and keep his commandments, for this is the whole
duty of man." (Ecclesiastes 12:13)

IDEAS ARE POWERFUL. JOHN Maynard Keynes once said this about some of
them:

> The ideas of economists and political philosophers, both when
> they are right and when they are wrong, are more powerful
> than is commonly understood. Indeed the world is ruled by
> little else. Practical men, who believe themselves to be quite
> exempt from any intellectual influences, are usually the
> slaves of some defunct economist. Madmen in authority . . .
> are distilling their frenzy from some academic scribbler of a
> few years back. I am sure that the power of vested interests is
> vastly exaggerated compared with the gradual encroachment
> of ideas, . . . soon or late, it is ideas, not vested interests, which
> are dangerous for good or evil.[552]

Keynes is writing here about the way in which many people are unaware
of the disputed nature of reality—in this instance, when it comes to eco-
nomics. They do not comprehend the way in which each of us is inevitably caught up in the "war of myths" that I began to discuss in chapter 1.
Keynes refers to these unaware people as "practical men (and women)"—
those who simply "take the world as they find it" (to coin a phrase) and
get on with their lives without reflecting too much about them. They tend
simply to assume that it's obvious what is true about reality, and about
right and wrong. They are in fact often suspicious of, and hostile toward,
those who suggest otherwise—"impractical" people with their heads in
the clouds, like philosophers or religious teachers, who make things more

difficult than they need to be. The consequence is that these "practical people" never ask questions about their own story, because they do not *see* it as a story. They see it simply as "the way things are."

The fact of the matter, though—and I hope this book has underlined this truth—is that every one of these "practical people" lives in a world that has been profoundly shaped by other people's ideas about what is true and right. No one is "exempt from . . . intellectual influence," nor indeed from moral influence. This is true whether they are ordinary folk, or people possessing considerable power ("madmen in authority"). There is no one who does not live inside an (inevitably disputable) story, recounted to them in the first instance by other people (chapter 3). Human beings are always "storied" in this way, whether or not they reflect upon this fact, just as they are always "political," whether or not they vote. "The world is indeed ruled by little else" than powerful ideas, "both when they are right and when they are wrong." You and I can do no other than find ourselves in a story, shaped by ideas. The only question is this: are we going to make any effort to ensure that we inhabit a true and a good story, shaped by *good* ideas, rather than a false and possibly dangerous one?

If this is indeed our commitment—and certainly it must be a *Christian person's* commitment—then of course we're going to need to understand which *are* the dominant stories of our time and place, and how they challenge and seek to undermine our own. This is no less true of the business of "being human" than of any other business. We need to understand what a properly Christian anthropology looks like—and we also need to understand competing ideas about human nature and where they come from.

This book has been an attempt to help Christians in both respects, at a moment in history when the church finds itself in crisis concerning "the human question." In the course of making my argument, I have explored first what Holy Scripture teaches about the fundamentals of a Christian anthropology and what are some of the major implications of these fundamentals. I have also introduced you, secondly, to a number of cuckoos in the Christian nest, explaining why as followers of Christ we should not (cannot) listen to the songs of these foreign bodies in our midst. There have been two aspects to this second part of the argument. In *all* cases I have tried to show the incompatibility with biblical teaching of what a particular cuckoo is singing about. And then in *many* cases I have also commented on the internal incoherence of the foreign ideas—how the ideas, in themselves, do not make good sense. Although I have not had the space to do this very extensively, and in some cases I have not been able to do it at all, I commend this second task as an important one that you should take on further for yourselves. For one of the challenges facing anyone holding a minority view in a majority culture is that the latter's core ideas can be experienced as intimidatingly powerful. Obviously (we tend to feel) they must be true—otherwise how could so many people *hold* them to be true? But when we begin through critical enquiry to understand their weakness, we also begin to see that *we* are not the ones who are unwise in *rejecting* them. It is *other people* who are unwise in uncritically *accepting* them.

For example—and I said in chapter 48 that I would return to this issue—it is one thing to realize that the postmodern view of justice stands so greatly in tension with biblical ideas. This is already a sufficient reason for rejecting it. However, it certainly strengthens our resolve to reject it when we realize that it is also intrinsically, intellectually and morally, *incoherent*. Postmodern theorists would have us believe, at one and the same time, that all truth-claims and justice-agendas are merely socially constructed in order to legitimate power, *and* somehow that their own truth-claims and justice-agendas are not. For they are vociferously, almost religiously, in favor of what they consider to be morally *right*—the liberation of the oppressed—even while asserting that all other moral claims are merely social constructs. But if *everyone* is blinded by class-consciousness and social location, why aren't *they*?

Likewise, intersectionality claims that oppressed people see things more clearly than anyone else—but how can this be true, if social forces make us wholly what we are, and if they control how we understand reality? Furthermore, if all people in possession of power inevitably use it for domination, then surely this is exactly what the postmodern theorists would do if they were able to replace the current "oppressors" at the top of society, as they so clearly desire to do. This is in fact what has happened in Marxist states all over the world in the course of the last one hundred years or so, as leftist revolutionaries have worked out in practice a very similar constructionist philosophy. George Orwell's novel *Animal Farm* is only one literary work among many that has shone a bright light on the dynamics involved in that process.[553] It is naïve to assume that powerful elites will not arise immediately out of the civilizational rubble created by revolution. They are always with us. The only question is, "Which kinds of people should we be most worried about having at the top of the pile?" Should it be liberal people who at least believe in objective law and justice, for example, or should it be those who have openly expressed contempt for such ideas?

And so we arrive at the "end of the matter" (Ecclesiastes 12). With respect to all "personal matter," this is that "end": "fear God and keep his commandments."[554] And because you want to continue doing both, be sure to identify and deal decisively with the cuckoos in your Christian nest. For each of them is one of the wiles of the devil, who wants to destabilize true

Christian faith in any way that he can. He desires this precisely because he hates "personal matter"—which is why "dis-incarnation" lies at the heart of his agenda.

We have seen this theme emerge again and again in this book, and not just in explicitly religious or spiritual ways (e.g., in Gnosticism or similar systems). I began in our *first* chapter, in fact, by introducing one influential person among many worldwide who are currently intent on creating a brave new world in which "the human problem" is solved by advanced technology, particularly artificial intelligence. As we come toward the end of this *final* chapter, let me mention an entire organization—the exceedingly influential World Economic Forum—whose (totalitarian) plans for our lives are premised precisely on the emergence of this brave new world, with its fusion of "the physical, digital and biological worlds, impacting all disciplines, economies and industries, and even challenging ideas about what it means to be human."[555] The WEF was founded by Klaus Schwab, whose various musings are those, not of "some *defunct* economist," but of a very active one who has the ear of global elites all over the world. And his ideas are obviously not simply economic in nature. They are, among other things, clearly "anthropological."

Dis-incarnation lies at the heart of the devil's assault on humanity. Incarnation must conversely lie at the heart of our Christian response—across the whole spectrum of our lives. This includes how we worship, how we educate, and (indeed) how we eat—insisting with Capon (chapter 8) on the breaking of "real bread" whereby we also "break the loveless hold of hell upon the world, and . . . set the secular free." With all this in mind, I want to conclude with a quote along the same lines from Eugene Peterson that gets right to heart of many of my concerns in this book:

> It is not possible to have a Christian gospel apart from place and person. The gospel is not an idea or a plan or a vision. It works exclusively in creation and incarnation, in things and people. Disincarnation is the work of the devil. . . . We need to rub our noses in the stuff of this world, inhale its fragrance, press our hands into the clay, listen to the songs and stories. God is out recruiting every writer, artist, musician, pastor, child, and parent he can find to help us do just that so that we can worship the Lord in the beauty of holiness.[556]

Endnotes

1   *Amsterdam*, directed by David O. Russell, featuring Christian Bale, Margot Robbie, and John David Washington. 20th Century Studios, 2022.

2   Arthur Conan Doyle, "A Scandal in Bohemia," in *The Adventures of Sherlock Holmes* (1892), https://etc.usf.edu/lit2go/32/the-adventures-of-sherlock-holmes/345/adventure-1-a-scandal-in-bohemia/, accessed February 26, 2023.

3   See further my *1 & 2 Kings*, 136–42.

4   Discover Wildlife, "Cuckoo Guide."

5   Woodland Trust, "Cuckoo."

Chapter 1

6   On the content of this chapter, see further my *Seriously Dangerous Religion*, 1–20, which reflects on the disputed nature of reality and the "stories" people tell about it.

7   Klein, "Screen New Deal."

8   Bilek, "The Billionaire Family."

9   Bilek, "The Billionaire Family."

10 Myers, *Binding the Strong Man*, 14–20.

Chapter 2

11 On the content of this chapter, see further my *Seriously Dangerous Religion*, 347–77, which reflects on the question of truth.

12 John 18:38.

13 Goldman, "The Comet Ping Pong Gunman."

Chapter 3

14 On the content of this chapter, see further our *A Biblical History of Israel*, 38–58, which elaborates on the role of trust in gaining knowledge.

15   Coady, *Testimony*.

16   Coady, *Testimony*, vii.

17   Coady, *Testimony*, 176.

Chapter 4

18   As in chapter 3, see further on the content of the present chapter our *A Biblical History of Israel*, 38–58, which elaborates on the role of trust in gaining knowledge.

19   I'm borrowing language here from my friend Brett Landry.

Chapter 5

20   On the content of this chapter, see further my *Seriously Dangerous Religion*. Throughout that volume I engage with various philosophers and religious teachers who have claimed to speak truthfully about the metaphysical realm.

21   Dawkins, *God Delusion*.

22   Weber, "Science as a Vocation," 17–18.

Chapter 6

23   On the content of this chapter, see further my *Seeking What Is Right*, 3–45, where I lay out in more detail the foundations for a specifically Christian approach to ethics, and my *Reformation and the Right Reading of Scripture*, 27–53, which concerns the nature of Holy Scripture as the Christian "rule of faith."

24   John 14:6.

25   John 8:58.

26   John 8:12.

27   John 8:39, 41–42.

28   John 8:51.

29   Exodus 3:14.

30   John 8:59.

31   Matthew 28:20.

32   John 20:28.

33   E.g., Provan, *Seeking What Is Right*, 17–28.

34   The apostle Paul in 2 Timothy 3:16–17.

35   Adams, *Hitchhiker's Guide to the Galaxy*.

Chapter 7

36 On the content of this chapter, see further my *Seriously Dangerous Religion*, 21–46 and some of 309–46, which discuss creation.

37 Deuteronomy 4:28.

38 Psalm 104:14–15.

39 The occasion was Melvyn's Bragg's *In Our Time* program aired on May 6, 2010.

40 Goff, "Our Improbable Existence."

41 Leman, "Aliens Created Our Universe."

42 I'm referring to specifically to the domains on the earth rather than in the heavens—for "angels" and the like are not the concern of this book, any more than aliens are.

43 Kass, *Wisdom*, 47–48.

44 Exodus 20:8–11.

45 Genesis 2:7, 19.

46 John 1:1–5.

47 John 1:14.

48 Colossians 1:16.

Chapter 8

49 On the content of this chapter, see further my *Seriously Dangerous Religion*, 77–103 and some of 309–46, which discuss human creation.

50 Genesis 2:19.

51 The ESV unfortunately obscures this close connection between verses 29 and 30 by translating the same Hebrew *rûaḥ* first as "breath" and then as "Spirit." See further my next chapter.

52 We say this aloud as "nefesh," with the vowels and the emphasis being the same as "better."

53 U2, "Yahweh," from their 2004 album, *How to Dismantle an Atomic Bomb*.

54 1 Timothy 4:3–4.

55 Capon, *Supper of the Lamb*, 114–15.

56 Chaze, "A Mayday Call."

57 Psalm 103:1–5.

58 Proverbs 10:3; 25:25.

59 Wolff, *Anthropology*, 24–25.

Chapter 9

60   On the content of this chapter, see further my *Seriously Dangerous Religion*, 279–307 and some of 309–46, which discuss biblical hope regarding our physical embodiment. See also my *Reformation and the Right Reading of Scripture*, 178–83, 210–13.

61   We say this aloud as "bah-saar" (with the emphasis on the second syllable).

62   E.g., Leviticus 26:29; Isaiah 22:13.

63   Psalm 56:4–11.

64   Wolff, *Anthropology*, 26–31.

65   Jeremiah 17:5–7.

66   Genesis 6:12.

67   Psalm 65:2–3.

68   Genesis 2:24.

69   Genesis 2:23.

70   Wolff, *Anthropology*, 8.

71   Genesis 41:8. We say this aloud as "roo-ach" (with the emphasis on the first syllable and the "ch" pronounced as in "loch").

72   Isaiah 42:5. We say *nəšāmâ* aloud as "ne-shah-maa" (with the emphasis on the third syllable).

73   Psalm 104:29–30.

74   E.g., Judges 3:10; 1 Samuel 10:6; Jeremiah 51:11; Ezekiel 11:5.

75   1 Kings 10:5; 21:4–5.

76   Wolff, *Anthropology*, 44.

77   Proverbs 17:22.

78   Proverbs 15:14; cf. Deuteronomy 29:4.

79   1 Kings 4:29, 32–33. See my *1 & 2 Kings*, 58–61.

80   Proverbs 24:30.

81   Wolff, *Anthropology*, 51.

82   Psalm 22:26.

83   H. Vorländer, "*Anthropos*," *NIDNTT* 2:564–7.

84   J. Stafford Wright, "The New Testament and Modern Psychology," *NIDNTT* 2:567–69 (567).

85   1 Corinthians 15:18; 2 Corinthians 5:8.

86   Romans 8:11, 22–23.

Chapter 10

87   On the content of this chapter, see further my *Seriously Dangerous Religion*, 77–103, and some of 309–46, which discuss human creation, along with *Discovering Genesis*, 59–78.

88   Walton, *Ancient Near Eastern Thought*, 113–8.

89   Deuteronomy 4:28.

90   Exodus 20:4–5.

91   The Hebrew used for the heavenly "lights" in Genesis 1:14–16 is *mā' ôr* ("mah-oar," with the emphasis on the second syllable)—as in later descriptions of the tabernacle (e.g., Exodus 35:14, 28; 39:37; Numbers 4:9).

92   Genesis 3:24; Exodus 25:18–22; 1 Kings 6:23–28.

93   Genesis 2:9; Exodus 25:31–40.

94   "Adam," *DBI*, 9.

95   Psalm 8:4.

96   Psalm 8:5—my own translation. The ESV renders the first part of the line in this way: "you have made him a little lower than the heavenly beings."

97   E.g., Exodus 33:18; Psalm 96:6; Psalm 145:5.

98   2 Corinthians 4:4; Colossians 1:15.

99   Romans 8:29; 1 Corinthians 15:49.

100   Colossians 3:10; cf. 2 Corinthians 3:18.

Chapter 11

101   On the content of this chapter, see further my *Seriously Dangerous Religion*, 47–75 (on the biblical idea of God), and *Ecclesiastes and Song of Songs*, 290–96 (on beauty).

102   Numbers 23:19.

103   1 Kings 8:23.

104   Genesis 1:4, 10, 12, 18, 21, 25, 31.

105   Matthew 4:4.

106   E.g., Genesis 12:11–14; 24:16; 29:17; 1 Samuel 25:3; 2 Samuel 11:2; 14:25, 27.

107   See further my *Ecclesiastes and Song of Songs*, 282–89.

108   Isaiah 28:1; 40:6–8.

109   Proverbs 11:22; cf. also Matthew 23:27.

110   1 Peter 3:1–6; Proverbs 31:30, noting the emphases more generally throughout Proverbs 31:10–31.

111   Lewis, "On Being Human."

112   Revelation 21–22.

113   1 Corinthians 15:35–49.

Chapter 12

114 On the content of this chapter, see further my *Convenient Myths*, 107–19, *Seriously Dangerous Religion*, 221–49, and *Seeking What Is Right*, 265–83, all of which discuss biblical "dominion."

115 E.g., 1 Kings 4:24; Isaiah 14:2; Jeremiah 5:31; Psalm 49:14.

116 E.g., Numbers 32:22, 29; Joshua 18:1; 2 Samuel 8:11.

117 A notable biblical example is found in 1 Kings 3:16–28. See further my *1 & 2 Kings*, 50–52.

118 Psalm 72:2–4.

119 Psalm 24:1.

120 We say this aloud as "hah-daar" (with the emphasis on the second syllable).

121 Psalm 104:1–4.

122 Psalm 8:5.

123 Psalm 104:19.

124 Psalm 104:20–22.

125 Psalm 104:25–35.

126 Psalm 147:7–9.

127 Psalm 147:16–17.

128 Psalm 19:1.

129 Psalm 148:7–13, noting especially verse 11.

130 Psalm 148:13.

131 Philippians 2:5–11.

132 Romans 8:17.

133 Matthew 20:25–28.

Chapter 13

134 On the content of this chapter, see further my *Convenient Myths*, 107–19, *Seriously Dangerous Religion*, 221–49, and *Seeking What Is Right*, 265–83, which discuss biblical "dominion."

135 Numbers 6:24–26.

136 Numbers 3:7–8.

137 We say these words aloud as "ah-vaad" and "shah-maar" (with the emphasis in both cases on the second syllable).

138 E.g., Judges 9:28; Exodus 3:12.

139 Genesis 6:19–20.

140 Romans 11:36; 1 Corinthians 10:26; cf. Revelation 4:11.

141 Colossians 1:15–20.

142 Colossians 1:19.

143 Romans 8:19, 22.

144 Genesis 1:28.

145 Genesis 8:22.

146 Genesis 9:20–21.

147 We say this aloud as "shah-loam" (with the emphasis on the second syllable).

148 Bauckham, *Bible and Ecology*, 6.

149 E.g., Calvin, *Genesis*, 57, 125–6; and *Institutes*, 3.10.1, where he notes in reference to 1 Corinthians 7:31 that "Paul . . . admonishes us to use this world without abusing it."

Chapter 14

150 On the content of this chapter, see further my *Seriously Dangerous Religion*, 163–90, and some of 309–46, which discuss our human relationship with God.

151 Psalm 86:5; 100:5.

152 Lamentations 3:22; cf. Psalm 106:1.

153 Psalm 36:5; cf. Exodus 34:6.

154 Micah 7:18.

155 Psalm 94:1–3.

156 Exodus 34:5–7.

157 Genesis 15:6.

158 E.g., in Hebrews 11:8–10.

159 Romans 8:31.

160 Jeremiah 31:3; Deuteronomy 6:4–5.

161 Deuteronomy 6:6–9.

162 Galatians 6:2.

163 Psalm 1:2.

164 Psalm 19:7–9.

165 Psalm 119:44–47.

166 Psalm 105:1–2.

167 Psalm 30:2–3.

168 Psalm 88:16–18.

169 Psalm 22:1–2.

170 Consider, e.g., Psalms 120–134, which develop the idea of pilgrimage through a strange land (cf. Psalm 23).

171   In the first category, e.g., Luke 1:68; Acts 4:24–30; 2 Corinthians 1:3; Ephesians 1:3; 1 Peter 1:3; in the second, Luke 2:38; Hebrews 13:15; Revelation 11:17–18, and then Romans 1:8; Philippians 4:6; Colossians 4:2; 1 Thessalonians 5:16–18.

172   Ephesians 3:18.

173   1 Corinthians 1:9.

174   Ephesians 2:4; 2 John 3.

175   Matthew 22:34–40.

176   John 14:20–21.

177   John 14:23–24; Hebrews 5:9; 1 John 2:3–6.

Chapter 15

178   On the content of this chapter, see further my *Seriously Dangerous Religion*, 191–219, and some of 309–46, which discuss human community.

179   Genesis 1:31.

180   Genesis 1:27.

181   Genesis 2:7. We say ' *ādām* aloud as "ah-daam" (with the emphasis on the second syllable), and ' *ădāmâ* as "ah-dam-aah" (with the emphasis on the third syllable).

182   Genesis 2:7–17.

183   Genesis 2:18–20. The ESV translates verse 19 as "the Lord God had formed every beast of the field and every bird of the heavens," implying that this had already happened at some prior point. It is much more likely, however, that the idea is that God first announces the search for a companion in verse 18 and then launches it in verse 19.

184   Genesis 2:19–20.

185   Walton, *Ancient Near Eastern Thought*, 87–92, 188–90.

186   Genesis 4:3–9.

187   Psalm 121:7.

188   Genesis 38:12; Song of Songs 5:16; Jeremiah 3:20; 1 Samuel 15:28. We say *rēaʿ* aloud as "ray-ah" (with the emphasis on the first syllable).

189   Proverbs 25:21.

190   Notice, e.g., 1 Samuel 24:11–13.

191   Job 31:29–30.

192   Genesis 9:6.

193   Philippians 2:4.

194   Matthew 22:36–40.

195   Luke 10:25–37.

196   Matthew 5:43–48.

Chapter 16

197 On the content of this chapter, see further my *Seriously Dangerous Religion*, 77–103, 309–46, and *Seeking What Is Right*, 223–43, which discuss male and female in more depth.

198 Genesis 2:19, cf. 2:7.

199 Genesis 2:20–24.

200 The Hebrew word *ṣēlā'* ("tsay-lah," with the emphasis on the first syllable) typically refers elsewhere in the OT to one side of something over against the other. Interestingly, the earliest OT translations in Aramaic, Greek, and Latin all choose words to translate it that allow for this interpretation (while also allowing for "rib").

201 Genesis 2:23; 29:14.

202 Genesis 2:24.

203 Genesis 2:18; cf, e.g., Hosea 13:9.

204 We say the Hebrew aloud as "ke-negg-doe" (with the emphasis on the third syllable).

205 Kass, *Wisdom*, 73.

206 Genesis 1:28.

207 Ephesians 5:31–33, quoting Genesis 2:24.

208 1 Corinthians 6:16–18.

209 Matthew 5:28.

210 1 Corinthians 6:9–10; cf. Romans 1:26–27.

211 1 Timothy 1:9–11.

212 See further Hill, *Washed and Waiting*; Yarhouse and Zaporozhets, *Costly Obedience*.

Chapter 17

213 On the content of this chapter, see further my *Seriously Dangerous Religion*, 105–61, and *Discovering Genesis*, 79–94, which reflect in more depth on the nature of "the fall."

214 Genesis 3:2–5.

215 Genesis 2:16.

216 Deuteronomy 1:39; cf. 1 Kings 3:7–9.

217 Notice, e.g., Isaiah 31:1–3, where Israel's military reliance on Egypt is akin to abandoning the true God and treating the Egyptians as if they were divine. In truth, however, "the Egyptians are men and not God" (verse 3).

218 Exodus 20:4–5.

219 1 Kings 8:10–12, 27.

220   Romans 1:19–23.

221   Genesis 3:9–13.

222   Genesis 3:16–17.

223   Genesis 1:27–28, 2:20–23.

224   Genesis 3:16; Psalm 8:6. We say this word aloud as "mah-shaal" (with the empha-
      sis on the second syllable).

225   When Genesis 3:16 speaks of the woman's "desire," we should interpret this
      with the help of the same word in Genesis 4:7, where it is used of sin's desire to
      devour Cain.

226   Hebrews 3:12.

227   John 14:30; 2 Corinthians 4:4.

228   1 John 5:19.

229   Matthew 15:19.

230   Romans 1:29–31.

231   James 4:1–2.

232   Galatian 5:14–15.

Chapter 18

233   On the content of this chapter, see further my *Seriously Dangerous Religion*,
      279–307, and some of 309–46, which reflect on biblical hope.

234   Genesis 9:6.

235   Genesis 9 also describes one of the consequences of this truth: the human assault
      on "the wild" (verses 2–3). See further my *Discovering Genesis*, 120–24.

236   Genesis 9:9–11.

237   We say this word aloud as "bih-reeth" (with the emphasis on the second syllable).

238   Genesis 9:1, 7.

239   Genesis 11:8.

240   Genesis 12:1–3.

241   Exodus 2:23–25.

242   Exodus 19:4–6.

243   Exodus 12:1–14.

244   Exodus 12:12–13.

245   2 Samuel 7:12–16.

246   2 Samuel 7:16.

247   Matthew 1:1; 2:2; 21:9; 27:11; 27:29, 37.

248   Revelation 5:5.

249 Revelation 11:15.

250 Acts 3:25–26.

251 Galatians 3:14.

252 Hebrews 5:9.

253 1 Corinthians 15:3.

254 Luke 22:20.

255 Matthew 9:2.

256 Romans 8:19.

257 Romans 8:21, 23.

258 1 Peter 2:9.

Chapter 19

259 On the content of this chapter, see further my *Seriously Dangerous Religion*, 279–307, and some of 309–46, which reflect on biblical hope.

260 Romans 8:31–39.

261 Psalm 22:6.

262 Psalm 22:1–2, 7–8, 11–18.

263 Psalm 22:22–31.

264 Isaiah 66:22; 2 Peter 3:13; Revelation 22:1.

265 Ezekiel 36:26–27.

266 Jeremiah addresses the same reality in terms of a new *covenant* written on the heart (Jeremiah 31:31–34), whereby God's law becomes part of the fabric of the human person and obedience follows naturally.

267 Isaiah 19:23–25.

268 Colossians 2:13.

269 Ezekiel 34:22–24; cf. Jeremiah 33:15; Zechariah 9:9–10.

270 Isaiah 11:1–5; cf. Zechariah 12:1–9.

271 Zechariah 8:20–23; cf. Isaiah 2:2–4; 66:18–23.

272 Ephesians 2:13–16.

273 Ezekiel 36:8–9, 11, 29–30, 34–35; Hosea 2:18.

274 Isaiah 11:1–9.

275 Colossians 1:19–20.

276 Daniel 12:2.

277 Isaiah 26:19.

278 Romans 2:7.

279 2 Timothy 1:10.

280   John 20:1–9, 24–31.

281   John 6:40.

282   Romans 8:37.

Chapter 20

283   Deuteronomy 6:5.

284   Ephesians 4:15.

285   Romans 12:1–2.

286   Romans 1:21, 24, 26, 28.

287   Barrett, *Romans*, 215.

288   Barrett, *Romans*, 215.

Chapter 21

289   Jeremiah 31:3; Deuteronomy 6:5.

290   Hebrews 12:28.

291   See chapter 40 for a brief description of the Stoic worldview.

292   Bratt, *Centennial Reader*, 488.

293   Genesis 2:15; Numbers 3:7–8.

294   Hebrews 13:16.

295   Several NT texts suggest that the singing or chanting of hymns of praise was an important part of Christian worship from the beginning (1 Corinthians 14:15, 26; Colossians 3:16; Ephesians 5:19; cf. Acts 16:25).

296   Augustine, *Confessions*, 9.7.15.

297   1 Timothy 4:13.

298   Justin Martyr, *First Apology*, 67.

Chapter 22

299   On the content of this chapter, see further my *Seeking What Is Right*, which offers a wide-ranging discussion of Christian ethics in which the question of "rights" is prominent.

300   Deuteronomy 20:19–20.

301   Genesis 9:3; see further my *Discovering Genesis*, 120–24.

302   This is guaranteed by draining its blood from its carcass: "You shall not eat flesh with its life, that is, its blood [in it]" (Genesis 9:4).

303   Leviticus 17:3–4; cf. Leviticus 17:11; Deuteronomy 12:23.

304   1 Samuel 8:13–18.

305   Exodus 21:1–6; Deuteronomy 15:12–18.

306   Exodus 20:10; Deuteronomy 12:12, 18.

307   Exodus 21:26–27; Deuteronomy 23:15–16.

308   Genesis 9:5–6.

309   Genesis 4:10.

310   Matthew 23:31–35.

311   2 Kings 16:3; 17:17, 31.

312   1 Kings 21:3; see further my *1 & 2 Kings*, 157–60.

313   1 Kings 21:21.

314   Deuteronomy 14:28–29.

315   Job 22:7–11.

316   See McLaughlin, *Secular Creed*.

317   The quoted words are from the Declaration's Preamble.

318   Among the biblical ideas are the Preamble's reference to "the inherent dignity and of the equal and inalienable rights of all members of the human family"; and the declarations that "everyone has the right to life" (Article 3), that "everyone has the right to recognition everywhere as a person before the law" (Article 6), that "men and women of full age, without any limitation due to race, nationality or religion, have the right to marry and to found a family," and "the family is the natural and fundamental group unit of society and is entitled to protection by society and the State" (Article 16), and that "no one shall be arbitrarily deprived of his property" (Article 17).

319   Féron, "Human Rights and Faith."

Chapter 23

320   On the content of this chapter, see further my *Seeking What Is Right*, 301–23, which discusses abortion.

321   Psalm 100:3.

322   Isaiah 64:8.

323   Job 10:10–11.

324   Jeremiah 1:5.

325   Psalm 139:13–16. We say the Hebrew *sākak* aloud as "sah-kaak."

326   Ecclesiastes 11:5.

327   Greasley and Kaczor, *Abortion Rights*, 27, 40–41.

328   Giubilini and Minerva, "After-Birth Abortion."

329   Lévesque, "Quebec College of Physicians Slammed."

330   Greasley and Kaczor, *Abortion Rights*, 141, quoting Steven Pinker.

331   Westermarck, *Origin*, 1:415.

332   Seneca, *De Ira*, 1.15, in *Seneca: Moral Essays*, 145, which translates the Latin in this way: "We drown even children who at birth are weakly and abnormal. Yet it is not anger, but reason that separates the harmful from the sound."

333   *Didache* 2.2.

334   *Epistle of Barnabas*, 19.5.

335   See further Greasley and Kaczor, *Abortion Rights*, 155–57.

Chapter 24

336   On the content of this chapter, see further my *Seeking What Is Right*, 301–23, which discusses suicide.

337   Ecclesiastes 12:7.

338   "Suicide," in the *Catechism of the Catholic Church*, §2280. See further Pope John Paul II, *Evangelium Vitae*.

339   Judges 9:52–54.

340   1 Samuel 31:4–5.

341   2 Samuel 17:23.

342   1 Kings 16:15–20. See my *1 & 2 Kings*, 128–31.

343   Matthew 27:3–5.

344   Plato, *Phaedo: The Last Hours of Socrates*.

345   Acts 16:27–29.

346   Romans 14:7–8.

347   1 Corinthians 6:19–20.

348   Romans 5:3–5.

349   Tertullian, *De Fuga in Persecutione*, 13.2.

350   *Catechism of the Catholic Church*, §2282.

351   Kass, "No Deadly Drug," 32.

352   Kass, "No Deadly Drug," 35.

353   Foley, "Compassionate Care, Not Assisted Suicide," 297. See further Canadian Society of Palliative Care Physicians, http://www.cspcp.ca/cspcp-key-messages-re-hastened-death/, and Christian Medical and Dental Society of Canada, www.cmdscanada.org, for many resources, including a video (*The Gift*).

354   Van Maren, "Canada's Killing Regime."

355   Callahan, "Physician-Assisted Suicide," 63–4.

356   Somerville, *Death Talk*, 23.

Chapter 25

357   On the content of this chapter, see further my *Seeking What Is Right*, 325–65, which discusses at length the question of human identity.

358   Byrne, "Is Sex Binary?"

359   Byrne, "Is Sex Binary?"

360   Wright, "The New Evolution Deniers."

361   *Merriam-Webster*, s.v. "Gender Identity."

362   *Merriam-Webster, s.v.* "Transgender."

363   "The majority of children with suspected gender dysphoria don't have the condition once they reach puberty." https://www.nhs.uk/conditions/gender-dysphoria/treatment/, accessed July, 8, 2019.

364   A Path, "63 Genders."

365   See further Roberts, *Transgender*, and Evangelical Alliance, *Trans Formed*.

366   E.g., The Gender Dysphoria Alliance at https://www.genderdysphoriaalliance.com/, which endorses "the realities of biological sex" and believes that "clinical practices should be based on peer-reviewed evidence, not activism or ideology."

367   Many historical examples of such "contagion" can be cited—for example, the "wave of suicides" that swept across Europe in the late eighteenth century in the wake of Goethe's novel *Young Werther*, "as if the very act of suicide was somehow infectious." Marsden, "Social Contagion."

368   These quotes are drawn from an exhibition in the Bauhaus Museum in Weimar, Germany, that I visited in October 2022.

369   See, e.g., the Jordan Peterson interview with the courageous Chloe Cole at https://youtu.be/6O3MzPeomqs.

370   Shepherd, "The People Who Think They Are Made of Glass."

Chapter 26

371   Psalm 113:9.

372   Psalm 127:3; Proverbs 17:6.

373   Psalm 128:3.

374   Matthew 19:14.

375   Ephesians 6:4; Colossians 3:21; 1 Thessalonians 2:7.

376   Titus 2:4; 1 Timothy 3:4.

377   Ephesians 6:4.

378   Proverbs 22:6.

379   Proverbs 1:8.

380   Deuteronomy 4:9.

381   Exodus 12:26.

382   Deuteronomy 6:7 speaks of doing so "when you sit in your house, and when you walk by the way, and when you lie down, and when you rise."

383   E.g., 1 Samuel 16:11; 2 Kings 4:18; Mark 6:3. "In later Judaism, the parents' responsibility in teaching a profession to their children was underlined by the maxim: 'Who does not teach a profession to his son teaches him brigandage' (b. Qidd. 29a)." Lemaire, "Education," 307.

384   For example, recent research has suggested that the birth of a child impacts a father's brain size. See "Dads' Brains Change Size."

385   Proverbs 22:6.

Chapter 27

386   On the content of this chapter, see further my *Seeking What Is Right*, 349–65, which describes the educational culture that many of us are currently engaging.

387   Ephesians 6:4.

388   Article 16.

389   Article 16.

390   Article 12.

391   Article 26.

392   1 Kings 4:33; cf. 1 Kings 11.

393   See Government of British Columbia "More Students Supported by SOGI-Inclusive Education."

394   From the "For Parents" page on the SOGI 123 website at https://www.sogieducation.org/parents.

395   See, e.g., Blackwell, "How Canadian Schools Aid Students' Gender Transition."

Chapter 28

396   On Hannah Arendt see further my essay "On Refusing to Be Persons."

397   Cherry, "Asch Conformity Experiments."

398   Arendt, *Origins of Totalitarianism*.

399   Passerin d'Entreves, "Arendt."

400   McGowan, *Arendt*, 60.

401   Lessing, *Prisons We Choose*, 13.

402   Romans 12:2.

403   McGowan, *Arendt*, 37.

404   Hebrews 10:24–25.

405   Romans 12:1.

Chapter 29

406 Galatians 3:28.

407 Galatians 3:28; Colossians. 3:11; James 2:1–4.

408 1 Corinthians 12:13; Galatians 3:27.

409 Philemon 16.

410 Matthew 28:19–20.

411 Revelation 7:9.

412 Galatians 3:27; Matthew 28:20.

413 1 Timothy 1:10.

414 Colossians 3:5–9.

415 Colossians 3:10–11.

416 E.g., Romans 12:13; 1 Timothy 3:2; 5:10; Titus 1:8; Hebrew 13:2; 1 Peter 4:9.

417 Philippians 2:15–16.

418 1 Corinthians 5:1–13.

419 Romans 16:3–23.

Chapter 30

420 Genesis 3:16–19. The common translation "childbearing" in Genesis 3:16 is misleading and should be avoided. See my *Seriously Dangerous Religion*, 117–19.

421 Exodus 19:6.

422 Deuteronomy 17:14–20.

423 Exodus 35:31–33.

424 Exodus 36:1.

425 Ephesians 5:11.

426 Romans 15:17.

Chapter 31

427 Ephesians 4:12–13; cf. Hebrews 6:10.

428 Romans 11:13; 1 Corinthians 16:15; 2 Corinthians 3:8, 9; 4:1; 5:18; 6:3; Colossians 4:17.

429 2 Corinthians 6:4–5.

430 Colossians 1:10; 2 Thessalonians 2:16–17.

431 1 Thessalonians 1:3.

432 2 Thessalonians 3:7–8.

433 Cf. also 1 Thessalonians 2:9.

434   Acts 18:3; 19:12; 20:33–35; 1 Corinthians 4:12.

435   Ephesians 4:2; cf. 1 Thessalonians 4:11.

436   1 Thessalonians 3:11–12.

437   2 Thessalonians 3:10.

438   2 Thessalonians 3:8; 1 Timothy 5:6–18.

439   Ephesians 4:2; cf. 1 Timothy 5:10; 6:18; Titus 3:14.

440   *Didache* 12.2–5.

441   Colossians 3:22–24.

442   See Mark 6:8–9 for one of the key texts.

443   Proverbs 28:19.

444   Deuteronomy 7:13.

445   Smiley, "American Agriculture."

446   1 Timothy 6:10.

Chapter 32

447   On the content of this chapter, see further my *Convenient Myths*, 107–19, *Seriously Dangerous Religion*, 221–49, and *Seeking What Is Right*, 265–83, which discuss creation care. For further reading see Moo and Moo, *Creation Care*.

448   Benzoni, "Thomas Aquinas and Environmental Ethics," 446.

449   Calvin, *Genesis*, 64–65, 96.

450   The full text can be found at https://genius.com/U2-yahweh-lyrics, accessed April 24, 2019.

451   2 Peter 3:10–11.

452   Wolf, "God, James Watt, and the Public Land," 65.

453   Romans 8:19–23.

454   Dunn, *Romans 1–8*, 471.

455   Hebrews 1:10–12; 12:26–29.

456   2 Peter 3:13.

457   Revelation 5:10.

458   Proverbs 12:10; cf. Deuteronomy 22:1–6.

459   So, e.g., Kumar and Yashiro, "The Marginal Poor."

460   See NASA, "Climate Change," with references to the academic literature. Many people who were previously unconvinced have now changed their minds. This includes, e.g., the UK peer Lord Lilley, "one of only five MPs to oppose the Climate Change Act in 2008 and was once vice-chairman of an oil and gas company," who has recently agreed that "the science that proves global warming is 'robust.'" Gatten, "Use Covid-Style Messaging."

461 Natter, "Republicans Who Couldn't Beat Climate Debate." See further Hanchett, "Polls suggest less environmentalism."

Chapter 33

462 1 Corinthians 5:5. See further on exclusion for the good of all 2 Thessalonians 3:6–15; 1 Timothy 1:20; Titus 3:10. The ideal is, of course, that confronting the sin will bring about "godly grief [that] produces a repentance" (2 Corinthians 7:10; 2 Timothy 2:25).

463 Luke 10:27.

464 Matthew 10:16.

465 *Convenient Myths*, 29–39.

Chapter 34

466 On the content of this chapter, see further my engagement with politics in *Seriously Dangerous Religion*, 251–78, and *Seeking What Is Right*, especially 125–201.

467 Philippians 2:4.

468 Jeremiah 29:7.

469 1 Peter 2:9–12.

470 Genesis 50:20.

471 Leviticus 11:44; Matthew 5:48.

472 Eliot, *Middlemarch*, 896.

473 McTaggart, "Greta Thunberg."

Chapter 35

474 Watson, "Television in Canada."

475 Solon, "Sean Parker."

476 Interview in *Consume This Movie*, directed by Gene Brockhoff. Well Crafted Films, 2008.

477 James 1:6–8.

478 Deuteronomy 6:7.

479 Deuteronomy 6:7; Romans 12:2.

480 Adams, *Hitchhiker's Guide to the Galaxy*.

Chapter 36

481 On the content of this chapter, see further my *Reformation and the Right Reading of Scripture*, 313–413, which describe the displacement of Christian faith from the center of Christendom in the course of the rise of modernity and modern science.

482   Zagorin, *Religious Toleration*, 290.

483   I am grateful to my friend Eddie Larkman for mentioning this line to me.

Chapter 37

484   Dickens, *Hard Times*, 13.

485   Van Liere, "On the Brink," 264.

486   Reventlow, "Towards the End of the 'Century of Enlightenment,'" 1045.

487   Wordsworth, "The Tables Turned."

488   Mayo Clinic, "Narcissistic Personality Disorder."

Chapter 38

489   See the text of the Manifesto at: https://www.marxists.org/archive/marx/
       works/1848/communist-manifesto/cho2.htm#:~:text=Your%20very%20
       ideas%20are%20but,of%20existence%20of%20your%20class, accessed Novem-
       ber 1, 2022.

Chapter 39

490   For a website devoted to keeping the real science in public view, see Reality's
       Last Stand, which is run by evolutionary biologist Colin Wright (https://drcolin-
       wright.com/) and publishes "weekly news, articles, and other content about gen-
       der ideology and the science of sex differences."

491   Dixon, "Most Children."

492   Government of Canada, "Canada's New Medical Assistance in Dying (MAID)
       Law."

493   Lilley, "Intolerant Trudeau."

Chapter 40

494   Arizona Christian University, "Counterfeit Christianity."

495   O'Keefe, *Epicureanism*, 117.

496   O'Keefe, *Epicureanism*, 130.

Chapter 41

497   On the content of this chapter, see further my *Seriously Dangerous Religion*,
       which discusses throughout its length various non-biblical alternatives for think-
       ing about bodies and souls, and about other anthropological matters.

498   Acts 17:16–34.

499   Acts 17:32.

Chapter 42

500   On the content of this chapter, see further my *Reformation and the Right Reading of Scripture*, 517–47, which engages with postmodern "constructionism" in literature.

501   A fairly recent, readable book that explores further the connection between mathematics and beauty is Livio, *Golden Ratio*. The author is an astrophysicist heading up the science division at the Hubble Space Telescope Science Institute in the USA.

502   Van Simson, *Gothic Cathedrals*, 20–39.

503   This is a much-quoted line, and it appears to have come down us by way of Johann Nikolaus Forkel's biography, *On Johann Sebastian Bach's Life, Genius and Works* (1802). Forkel's sources were Bach's obituary along with materials obtained from Bach's sons, Carl Philipp Emanuel and Wilhelm Friedemann.

504   Both quotes are drawn from an exhibition at the Bach House in Eisenach, Germany, which I visited on October 28, 2022.

505   Friedmann, "Beauty before Content."

Chapter 43

506   On the content of this chapter, see further my *Convenient Myths*, 41–127, which engages at length with Romantic myths about the past.

507   Genesis 4:23.

508   Exodus 21:23–25.

509   Ellingson, *Myth*, 36.

510   Hazard, *European Mind*, 14. See further Ellingson, *Myth*, 64–76.

511   LeBlanc, *Battles*, 150–51.

512   LeBlanc, *Battles*, 6.

513   LeBlanc, *Battles*, 8.

514   Headland, "Revisionism," 607.

515   Letter to his sister-in-law, Caroline von Beulwitz, on December 10, 1788. Friedrich Schiller Archive, accessed November 26, 2022, https://www.friedrich-schiller-archiv.de/briefe-schillers/an-caroline-von-beulwitz/schiller-an-caroline-von-beulwitz-10-dezember-1788/.

516   Romans 1:21.

517   1 John 1:8–9.

Chapter 44

518   Proverbs 4:7.

519   Briggs, "Bacon's Science and Religion."

520 Kissinger, "How the Enlightenment Ends."

521 Brecht, *Martin Luther*, 33.

522 Mitchell, *American Awakening*, 162–64.

523 Kronman, *Education's End*, 49.

Chapter 45

524 Matthew 18:20.

525 Hebrews 10:24–25.

526 Bonhoeffer, *Life Together*. For a great book that develops the implications for us nowadays of Bonhoeffer's thinking (and is particularly perceptive about the threat of "online education"), see House, *Bonhoeffer's Seminary Vision*.

527 Mitchell, *American Awakening*, 162–64.

528 As I revised this paragraph for the last time, I came across this article about a some developments at my *alma mater*: Clarence-Smith, "Cambridge Scholars Face Student Backlash." It seems that professors at the University of Cambridge have done something unconscionable. Concerned about declining in-person, student attendance at lectures, they have scrapped recorded lectures. Numerous students have responded by claiming that this attempt to "force" them to attend lectures "reflects a paternalistic view of students in which they are not afforded the agency to make decisions about their own learning," alleging that this move could "damage students' wellbeing." This is precisely the kind of trouble you ask for when you turn the field of education into a consumer marketplace.

529 Zechariah 2:7.

Chapter 46

530 1 Timothy 4:13.

Chapter 47

531 Underlying my treatment of justice in this chapter and the next is the helpful paradigm provided by Timothy Keller, "A Biblical Critique of Secular Justice and Critical Theory."

532 Micah 6:8.

533 Proverbs 31:8–9.

Chapter 48

534 Center for Intersectional Justice, "What Is Intersectionality?"

535 Keller, "A Biblical Critique."

536 Recently, e.g., I read this: Pollard, "Amnesty International Has Become a Woke Joke." Another originally apolitical organization, noted for championing freedom of thought and expression, has capitulated to woke partisanship.

537 Volf, *Exclusion and Embrace*, 124.

538 Admissions is currently a hot topic in various countries, with numerous educational institutions arguing that they are not actually discriminating by favoring, e.g., Black, Hispanic, and Native American applicants over white and Asian ones. They clearly are. See, e.g., Liptak, "Race-Based College Admissions." In the same way, employers regularly argue nowadays that they are not discriminating by favoring people in certain groups, because discrimination is not discrimination in such cases, because—well, because the victims of it are indeed members of *other* groups, which deserve what is happening to them.

Chapter 49

539 On the content of this chapter, see further my *Convenient Myths*, 107–19, *Seriously Dangerous Religion*, 221–49, and *Seeking What Is Right*, 265–83, which discuss environmental issues,.

540 Bauckham, *Bible and Ecology*, 6.

541 White, "Ecologic Crisis."

542 White, "Ecologic Crisis," 25.

543 Cited in Taylor, *Dark Green Religion*, 36.

544 See my *Convenient Myths*, 41–82.

545 Doyle, "A Friedrich for the National Gallery," 109.

546 Low, "Ecology," 356.

547 Low, "Ecology," 368.

548 Neumann, "Prehistoric Peoples," 143.

549 Low, "Ecology," 355.

550 Low, "Ecology," 355.

551 See *Convenient Myths*, 121–27.

Chapter 50

552 Keynes, *General Theory of Employment*, 383–84.

553 Orwell, *Animal Farm*.

554 Ecclesiastes 12:13.

555 World Economic Forum, "The Fourth Industrial Revolution, by Klaus Schwab."

556 Peterson, *As Kingfishers Catch Fire*, 81.

Select Bibliography

A Path. "63 genders . . . now 81 genders." March 20, 2000, accessed July 9, 2019. https://apath.org/63-genders/.

Adams, Douglas. *The Hitchhiker's Guide to the Galaxy*. London: Pan, 1979.

Arendt, Hannah. *The Origins of Totalitarianism*. New York: Harcourt Brace Jovanovich, 1973.

Arizona Christian University. "Counterfeit Christianity: 'Moralistic Therapeutic Deism' Most Popular Worldview in U.S. Culture." April 27, 2021, accessed October 22, 2022. https://www.arizonachristian.edu/2021/04/27/counterfeit-christianity-moralistic-therapeutic-deism-most-popular-worldview-in-u-s-culture/.

Augustine, *Confessions*. *NPNF* 1.

Barrett, C. K. *The Epistle to the Romans*. Rev. ed. Peabody, MA: Hendrickson, 1991.

Bauckham, Richard. *Bible and Ecology: Rediscovering the Community of Creation*. London: Darton, Longman and Todd, 2010.

Benzoni, Francisco. "Thomas Aquinas and Environmental Ethics: A Reconsideration of Providence and Salvation." *JR* 85 (2005) 446–76.

Bilek, Jennifer. "The Billionaire Family Pushing Synthetic Sex Identities SSI." *Tablet*, June 15, 2022, accessed September 16, 2022. https://www.tabletmag.com/sections/news/articles/billionaire-family-pushing-synthetic-sex-identities-ssi-pritzkers.

Blackwell, Tom. "How Canadian Schools Aid Students' Gender Transition without Family Consent." *National Post*, January 5, 2023, accessed January 5, 2023. https://nationalpost.com/news/schools-consent-transgender-gender-transition.

Bonhoeffer, Dietrich. *Life Together: The Classic Exploration of Christian Community*. New York: HarperOne, 1978.

Bratt, James D., ed. *A Centennial Reader*. Grand Rapids: Eerdmans, 1998.

Brecht, Martin. *Martin Luther: His Road to Reformation 1483–1521*. Translated by James L. Schaaf. Philadelphia: Fortress, 1985.

Briggs, John C. "Bacon's Science and Religion." In *The Cambridge Companion to Bacon*, edited by Markku Peltonen, 172–99. Cambridge: Cambridge University Press, 1996.

Byrne, Alex. "Is Sex Binary?" ARC Digital, November 1, 2018, accessed July 8, 2019. https://arcdigital.media/is-sex-binary-16bec97d161e.

Callahan, Daniel. "Reason, Self-Determination, and Physician-Assisted Suicide." In *The Case against Assisted Suicide*, edited by K. Foley and H. Hendin, 52–68. Baltimore: Johns Hopkins University Press, 2002.

Calvin, John. *Commentaries on the First Book of Moses Called Genesis*. Edited and translated by John King. CalC 1. 1847. Reprint, Grand Rapids: Baker, 1981.

———. *Institutes of the Christian Religion*. 2 vols. Translated by Henry Beveridge. Grand Rapids: Eerdmans, 1989.

Capon, Robert Farrar. *The Supper of the Lamb: A Culinary Reflection*. New York: The Modern Library, 2002.

Chaze, Emmanuelle. "A Mayday Call, a Dash across the Mediterranean . . . and 130 Souls Lost at Sea." *The Guardian*, April 25, 2021, accessed September 16, 2022. https://www.theguardian.com/global-development/2021/apr/25/a-mayday-call-a-dash-across-the-ocean-and-130-souls-lost-at-sea.

Center for Intersectional Justice. "What Is Intersectionality?" Accessed November 1, 2022. https://www.intersectionaljustice.org/what-is-intersectionality.

Cherry, Kendra. "The Asch Conformity Experiments." Verywellmind, May 10, 2022, accessed October 5, 2022. https://www.verywellmind.com/the-asch-conformity-experiments-2794996.

Clarence-Smith, Louisa. "Cambridge Scholars Face Student Backlash over Scrapping Recorded Lectures." *The Telegraph*, January 3, 2023, accessed on January 3, 2023. https://www.telegraph.co.uk/news/2023/01/03/cambridge-scholars-face-student-backlash-scrapping-recorded/.

Coady, C. A. J. *Testimony: A Philosophical Study*. Oxford: Clarendon, 1992.

Dawkins, Richard. *The God Delusion*. 10th anniversary ed. San Francisco: Black Swan, 2016.

Dickens, Charles. *Hard Times*. Norton Critical Editions. New York: Norton, 1966.

Discover Wildlife. "Cuckoo Guide." Accessed November 4, 2022. https://www.discoverwildlife.com/animal-facts/birds/facts-about-cuckoos/.

Dixon, Hayley. "Most Children Who Think They're Transgender Are Just Going through a 'Phase', says NHS." *The Telegraph*, October 23, 2022, accessed October 23, 2022. https://www.telegraph.co.uk/news/2022/10/23/children-who-think-transgender-just-going-phase-says-nhs/.

Doyle, Margaret M. "A Friedrich for the National Gallery of Art, Washington." *BurM* 148 (2006) 109–12.

Dunn, James D. G. *Romans 1–8*. Word Biblical Commentary 38A. Dallas: Word, 1988.

Eliot, George. *Middlemarch*. Edited by W. J. Harvey. Harmondsworth, UK: Penguin, 1965.

Ellingson, Ter. *The Myth of the Noble Savage*. Berkeley: University of California Press, 2001.

Epistle of Barnabas. ANF 1.

Evangelical Alliance. *Trans Formed*. London: Evangelical Alliance, 2018.

Féron, Henri. "Human Rights and Faith: A 'World-Wide Secular Religion'?" *EGP* 7.4 (2014) 181–200. DOI: 10.3402/egp.v7.26262.

Foley, Kathleen. "Compassionate Care, Not Assisted Suicide." In *The Case against Assisted Suicide*, edited by K. Foley and H. Hendin, 293–309. Baltimore: Johns Hopkins University Press, 2002.

Foley, Kathleen M., and Herbert Hendin, eds. *The Case against Assisted Suicide: For the Right to End-of-Life Care*. Baltimore: Johns Hopkins University Press, 2002.

Friedmann, Jonathan L. "Beauty before Content." Thinking on Music, accessed November 5, 2022. https://thinkingonmusic.wordpress.com/tag/richard-dawkins/.

Gatten, Emma. "Use Covid-Style Messaging to Get People Onboard with Net Zero, Says 'Bossy' Lords Report." *The Telegraph*, October 12, 2022, accessed October 12. 2022, https://www.telegraph.co.uk/environment/2022/10/12/use-covid-style-mess aging-get-people-onboard-net-zero-says-bossy/.

Giubilini, Alberto, and Francesca Minerva. "After-Birth Abortion: Why Should the Baby Live?" *JME* 39 (2013) 261–63.

Goff, Philip. "Our Improbable Existence Is No Evidence for a Multiverse." *Scientific American*, January 10, 2021, accessed November 3, 2022. https://www. scientificamerican.com/article/our-improbable-existence-is-no-evidence-for-a-multiverse/.

Goldman, Adam. "The Comet Ping Pong Gunman Answers Our Reporter's Questions." *New York Times*, December 7, 2016, accessed September 16, 2022. https://www. nytimes.com/2016/12/07/us/edgar-welch-comet-pizza-fake-news.html.

Government of British Columbia. "More Students Supported by SOGI-Inclusive Education." May 17, 2019, accessed July 11, 2019. https://archive.news.gov.bc.ca/ releases/news_releases_2017–2021/2019EDUC0040–000975.htm.

Government of Canada. "Canada's New Medical Assistance in Dying MAID Law." Accessed October 20, 2022. https://www.justice.gc.ca/eng/cj-jp/ad-am/bk-di. html.

Greasley, Kate, and Christopher Kaczor. *Abortion Rights: For and Against*. Cambridge: Cambridge University Press, 2017.

Hanchett, Jim. "Polls Suggest Less Environmentalism among U.S. Christians." *Futurity*, February 1, 2018, accessed February 18, 2020. https://www.futurity.org/christians-environment-opinion-1670122./.

Hazard, Paul. *The European Mind 1680–1715*. London: Hollis and Carter, 1953.

Headland, Thomas. "Revisionism in Ecological Anthropology." *CAnth* 38 (1997) 605–9.

Hill, Wesley. *Washed and Waiting: Reflections on Christian Faithfulness and Homosexuality*. Grand Rapids: Zondervan, 2010.

House, Paul R. *Bonhoeffer's Seminary Vision: A Case for Costly Discipleship and Life Together*. Wheaton, IL: Crossway, 2015.

Justin Martyr. *First Apology*. ANF 1.

Kass, Leon R. *The Beginning of Wisdom: Reading Genesis*. New York: Free, 2003.

———. "I Will Give No Deadly Drug: Why Doctors Must Not Kill." In *The Case against Assisted Suicide*, edited by K. Foley and H. Hendin, 17–40. Baltimore: Johns Hopkins University Press, 2002.

Keller, Timothy. "A Biblical Critique of Secular Justice and Critical Theory." Accessed November 1, 2022. https://quarterly.gospelinlife.com/a-biblical-critique-of-secular-justice-and-critical-theory/.

Keynes, John Maynard. *The General Theory of Employment, Interest, and Money*. New York: Harcourt, Brace, 1936.

Kissinger, Henry A. "How the Enlightenment Ends." *The Atlantic*, June 2018, accessed October 27, 2022. https://www.theatlantic.com/magazine/archive/2018/06/henry-kissinger-ai-could-mean-the-end-of-human-history/559124/.

Klein, Naomi. "Screen New Deal." *The Intercept*, May 8, 2020, accessed September 16, 2022, https://theintercept.com/2020/05/08/andrew-cuomo-eric-schmidt-coronavirus-tech-shock-doctrine/.

Kronman, Anthony T. *Education's End: Why Our Colleges and Universities Have Given Up on the Meaning of Life*. New Haven, CT: Yale University Press, 2008.

Kumar, Pushpam, and Makiko Yashiro. "The Marginal Poor and Their Dependence on Ecosystem Services: Evidence from South Asia and Sub-Saharan Africa." In *Marginality: Addressing the Nexus of Poverty, Exclusion and Ecology*, edited by Joachim von Braun and Franz W. Gatzweiler, 169–80. Dordrecht: Springer, 2014.

LeBlanc, Steven. *Constant Battles: The Myth of the Peaceful, Noble Savage*. New York: St. Martin's Press, 2003.

Lemaire, André. "Education: Ancient Israel." *AYBD* 2:305–312.

Leman, Jennifer. "Aliens Created Our Universe in a Lab, Scientist Suggests." Popular Mechanics, April 25, 2022, accessed November 3, 2022. https://www.popular mechanics.com/space/deep-space/a39797483/aliens-created-our-universe-in-a-lab/.

Liptak, Adam. "Supreme Court Seems Ready to Throw Out Race-Based College Admissions." *New York Times*, October 31, 2022, accessed November 2, 2022, https://www.nytimes.com/2022/10/31/us/supreme-court-harvard-unc-affirmative-action.html.

Lessing, Doris. *Prisons We Choose to Live Inside*. 1986. Reprint, Toronto: Anansi, 2006.

Lévesque, Catherine. "Quebec College of Physicians Slammed for Suggesting MAID for Severely Ill Newborns." *National Post*, October 11, 2022, accessed November 4, 2022. https://nationalpost.com/news/quebec-college-of-physicians-slammed-for-suggesting-maid-for-severely-ill-newborns.

Lewis, C. S. "On Being Human." http://famouspoetsandpoems.com/poets/c__s__lewis/poems/2362.

Lilley, Brian. "Intolerant Trudeau Divides Canadians While O'Toole Shows Understanding." *Toronto Sun*, January 27, 2022, accessed October 20, 2022. https://torontosun.com/opinion/columnists/lilley-intolerant-trudeau-divides-canadians-while-otoole-shows-understanding.

Livio, Mario. *The Golden Ratio: The Story of Phi, the World's Most Astonishing Number*. New York: Crown, 2003.

Low, Bobbi S. "Behavioral Ecology of Conservation in Traditional Societies." *HN* 7 (1996) 353–79.

Marsden, Paul. "Memetics and Social Contagion: Two Sides of the Same Coin?" *JMem* 2 (1998) 171–85.

Mayo Clinic. "Narcissistic Personality Disorder." Accessed October 19, 2022. https://www.mayoclinic.org/diseases-conditions/narcissistic-personality-disorder/symptoms-causes/syc-20366662#:~:text=Overview,lack%20of%20empathy%20for%20others.

McGowan, John. *Hannah Arendt: An Introduction*. Minneapolis: University of Minnesota Press, 1998.

McLaughlin, Rebecca. *The Secular Creed: Engaging Five Contemporary Claims*. Austin, TX: Gospel Coalition, 2021.

McTaggart, India. "Greta Thunberg: It's Time to Overthrow the West's Oppressive and Racist Capitalist System." *The Telegraph*, November 2, 2022, accessed November 2, 2022. https://www.telegraph.co.uk/news/2022/11/02/greta-thunberg-time-over throw-wests-oppressive-racist-capitalist/.

Merriam-Webster Online. "Gender Identity." Accessed July 4, 2019. https://www.merriam-webster.com/dictionary/gender%20identity.

———. "Transgender." Accessed July 4, 2019. https://www.merriam-webster.com/dictionary/transgender.

Mitchell, Joshua. *American Awakening: Identity Politics and Other Afflictions of Our Time*. New York: Encounter, 2020.

Moo, Douglas J., and Jonathan A. Moo. *Creation Care: A Biblical Theology of the Natural World*. Biblical Theology for Life. Grand Rapids: Zondervan, 2018.

Myers, Ched. *Binding the Strong Man: A Political Reading of Mark's Story of Jesus*. Maryknoll, NY: Orbis, 1988.

NASA. "Climate Change: How Do We Know?" Accessed February 18, 2020. https://climate.nasa.gov/evidence/.

Natter, Ari. "Republicans Who Couldn't Beat Climate Debate Now Seek to Join It." *Bloomberg*, March 5, 2019, accessed February 18, 2020. https://www.bloomberg.com/news/articles/2019-03-05/republicans-who-couldn-t-beat-climate-debate-now-seek-to-join-it.

Neumann, Thomas W. "The Role of Prehistoric Peoples in Shaping Ecosystems in the Eastern United States: Implications for Restoration Ecology and Wilderness Management." In *Wilderness and Political Ecology: Aboriginal Influences and the Original State of Nature*, edited by Charles E. Kay and Randy T. Simmons, 141–78. Salt Lake City: University of Utah Press, 2002.

O'Keefe, Tim. *Epicureanism*. Berkeley: University of California Press, 2010.

Orwell, George. *Animal Farm*. London: Collins, 2021.

Passerin d'Entreves, Maurizio. "Hannah Arendt." *The Stanford Encyclopedia of Philosophy*, edited by Edward N. Zalta, Fall 2019. Accessed October 5, 2022. https://plato.stanford.edu/archives/fall2019/entries/arendt/.

Plato, *Phaedo: The Last Hours of Socrates*. Translated by Benjamin Jowett. Project Gutenberg, January 15, 2013, accessed November 4, 2022. https://www.gutenberg.org/files/1658/1658-h/1658-h.htm.

Pollard, Stephen. "Amnesty International Has Become a Woke Joke." *The Telegraph*, October 30, 2022, accessed November 2, 2022. https://www.telegraph.co.uk/news/2022/10/30/amnesty-international-has-become-woke-joke/.

Pope John Paul II. *Evangelium Vitae*. Accessed November 30, 2019. http://www.vatican.va/content/john-paul-ii/en/encyclicals/documents/hf_jp-ii_enc_25031995_evangelium-vitae.html.

Peterson, Eugene H. *As Kingfishers Catch Fire: A Conversation on the Ways of God Formed by the Words of God*. Colorado Springs: Waterbrook, 2017.

Provan, Iain. *1 & 2 Kings*. Understanding the Bible. Grand Rapids: Baker, 1995.

———. *Convenient Myths: The Axial Age, Dark Green Religion, and the World That Never Was*. Waco, TX: Baylor University Press, 2013.

———. *Discovering Genesis: Content, Interpretation, Reception*. Grand Rapids: Eerdmans, 2016.

———. *Ecclesiastes and Song of Songs*. NIV Application Commentary. Grand Rapids: Zondervan, 2001.

———. "On Refusing to Be Persons: Hannah Arendt in Christian Perspective." In *Offering the Light: Essays in Honour of Philip E. Satterthwaite on the Occasion of his Retirement*, edited by Tze-Ming Quek, Kiem-Kiok Kwa, and Wen-Pin Leow, 120–37. Singapore: Graceworks, 2022.

———. *The Reformation and the Right Reading of Scripture*. Waco, TX: Baylor University Press, 2017.

———. *Seeking What Is Right: The Old Testament and the Good Life*. Waco, TX: Baylor University Press, 2020.

————. *Seriously Dangerous Religion: What the Old Testament Really Says, and Why It Matters*. Waco, TX: Baylor University Press, 2014.

Provan, Iain, V. Philips Long, and Tremper Longman III. *A Biblical History of Israel*. 2nd ed. Louisville, KY: Westminster John Knox, 2015.

Reventlow, Henning G. "Towards the End of the 'Century of Enlightenment': Established Shift from *Sacra Scriptura* to Literary Documents and Religion of the People of Israel." *HBOT* 2:1024–63, 1045.

Roberts, Vaughan. *Transgender*. Epsom, UK: Good Book Company, 2016. Kindle edition.

Roman Catholic Church. *Catechism of the Catholic Church*. 2nd ed. Vatican: Libreria Editrice Vaticana, 2012.

Shepherd, Victoria. "The People Who Think They Are Made of Glass." BBC, accessed September 29, 2022. https://www.bbc.com/news/magazine-32625632.

Seneca. *De Ira*. In *Seneca: Moral Essays*. Translated by John W. Basor. Cambridge: Harvard University Press, 1923.

Smiley, Jane. "What's Wrong with American Agriculture?" Accessed 22 October 2007. http://www.organicconsumers.org/articles/article_1784.cfm.

Solon, Olivia. "Ex-Facebook President Sean Parker: Site Made to Exploit Human 'Vulnerability.'" *The Guardian*, November 9, 2017, accessed August 3, 2019. https://www.theguardian.com/technology/2017/nov/09/facebook-sean-parker-vulnerability-brain-psychology.

Somerville, Margaret A. *Death Talk: The Case against Euthanasia and Physician-Assisted Suicide*. 2nd ed. Montreal: McGill-Queen's University Press, 2014.

Taylor, Bron. *Dark Green Religion: Nature Spirituality and the Planetary Future*. Berkeley: University of California, 2010.

The Teaching of the Twelve Apostles, Commonly Called the Didache. In *Early Christian Fathers*, edited by Cyril Charles Richardson, 177–78. LCC 1. New York: Macmillan, 1970.

The Telegraph. "Dads' Brains Change Size When Their Babies Are Born." October 9, 2022, accessed October 10, 2022. https://www.telegraph.co.uk/news/2022/10/09/dads-brains-change-size-when-babies-born/.

Tertullian. *De Fuga in Persecutione* [Flight in Time of Persecution]. *ANF* 4.

Van Liere, Eldon N. "On the Brink: The Artist and the Sea." In *Poetics of the Elements in the Human Condition: The Sea*, edited by Anna-Teresa Tymieniecka, 269–86. Analecta Husserliana 19. Dordrecht: Reidel, 1985.

Van Maren, Jonathon. "Canada's Killing Regime." *First Things*, October 18, 2022, accessed November 4, 2022. https://www.firstthings.com/web-exclusives/2022/10/canadas-killing-regime.

Van Simson, Otto Georg. *The Gothic Cathedrals: Origins of Gothic Architecture and the Medieval Concept of Order*. New York: Harper & Row, 1964.

Volf, Miroslav. *Exclusion and Embrace: A Theological Exploration of Identity, Otherness, and Reconciliation*. Nashville: Abingdon, 1996.

Walton, John. *Ancient Near Eastern Thought and the Old Testament: Introducing the Conceptual World of the Hebrew Bible*. Grand Rapids: Baker Academic, 2006.

Watson, Amy. "Television in Canada—Statistics & facts." Statista, May 17, 2019, accessed August 2, 2019, https://www.statista.com/topics/2730/television-in-canada/.

Weber, Max. "Science as a Vocation." In *Science as a Vocation*, translated by M. John, edited by Peter Lassman and Irving Velody, 3–31. London: Unwin Hyman, 1989.

Westermarck, Edward. *The Origin and Development of the Moral Ideas*. 2 vols. 2nd ed. London: Macmillan, 1924.

White, Lynn. "The Historical Roots of Our Ecologic Crisis." Reproduced in *Western Man and Environmental Ethics*, edited by Ian G. Barbour, 18–30. Reading, UK: Addison-Wesley, 1973.

Woodland Trust. "Cuckoo." Accessed November 4, 2022. https://www.woodlandtrust. org.uk/trees-woods-and-wildlife/animals/birds/cuckoo/#:~:text=A%20 cunning%20master%20of%20misdirection,brought%20up%20by%20the%20 host.&text=Other%20birds%20are%20tricked%20into%20caring%20for%20 the%20cuckoo's%20young.&text=Cuckoos%20leave%20the%20nest%20 after%20around%2020%20days.

Wolf, Ron. "God, James Watt, and the Public Land." *Audubon* 83 (1981) 58–65.

Wolff, Hans Walter. *Anthropology of the Old Testament*. Translated by Margaret Kohl. London: SCM, 1974.

Wordsworth, William. "The Tables Turned." In *Selected Poetry*, edited by Mark Van Doren, 82–83. New York: Modern Library, 1950.

World Economic Forum. "The Fourth Industrial Revolution, by Klaus Schwab." Accessed November 24, 2022. https://www.weforum.org/about/the-fourth-industrial-revolution-by-klaus-schwab#:~:text=This%20Fourth%20Industrial%20 Revolution%20is,it%20means%20to%20be%20human.

Wright, Colin "The New Evolution Deniers." *Quillette*, November 30, 2018, accessed July 18, 2019. https://quillette.com/2018/11/30/the-new-evolution-deniers/.

Yarhouse, Mark, and Olya Zaporozhets. *Costly Obedience: What We Can Learn from the Celibate Gay Christian Community*. Grand Rapids: Zondervan, 2019.

Zagorin, Perez. *How the Idea of Religious Toleration Came to the West*. Princeton: Princeton University Press, 2003.

Made in the USA
Monee, IL
26 September 2024

66703033R00152